SPIRITUAL EDUCATION

SPIRITUAL EDUCATION

THE EDUCATIONAL THEORY AND PRACTICE OF THE LUBAVITCHER REBBE RABBI MENACHEM M. SCHNEERSON

ARYEH SOLOMON

A Herder & Herder Book
The Crossroad Publishing Company
New York

A Herder & Herder Book
The Crossroad Publishing Company
www.crossroadpublishing.com

© 2020 by Aryeh Solomon

In continuation of our 200-year tradition of independent publishing, The Crossroad Publishing Company proudly offers a variety of books with strong, original voices and diverse perspectives. The viewpoints expressed in our books are not necessarily those of The Crossroad Publishing Company, any of its imprints or of its employees, executives, or owners. Although the author and publisher have made every effort to ensure that the information in this book was correct at press time, the author and publisher do not assume and hereby disclaim any liability to any party for any loss, damage, or disruption caused by errors or omissions, whether such errors or omissions result from negligence, accident, or any other cause. No claims are made or responsibility assumed for any health or other benefits.

The text of this book is set in 12/15 Adobe Garamond Pro.

Composition by Rachel Reiss
Cover design by Sophie Appel
Index by Puddingburn Publishing Services, Australia
Cover photo from the photo archives of Rabbi Velvil Schildkraut

Library of Congress Cataloging-in-Publication Data
available upon request from the Library of Congress.

ISBN 978-0-8245-9958-4 paperback
ISBN 978-0-8245-9959-1 cloth
ISBN 978-0-8245-9960-7 ePub
ISBN 978-0-8245-9961-4 mobi

Books published by The Crossroad Publishing Company may be purchased at special quantity discount rates for classes and institutional use. For information, please e-mail sales@crossroadpublishing.com.

RABBI MENACHEM M. SCHNEERSON
Lubavitch
770 Eastern Parkway
Brooklyn, N. Y. 11213

493-9250

מנחם מענדל שניאורסאהן
ליובאוויטש

770 איסטערן פּאַרקוויי
ברוקלין, נ. י.

By the Grace of G-d
Lag B'Omer, 5747
May 17, 1987
Brooklyn, N.Y.

His Excellency
President Ronald Reagan
The White House
Washington, D.C.

Greeting and Blessing:

Once again, dear Mr. President, it is a genuine
pleasure to acknowledge your kind felicitations on the
occasion of my recent birthday.

I was impressed with your meaningful Proclamation of
"Education Day, USA" in connection with the Joint Resolution
of the United States Congress, and I sincerely appreciate
your heading the roster of signatories to the "International
Scroll of Honor" affiliated with it. Its mention of
"the historical tradition of ethical values and principles,
which have been the bedrock of society from the dawn of
civilization when they were known as the Seven Noahide Laws,
transmitted through G-d to Moses on Mount Sinai," is a
clarion call vital to all mankind.

Furthermore, it is particularly gratifying that you use
this occasion to bring to the attention of the Nation and
of the International community the need of upgrading
education in terms of moral values, without which no true
education can be considered complete.

Consistent with your often declared position, that
"no true education can leave out the moral and spiritual
dimensions of human life and human striving," you,
Mr. President, once again remind parents and teachers, in
the opening paragraph of your Proclamation, that their
sacred trust to children must include "wisdom, love,
decency, moral courage and compassion, as part of everyone's
education." Indeed, where these values are lacking, education
is - to use a classical phrase - "like a body without a
soul."

With the summer recess approaching, one cannot help wondering
how many juveniles could be encouraged to use their free time
productively, rather than getting into mischief - if they were
mindful of - to quote your words - a Supreme Being and a Law
higher than man's.

I take this opportunity of again acknowledging very gratefully
your kind sentiments and good wishes.

With utmost esteem and blessing,

Cordially

CONTENTS

FOREWORD

As the leader of the Habad-Lubavitch Movement from 1951 to 1994, the Lubavitcher Rebbe, Rabbi Menachem Mendel Schneerson led a primarily educational organization that operated in over forty countries. For more than fifty years, he addressed a wide array of matters pertaining to education in his correspondence, essays, and public addresses. Most academic research on R. Schneerson has hitherto been sociological in orientation, focusing on his religious activism while ignoring the systematic and conceptual thought underlying it. The resulting literature has perpetuated a one-sided perception of R. Schneerson as an influential or charismatic religious leader who oversaw Habad's global outreach while largely overlooking his intellectual contribution.

This book closely examines Rabbi Schneerson's substantive educational corpus and identifies the cohesive and comprehensive educational philosophy contained in it. Rabbi Schneerson's educational corpus has been analyzed, its key elements isolated and thematically collated, thereby confirming the hypothesis that they comprise a significant educational philosophy. The consistency of these elements with Rabbi Schneerson's recommendations for educational practice and policy has been noted and their interconnections and the meta-themes to which they relate have been documented, thereby confirming Rabbi Schneerson's contribution to educational philosophy in general and educational practice in particular. Some of the major implications of Rabbi Schneerson's educational philosophy for current educational practice and policy, and for moral education in particular, are recorded.

Having uncovered a comprehensive educational philosophy within Rabbi Schneerson's corpus, *Spiritual Education* presents its original contribution by making explicit the pivotal elements of that philosophy. It demonstrates how Rabbi Schneerson has contributed a hitherto hidden educational philosophy that is of practical relevance and which frequently surpasses the limitations of popular educational thinking.

ACKNOWLEDGMENTS

This book is the result of the cooperation of a number of people whom I wish to acknowledge:

- Emeritus Professor Philip Wexler, editor of Herder and Herder's series on Jewish spirituality, who enthusiastically embraced the publication of this book.
- Dr. Ramon Lewis and Dr. Steven Stolz of the Graduate School of Education at Melbourne's La Trobe University who were of foremost influence on the doctoral research from which this book has evolved.
- Rabbi Naftali Loewenthal, Mrs. Louise Miller, and Michael Wexler, editors at various stages of the progression of this book who made invaluable suggestions.
- New York scholar of Habad Hasidism, Rabbi Michoel A. Seligson who shared his expertise on Rabbi Schneerson's writings.
- Canadian Habad educator, Rabbi Mordechai Berger, of blessed memory, who endorsed the fruits of my early research and encouraged my ongoing examination of Rabbi Schneerson's educational discourse.
- My parents of blessed memory who imbued me with a love of Jewish tradition at a tender age.
- On a very special note, I dedicate this work to my wife and companion, Edna, for her constant encouragement and sound counsel as well as to our children and grandchildren. May each of you grow to achieve the fullest actualization of your limitless spiritual potential, guided by the educational ideals presented in these pages.

- Finally, I wish to express my gratitude to Rabbi Schneerson. This work, like my previous book, germinated in 1975 in the privacy of Rabbi Schneerson's study, where he encouraged me to pursue post-graduate studies in education, expressing the hope that this study would contribute to the "furtherance of Jewish observance and the dissemination of the wellsprings of Hasidic wisdom." May this book serve to fulfill those expectations.

ABBREVIATIONS OF FREQUENTLY CITED SCHOLARS AND WORKS

BST   Rabbi Israel Baal Shem Tov (1698-1760)
RJIS   Rabbi Joseph Isaac Schneersohn (1880-1950)
RLY   Rabbi Levy Yitzchak Schneerson (1878-1944)
RSB   Rabbi Shalom DovBer Schneersohn (1860-1920)
RSZ   Rabbi Schneur Zalman of Liadi (1745-1813)

IK   *Igrot Kodesh* of Rabbi Menachem M. Schneerson
IK-RJIS   *Igrot Kodesh* of Rabbi Joseph Isaac Schneersohn
LD-RJIS   *Likkutei Dibburim* of Rabbi Joseph Isaac Schneersohn (1980 edition)
LS   *Likkutei Sichot* of Rabbi Menachem M. Schneerson
SH   *Sefer HaSichot* of Rabbi Menachem M. Schneerson
SH-RJIS   *Sefer HaSichot* of Rabbi Joseph Isaac Schneersohn
SK   *Sichot Kodesh* of Rabbi Menachem M. Schneerson
SM   *Sefer HaMa'amarim* of Rabbi Menachem M. Schneerson
SM-RJIS   *Sefer HaMa'amarim* of Rabbi Joseph Isaac Schneersohn
TAN-RSZ   *Tanya-Likkutei Amarim*
TM-HIT   *Torat Menachem—Hitva'aduyot* of Rabbi Menachem M. Schneerson

For Talmudic literature, the letters "a" or "b" after a page number refer to the particular side of the folio of a Talmudic text. In citing the works *Likkutei Torah* and *Torah Ohr*, letters "a" and "b" after a page number refer to the first and second columns on the first folio, while "c" and "d" refer to the first and second columns on the second folio. In utilizing translations of Rabbi Schneerson's writings, the transliteration of Hebrew terms has at times been standardized for the reader's convenience.

This book has been published with the kind assistance
of members of the community.

Most generously, help was given
in memory of
Reb Arel Serebryanski
an exemplary Chabad chasid, emissary and educator

The Traurig family in memory of their grandparents
Yosef Meir and Golda Markovitz

Shmuel Schapiro in memory of his grandfather
Rabbi Baruch Gopin

Helen, Ilana and Leon Mendels in loving memory of
David Michael Mendels

David Bleier in memory of his father
Yosef Bleier

Arnold and Daniel Levine in memory of their parents
Eliyohu and Rochel Levine

Yossi Solomon in memory of his grandmother
Miriam Hadassah Solomon

Chapter 1

THE SIGNIFICANCE OF RABBI SCHNEERSON'S EDUCATIONAL PHILOSOPHY

It is perhaps the case that R. Schneerson's fame as a leader, organizer, and innovator of communal projects has impeded a measured assessment of his originality as a thinker.
—Professor Jonathan Sacks, Emeritus Chief Rabbi of the British Commonwealth[1]

The Purpose of This Book

This book reveals the cohesive educational philosophy that exists within the vast literary corpus of Rabbi[2] Menachem Mendel Schneerson (1902-1994), the seventh dynastic leader or *Admor*[3] of the Habad[4] Hasidic Movement. As the seventh Lubavitcher Rebbe from 1951 to 1994, Rabbi Schneerson led a primarily educational organization that operated in over forty countries, addressing a wide array of matters pertaining to education in his correspondence, essays, and public addresses. In particular, it illustrates how R. Schneerson's recommendations for educational practice and policy are an expression of that educational philosophy as the elements of the philosophy are inter-related so that they establish a cohesive and comprehensive educational philosophy.

Despite the many understandings[5] within scholarly literature[6] regarding the prerequisite components of a comprehensive educational philosophy, this book has adopted elements of Professor Randall Curren's educational framework[7] as it easily identifies certain useful core elements of education for this exposition. Curren defines a systematic philosophy of education as:

> a unified, guiding perspective on education...that addresses all five normatively basic aspects of education itself, or *five basic questions* about the conduct of education: What are its aims? What authority does it rest on? What responsibilities does it entail? How, or in what manner, should it be carried out? What should its content be?[8]

While addressing these five criteria, attention is also paid to the nature of education, which Curren[9] and others[10] view as a pivotal concern of educational philosophy axiomatic to discussion of the other elements.

Consequently, R. Schneerson's educational corpus was analyzed with a view to establishing how it addresses the following questions:

(i)   What is the nature of education?
(ii)   What are the aims of education?
(iii) On what authority does education rest?
(iv)   What responsibilities does education entail?
(v)   How, or in what manner, should education be carried out?
(vi)   What should be the content of education?[11]

Moreover, the author has accepted the widespread contention[12] that for an educational discourse to be worthy of classification as educational philosophy, it must also have ramifications for educational practice and policy.[13] Hence, evidence of the transferral of R. Schneerson's theoretical educational positions into his recommendations for educational practice and policy further verifies the existence of a coherent educational philosophy within his corpus.[14]

A further criterion requires that a philosophy of education must be systematic and comprehensive with its various elements exhibiting internal consistency. The writer found a cogent and consistent educational position with practical ramifications in R. Schneerson's writings that embraces the expression of the major elements listed above. The conclusion reached is that R. Schneerson's educational discourse, rather than comprising a vast collection of disparate educational thoughts, deserves classification as a systematic educational philosophy.

The discovery of such a coherent educational philosophy, its ramifications for practice, and the disclosure of its distinctive dimensions in the context of the broader landscape of educational philosophy carry significant implications. Indeed, this book qualifies the view of R. Schneerson as an influential and charismatic religious leader who oversaw Habad's global outreach movement but which fails to recognize his intellectual contribution.[15] These works comprise a substantive body of academic literature and social analysis that has mainly focused on the religious activism set in motion by R. Schneerson, while largely ignoring the existence of the systematic and conceptual thought upon which such activity is predicated. Three admirable books by Fishkoff, Kraus, and Eliezrie[16] engage in extensive documentation of the impact of R. Schneerson's global religious activism and the influence of his emissaries' implementation of these outreach goals. However, none of these texts focuses on the ideology underlying the activity. Because a coherent educational philosophy has emerged from this study, the investigation has provided disclosure of the underlying inspiration for much of this religious activism. Also, as the research has established R. Schneerson to be an educational thinker of significance, it has exposed a dimension of his intellectual contribution largely eclipsed by his achievements.[17] This confirms Emeritus Chief Rabbi Dr. Jonathan Sacks' contention[18] that a preoccupation with documenting R. Schneerson's communal achievements has inevitably led to diminution of his significance as a writer and thinker.

R. Schneerson and Education

This book does not seek to focus on R. Schneerson's achievements. Nevertheless, to understand why investigation of R. Schneerson's educational philosophy is significant, we must first explain its importance in light of his extensive educational contribution and the acknowledgment of that achievement. The seventh Lubavitcher Rebbe, Rabbi Menachem Mendel Schneerson, was perhaps the twentieth century's most well-known Orthodox Jewish leader.[19] For over forty years, as spiritual leader of the Habad-Lubavitch Hasidic Movement, he devoted his energies to the worldwide reconstruction of post-Holocaust religious life that has deeply inspired an ongoing re-awakening of Jewish awareness and observance in as many as eighty-five countries,[20] and impacted on individuals formerly far removed from Jewish living. Moreover, his educational influence has been felt beyond the Jewish community,[21] his declared concerns including the education of humanity in general[22] and the prioritization of moral education.[23]

In 1978, R. Schneerson referred[24] to the Habad-Lubavitch school of the Hasidic movement which he led as one "which sees in education the cornerstone, not only of Jewish life, but of humanity at large and [one] which has been dedicated to this vital cause ever since its inception more than two hundred years ago." Through his educational recommendations, R. Schneerson constantly urged people to strive to meet the ideals expected by Judaism, even when such ideals demanded a code of morality more demanding than considered appropriate by society.[25]

R. Schneerson's educational initiatives included the establishment of many Jewish educational institutions worldwide, setting in motion informal educational activities, formal educational programs for tertiary students, and inaugurating global projects that promote religious education. He dispatched educational emissaries to remote communities and agitated for the upgrading of religious education for women, inauguration of education programs for the elderly, rehabilitation of former prisoners through education, and an educational outreach to Soviet Jewry, seeking to rectify the deprivation of religious education in the USSR under Communist oppression.[26] He oversaw educational publications in many languages and launched specific educational campaigns throughout his years of leadership.[27]

In the pursuit of awakening Jewish awareness, R. Schneerson's global efforts towards the post-Holocaust reconstruction and development of Jewish life began with educational initiatives.[28] The significance of education to R. Schneerson's agenda was ongoing, but in some years, it became not merely a high priority but the highest priority. Such years were designated by him as a year of "The Campaign for Jewish Education" (1976), "The Year of Jewish Education" (1977), and "The Year of the Jewish Child" (1981). Similarly, he agitated for education of the elderly (1980), and his campaigns for the promulgation of the Noahide Laws of morality (1983-1992) and the introduction of a "Moment of Reflection" at the start of the public school day (1962-1992) were continual.

Given the twentieth century's extraordinary technological advancements in the areas of travel and communication, R. Schneerson's endeavors in the field of Jewish education were undertaken on a global scale, with him seeking to inspire a worldwide renaissance of Jewish education and observance. Chief Rabbi of the British Commonwealth, Rabbi Lord Professor Jonathan Sacks[29] considered many of R. Schneerson's educational achievements, such as the *Baal Teshuvah* [Returnee] Movement, the Jewish day school movement, and the resuscitation of dying communities, to have so deeply shaped the development of post-war Judaism that they are no longer considered as solely Lubavitch. He cited the Jewish day school movement of which Habad-Lubavitch, under R. Schneerson's leadership, was one of the earliest pioneers, as a prime example of this phenomenon. Rabbi Sacks noted that "it has displaced across a wide spectrum the once prevalent ideology that Jewish education was a kind of dutiful appendage to the real business of acquiring a secular culture." He also commented that "If today we are familiar with the phenomena of *ba'alei teshuvah* [religious returnees] and

Jewish Outreach, it is almost entirely due to the pioneering work by Lubavitch, since adopted by many other groups within Orthodoxy."

The breadth of R. Schneerson's educational influence was such that US presidents acknowledged his contribution.[30] For example, on January 7, 1975, US president Gerald R. Ford wrote to R. Schneerson:

> On your twenty-fifth anniversary as Lubavitcher Rebbe, I want to join with those who applaud the dedication and wisdom that have characterized your leadership of this inspiring religious movement. Your efforts on behalf of education and your countless humanitarian endeavors have greatly benefited and strengthened our society. By giving direction to the movement's commitment to preserve Jewish tradition, you have portrayed a legacy that is a source of comfort and courage to many of our citizens. I whole-heartedly commend your quarter century of distinguished achievement and wish you continued satisfaction from your work in the years ahead...[31]

In addition, since 1978, the US Congress has annually proclaimed R. Schneerson's birthday as "Education Day, USA" and a "National Day of Reflection."[32] Upon declaring "Education Day, USA, 1989 and 1990," American President George H. W. Bush[33] cited R. Schneerson's global promulgation of the Noahide Laws[34] and the standards of conduct derived from them. Acknowledging R. Schneerson's significant contribution to society, President Bush commented that "we owe a tremendous debt to R. Schneerson and to all those who promote education that embraces moral and ethical values and [which] emphasizes their importance."[35] Several other US presidents have made similar affirmative public statements.[36]

Importantly, on September 12, 1994, R. Schneerson was posthumously awarded the Congressional Gold Medal[37] "in recognition of his outstanding contribution towards world education, morality and acts of charity."[38] On this special occasion, President Clinton

(1995) also stated, "With the awarding of the Medal, we recognize a revered leader who was a great moral inspiration, not only to the Lubavitch community and Jews around the world, but to people of all religions and faiths."[39] R. Schneerson's concern for the secular world and the lives of ordinary people was seen by the mayor of New York City, Rudolph Giuliani,[40] to be a highly significant aspect of his personality. Giuliani also considered R. Schneerson's many widespread acts of kindness and charity to have "enriched all and helped make the world a better place."

Arguing that "it would be hard to find an historical precedent for R. Schneerson's massive effort to re-ignite the flame of Judaism in a secular world," Rabbi Sacks[41] considered R. Schneerson's definitive contribution to be his transformation of "the religious landscape of Jewish life." His educational initiatives undertaken on a global scale were unique in serving to heighten Jewish awareness and observance worldwide.[42] In 2014, Rabbi Sacks reflected,

> There have been many great Jewish leaders in history. Some left a permanent mark on the Jewish mind by their contributions to Torah and the poetry and prose of the Jewish soul. Some created new communities, others revived flagging ones; some shaped the entire tenor of the region. But it would be hard to name an individual who, in his lifetime, transformed virtually every community in the world as well as created communities in places where none existed before. That is a measure of the achievement of the Lubavitcher Rebbe. He was not just a great leader—he was a unique one.[43]

Educational Writings

Before proceeding with further information, the body of R. Schneerson's writings that have been the subject of this investigation needs to be contextualized. Since his passing in June 1994 at the age of 92, there exists today his written legacy of over 200 volumes of scholarly writings that contain his lifetime's teachings and elaborations of Judaism.[44] To gain an insight into his teachings, we turn to these 200 Hebrew and Yiddish volumes that comprise his analyses of the Torah, the Talmud, discussions of Rashi, Maimonides, and other sages, Halachic responsa, discourses on Jewish mysticism, and a vast correspondence, addressed to both individuals and communities.

Since publication of an overview of R. Schneerson's 200-volume literary corpus in 2000 by Solomon,[45] further significant posthumous publication of several volumes of R. Schneerson's primary works as well as many anthologies and secondary works has occurred. A most valuable addition to his published corpus of primary works has been the publication of seven subsequent volumes of Hebrew-Yiddish correspondence, making available 2,652 hitherto-unpublished letters and hand-written replies (penned by R. Schneerson between 1968 and 1977), in addition to those twenty-five volumes published prior to the year 2000 (comprising letters penned by R. Schneerson between 1925 and 1968).[46] Between 2003 and 2017, Kehot has published four volumes of *Igrot Kodesh Meturgamot* ["Revered Correspondence Translated"] which present Hebrew translations of 1,415 items of R. Schneerson's Yiddish correspondence penned between September 1942 and August 1975, thus making these more accessible to an extended audience. As well, a thirty-ninth volume of *Likkutei Sichot* (R. Schneerson's *magnum opus*)[47] has been published.[48]

Since 1994, Kehot Publication Society has posthumously published six volumes of R. Schneerson's unedited scholarly notes and diary entries (entitled *Reshimot*), authored prior to his assuming Habad leadership and kept in diaries. These writings provide an invaluable insight into his intellectual preoccupations prior to assuming the leadership of Habad and indicate early expressions of the foundations of his religious thought.[49]

A further major development that has helped to render R. Schneerson's discourse accessible is the publication of over sixty-three volumes of *Torat Menachem-Hitva'aduyot*, comprising talks delivered by R. Schneerson between 1950 and 1971, in addition to the previously published forty-three volumes of talks delivered by R. Schneerson between 1981 and 1992. The scholar spearheading this initiative under Kehot Publication's imprint of Lahak Publications, Rabbi Chaim Shaul Brook, anticipates publication of approximately forty further volumes of talks delivered by R. Schneerson between 1971 and 1981. These volumes comprise a lucid and fully annotated Hebrew-language rendition of transcripts of his addresses. *Torat Menachem-Hitva'aduyot* rectifies previous omissions from the Yiddish-language transcripts by including emendations based on other accurate transcripts and provides footnotes to pertinent rabbinic literature and cross-references to other relevant addresses. *Torat Menachem-Hitva'aduyot* thus makes widely accessible a most authoritative, annotated Hebrew-language rendition of addresses that were formerly available only in Yiddish and without footnotes.[50] In 2012, Kehot Publication Society published Rabbi Michoel Aaron Seligson's *Sefer HaMafte'chot L'Sichot Kodesh 5695-5752* [*Indices to the Addresses of Rabbi Menachem M. Schneerson*]. By providing references to over 3,000 topics discussed in his public addresses, this comprehensive index is of invaluable assistance to research into R. Schneerson's contribution.

The Expectation of Finding an Educational Philosophy

It is well known that while a significant portion of R. Schneerson's writings deal with religious education in institutions under his jurisdiction, he also expressed his deep concern for education beyond the religious day school. Given the extent of his educational influence as well as the volume of his writings, few people today would be surprised to encounter isolated fragments of R. Schneerson's "educational thought," meaning that he contributed to educational discussions on a variety of issues. More than 3,500 of his Hebrew,

Yiddish, or English articles of correspondence, addresses, or discourses on matters of educational concern have been identified by the researcher. Besides these elements, there are many more texts that appear in educational anthologies and which are listed in indices to the thirty-two volumes of R. Schneerson's correspondence (*Igrot Kodesh*) under the entry of "education." This educational corpus provided the repository of data that were scrutinized for the central investigation. Given the sheer vastness of this corpus, its scrutinization for a cohesive philosophy of education is long overdue.

In addition, three further factors contribute to the need to investigate whether a pervasive educational philosophy exists within R. Schneerson's writings. First, unlike his immediate predecessors,[51] R. Schneerson did not attempt to collate a systematic formulation of his educational philosophy.[52] Rather, R. Schneerson spoke, wrote, and responded to the pressing educational concerns of the moment, leaving the collation of his educational writings largely to others, but endorsing and encouraging[53] their thematic collection.[54]

Second, in the absence of a systematic formulation, it is imperative that investigations engage in this thematic analysis, as its omission will inevitably uncover what appear, to the untrained eye, to be fragmented and unsystematic educational thoughts. Failure to pursue the process that enables detection of the comprehensive educational philosophy of which these individual ideas are crucial components may result in a lack of appreciation of just how the particular educational ideals and procedures are consistent with that comprehensive philosophy. However, given R. Schneerson's predecessors' enunciation of their educational philosophy, the presumption that an educational philosophy might be contained, albeit discreetly, within this educational corpus is a reasonable expectation.

Third, because many scholars of Hasidism are unfamiliar with the educational discussions occurring in the broader educational context, they are not equipped to detect any innovative dimensions permeating R. Schneerson's writing.

To investigate the possible existence of R. Schneerson's educational philosophy, the writer of this book used several sources. First, there was R. Schneerson's overt educational discourse, meaning his correspondence,[55] as well as edited transcripts of public addresses[56] and private audiences,[57] when he discusses an array of pressing educational concerns. The existence of such educational writings was unsurprising, given that he presided over a primarily educational movement[58] and saw education as his first priority.[59]

Moreover, the existence of R. Schneerson's educational philosophy was a distinct possibility when considering the educational legacy of the founder of Hasidism, R. Israel Baal Shem Tov, to which R. Schneerson was an inheritor. In an interview with Dr. Ramon Lewis in 2006, Dr. Lewis suggested that the Baal Shem Tov's educational contribution pre-empted Howard Gardner's "Multiple Intelligences"[60] by 200 years, with its emphasis on kinesthetic intelligence through dance, musical intelligence through *niggun* [melody without words], intra-personal intelligence through *hitbonnenut* [contemplation],[61] and interpersonal intelligence through the Hasidic[62] *farbrengen* [an intimate gathering for moral exhortation].[63] Indeed, the Baal Shem Tov's novel and unique educational contribution wished to make Judaism of the analytical "left-brain"[64] Talmudist also the possession of the "right-brain" artisan, mystic, and dreamer. Later, through Habad's educational revolution, Rabbi Schneur Zalman of Liadi wanted to make the intuitive and inspirational "right-brain" contribution of the Baal Shem Tov accessible to the logical-sequential "left-brain" learner; and under Habad's fifth Rebbe, this became the subject matter of a curriculum for teenagers, to be studied with the same rigor and intellectual engagement as the study of a Talmudic text.[65] It is especially noteworthy that R. Schneerson's predecessor, Rabbi Yosef Yitzchak Schneersohn, saw himself, first and foremost,[66] as an educator:[67] indeed, in the 1940s, Rabbi Yosef Yitzchak encouraged[68] special courses of pedagogical methodology conducted by Orthodox educationalist and world-renowned scholar of education, Professor William Brickman, for senior students at the Lubavitcher Yeshivah.[69]

Furthermore, some experts in educational philosophy[70] point out that an individual does not necessarily need to write or talk about education specifically to contribute to educational philosophy. For example, it has been observed[71] that while Rabbi Judah Loewe, (1525-1609), popularly known as the Maharal of Prague, may not have written specifically about education, his educational philosophy is discernible from his general writings. This principle suggests that evidence of a comprehensive educational philosophy may also possibly be confirmed through examination of R. Schneerson's analysis of certain elements of Rashi's commentary to the Torah,[72] as evident in an address where R. Schneerson enters the mind-set of the five-year-old child,[73] or through R. Schneerson's clarification of a *Mishnah* from *The Ethics of the Fathers* about the ideal approach to learning.[74] Similarly, R. Schneerson's cryptic gloss to a preliminary draft of a *Tzivot Hashem* magazine for children in which he objects to grotesque exaggeration of the human face and identifies this as an unacceptable educational technique[75] may provide evidence of an important aspect of a cogent educational philosophy. Finally, even an action by an educator can be utilized as evidence confirming an aspect of an educator's educational philosophy.[76]

This book is of particular contemporary relevance because R. Schneerson is being recast by many people as a charismatic leader, while his scholarship and creative intellectual contribution to a range of areas, specifically education, are largely overlooked. Other presentations of R. Schneerson include those that focus exclusively on his Messianism, his status as a miracle worker, and his influence as a religious leader. These claims, though worthy of analysis, are not examined here as they are beyond the focus of this book, which is solely about R. Schneerson's intellectual contribution in the area of education. Similarly, it is to be noted that this book has focused exclusively on identifying R. Schneerson's educational philosophy. The identification of his contribution to other subjects such as psychology and social theory, as well as his innovative approaches to areas of Jewish scholarship[77] dispersed throughout his writings, are beyond the scope of this research.

Throughout history, there have been many great educational thinkers whose writings may have contributed to particular areas of educational concern, but not all of them have contributed a compre-hensive educational philosophy.[78] This book will therefore investigate whether there exists an order, "a whole," that encompasses R. Schneer-son's educational thoughts and renders them a coherent educational philosophy greater than a mere conglomeration of educational writings and ideas. Moreover, knowledge of R. Schneerson's compre-hensive educational philosophy is more empowering to people than a familiarity with his disparate educational thoughts, as it allows for decisions in educational practice and parenting to be made that are consistent with his educational philosophy when a specific directive regarding a matter of educational practice is otherwise unavailable.

Previous research by Solomon (2000)[79] mapped the transferral of the pervasive themes of R. Schneerson's general discourse into his educational discourse, specifically drawing from his addresses. The research[80] was able to identify characteristic themes that pervaded the Rebbe's literary corpus and chartered their transferral into a sample of thirty-seven specific educational recommendations for educational practice.[81]

The individual educational thoughts uncovered in this earlier research are as follows:

Key Elements of Rabbi Schneerson's General Thought

Four clusters of themes were found throughout R. Schneerson's philosophy of education. These are: Torah as Instruction, the Positive View of the Individual, The Transformational Task, and Redemption. Sixteen sub-themes were identified within these four major themes as shown in the following synopsis and overview.

Torah as Instruction

- The eternal relevance of Torah as a source of contemporary instruction and the intrinsic unity of elements of Torah.

The Positive View of the Individual

- The limitless potential of the individual.
- The attainability of goals considered as a pre-ordained victory.
- Redeemability of the individual and the resultant error of despair.
- Every descent is for the sake of a subsequent ascent.
- Synthesis of opposites.
- Positive thought and speech.

The Transformational Task

- Self-transformation through the constant transcending of limitations.
- Self-transformation through *bittul* (self-abnegation), devotion and idealism.
- Transformation of one's fellow through moral education.
- Transformation through inclusivism.
- Transformation through an uncompromising presentation of ideals.
- Transformation of the physical universe.
- The primacy of deed.
- Empowering the learner.

Redemption

- Messianism.

Because the current research focuses on a close examination and systematic analysis of the elements of R. Schneerson's educational letters[82] and addresses, greater reference to R. Schneerson's educational correspondence in *Igrot Kodesh* is expected. In light of the direct application of R. Schneerson's correspondence to educational situations, with the letters' educational content largely divested of exegetical context, the *Igrot Kodesh* provides the ideal source for such a philosophy to be found. The thirty-two volumes of R. Schneerson's Hebrew-Yiddish correspondence published to date, as well as volumes of his English-language correspondence, comprise a vast, though largely unexamined repository of educational insight, a deficiency that this book aims to address.

The Process of the Current Research

In Stage 1, a rigorous search of R. Schneerson's 200-volume literary corpus was undertaken with a view to isolating all references to education or writings with direct implications for educational practice and philosophy. In addition, his extensive discourse was examined to isolate those documents of educational concern that comprise a repository of educational commentary and possible elements of a comprehensive educational philosophy. Where educational references were identified, they were isolated and a process of examination of this data begun with a view to their subsequent reorganization in a chronological table. This chronological arrangement avoided duplication of texts that appear in more than one primary source, such as letters that appear in both *Igrot Kodesh* and *Likkutei Sichot*, and also overcame the difficulty of tracking primary sources that receive partial citations in multiple secondary sources. The researcher also noted the educational themes contained in each document.

While many of these educational concepts appear to be repeated in several sources, a close examination notes subtle nuances and R. Schneerson's development of these themes in later citations. Because investigation of the identification of an overall educational framework was the purpose, overt connections between the themes were recorded and the logic whereby one theme is derived from another made explicit. This was important as an educational philosophy is distinguished by an overarching order that encompasses its individual components and thereby transforms them from clusters of disparate educational ideas into a holistic educational philosophy. Therefore, indications within the corpus that provided evidence of meta-themes which integrated the specific educational themes were also recorded.

IN CHAPTERS 2-7 there is a close analysis of the distinctive elements of R. Schneerson's educational corpus. This book reveals an analysis of the elements that refer to the nature and aims of education (Chapters 2 and 3), educational authority and responsibility (Chapters 4 and 5), as well as the methodology and content of education (Chapters 6 and 7) in order to record the crucial components that establish a comprehensive educational philosophy. R. Schneerson's contribution to these discussions as well as exemplification of the interrelatedness of these elements are documented.

CHAPTER 8 records transferral of the crucial elements of R. Schneerson's educational philosophy into the realm of practice and policy and how R. Schneerson's recommendations for practice represent his educational philosophy. This chapter contains the implications of R. Schneerson's educational philosophy for real-life situations and for educational practice. The chapter also documents the investigation into whether R. Schneerson has contributed a systematic educational philosophy which has implications for schooling and learning. The conclusion drawn confirms the consistency of R. Schneerson's educational philosophy and his recommendations for practice, given that an educational philosophy must be consistent with the recommendations for educational practice.

This book reveals the implications of this holistic educational philosophy for practice in both Jewish education and the wider educational context. Despite R. Schneerson's educational writings being based upon the classical rabbinic insights into education, including Biblical, Talmudic, Midrashic, Kabbalistic, as well as the teachings found in earlier Hasidic texts, there is evidence that he addressed the contemporary educational situation and its challenges, such as youth alienation and disenchantment, an over-preoccupation with materialism, and a questioning of the human being's universal significance. This book exposes R. Schneerson's broad approach to educational circumstances of all categories, which is not limited to Habad educational ideals or Jewish education alone.

IN CHAPTER 9, research is undertaken to identify additional characteristics of a respected educational philosophy. The first is that its elements exist in relationship to each other, thereby confirming the existence of a *holistic* educational philosophy rather than a conglomeration of unrelated elements. The second feature is that the elements are united by meta-themes from which they are derived and to which they pay homage. Third, the chapter also searches for the innovative dimension of R. Schneerson's educational philosophy when viewed against the backdrop of educational discussion throughout the ages.[83] R. Schneerson's creative insights which were unknown to educational theorists both within and beyond the Jewish community are made explicit. There is an examination of whether the elements of the newly disclosed educational philosophy differentiates it from current trends, and innovative dimensions are recorded. Identification of R. Schneerson's novel contribution provides evidence that in the realm of educational philosophy, at the very heart of educational debate, R. Schneerson has made a significant and innovative contribution. There is also a formal assessment of whether an educational philosophy has been identified.

It is to be noted that any demarcation between educational and non-educational texts is, by definition, blurred and ambiguous. While thousands of texts that fall unambiguously and exclusively within either the educational or non-educational categories exist, there is also a category of text which, though not specifically educational in orientation, has implications for the philosophy of education.[84] Therefore, while not exhaustive, given the volume of the sample of texts systematically analyzed for their educational content, coupled with the methodological rigor employed and the scrupulous analysis to which the texts were subjected, the author is confident that the results present a thorough and comprehensive investigation of whether a cohesive educational philosophy exists within R. Schneerson's corpus, accurately portraying its nature and content. This has been achieved in a way that far surpasses devotee anthologies, which make no attempt at a scholarly, objective analysis of R. Schneerson's corpus nor identify the existence of a comprehensive educational philosophy and thereafter assess its contribution.

Literature on Rabbi Schneerson's Educational Contribution

As early as 1954, R. Aaron Mordechai Zilbershtrom of Jerusalem had sought R. Schneerson's endorsement of his anthologizing educational material culled primarily from the writings of R. Schneerson's predecessor, R. Yosef Yitzchak Schneersohn. The proposal received R. Schneerson's endorsement, with him replying:

> I was delighted by your idea to collate the material currently dispersed through the *sichot* concerning matters of education and guidance, and may your application to this task be with the enthusiasm that befits it . . . [85]

Notwithstanding this endorsement, the project as originally envisaged did not immediately materialize.[86] It was only in the 1970s that Habad scholars began publishing anthologies of R. Schneerson's educational directives and those of his predecessors, in keeping with his approval. Thirty-one such anthologies of R. Schneerson's educational discourse have appeared between 1972 and 2017.

Reviewing the educational literature on R. Schneerson, one detects a view of his educational writings as a collection of disparate communications on a variety of education concerns with no reference to them forming a comprehensive educational philosophy. Indeed, in the popular anthologies of R. Schneerson's educational writings there has been a deflection from an accurate assessment of his intellectual contribution. Thus, although thirty-one works of secondary literature purporting to convey crucial aspects of R. Schneerson's educational discourse have been published, none of this literature has focused on examining the underlying unity of his educational thought or the possible existence of an overarching educational philosophy. An overview of these popular anthologies highlights the absence of prior analytical or evaluative research and confirms a tendency to communicate only fragmented elements of his educational writings but ignore the possibility of themes that might comprise an underlying cohesive and cosmic educational philosophy.

Several of these anthologies largely overlook prominent expressions of R. Schneerson's educational thought. In some instances such omissions are attributable to the anthology's publication predating the appearance of R. Schneerson's articulation of a particular theme.[87] In other instances, the self-imposed limitation of a publication has meant the omission of significant samples of R. Schneerson's educational discourse.[88] Thus, the resultant representation of R. Schneerson's educational thought that emerges from anthologies concerned only with matters pertaining to the norms of the Hasidic educational milieu will be incomplete and thus flawed.[89] Moreover, highly significant educational directives which are found in R. Schneerson's English correspondence are excluded from those anthologies due to their exclusive focus on R. Schneerson's Hebrew or Yiddish correspondence. Further examples of telling omissions from the anthologies are R. Schneerson's educational suggestions addressed to successive American presidents, his detailed response to those involved in special education who sought his perspective on the philosophy and practice of this educational challenge, and his rigorous defense of his various educational initiatives such as *Tzivot Hashem* for youth when it was challenged by those outside the Habad fraternity. R. Schneerson's addresses to children, the elderly, and the physically impaired, which contain highly significant educational material, are often omitted. The non-inclusion of R. Schneerson's recommendations for the education of the Down-syndrome child and his concerns for education within the public school system make many anthologies inadequate.

Notwithstanding their deficiencies, these anthologies provide a useful starting-point for an analysis of R. Schneerson's educational discourse as it applies to practice. This is relevant to the assessment of an educational philosophy, particularly in light of the requirement that it must emerge in educational experience and be prescriptive in its implications for educational policy and practice.[90] Indeed, noted Habad educationalist, Rabbi Naftali Roth of Jerusalem, who has facilitated the publication of several anthologies, has lamented[91] their fragmented and duplicative nature as well as the absence of what he termed *Torat HaChinuch B'Mishnat HaRabbi MiLubavitch* [Comprehensive Educational Philosophy in the Writings of the Lubavitcher Rebbe]. This book aims to address this shortcoming in the chapters that follow.

Notes

1. Sacks, 1980.
2. Throughout the thesis, to avoid repetition, the term "Rabbi" may be denoted by "R."
3. *Admor* (plural *Admorim*) is an acrostic for the initial letters of *Adoneinu Moreinu V'Rabbeinu*—meaning "our master, teacher and Rabbi." This is the term for a Hasidic master used in indirect speech (Jacobs, 1972:13). The Yiddish term *Rebbe* (derived from the Hebrew word *Rabi*, meaning "my teacher" or "my master") is an alternative term for a spiritual guide with a Hasidic following [Kaploun (*trans.*), 1987:314].
4. The word *Habad* is an acronym for the initials of the three Hebrew words *Hochmah, Binah,* and *Daat,* which refer to the three basic elements upon which the philosophy of Habad is founded, namely "wisdom," "understanding," and "knowledge" (Posner, 1994:118-9).
5. A. Edel (1956:126) referred to the unavailability of a "specific inventory of aims and contents for philosophy of education" and argued that there can never be a "definitive description of the philosophy of education." T.W. Moore (1982:1), himself a pre-eminent writer on the philosophy of education, observed that "philosophers are themselves forever in disagreement over the very nature of philosophy and the categories of enquiries that fall within their purview." Moore (*ibid.*) concluded that "there is little consensus about

what philosophers are doing or ought to be doing" and noted that amongst philosophers of education "there is quite considerable diversity about what exactly their task is or ought to be." Curren (2003:4) has similarly referred to philosophy of education's "disparate and scattered practitioners."

6. Many of the references to discussions of the components of educational philosophy and theory are to works published in the 1960s, 1970s and 1980s, as it was "in the 1960s and 1970s [that] philosophy of education in Great Britain developed a new look and was firmly put on the map as a branch of educational philosophy" (R.S. Peters, 1983:30). Barrow (1994:4445) has observed that "During the 1960s and 1970s analytic philosophers were prominent in educational debate." Similarly, D.C. Phillips (1994:4450) has commented that "The zenith of analytical philosophy of education seems not to have been reached until the 1960s and early 1970s, when the work of Peters, Hirst, Dearden and Wilson was dominant in the United Kingdom, and the work of Scheffler, Green, McClellan, and others achieved virtual hegemony in the United States."

7. Curren, 2007:3. A recent highly significant and comprehensive attempt to identify the prerequisite elements of a philosophy of education is that of Dr. Randall Curren who has "devoted two decades to attempting to define how philosophy of education can be organized and to surveying the attempts that others have made." (Email correspondence of December 16th, 2011 received by the researcher from Dr. Curren in response to questions posed to him.) As editor of two contemporary prestigious tomes on philosophy of education, *A Companion to the Philosophy of Education* (Blackwell Publishing, 2003) and *Philosophy of Education: An Anthology* (Blackwell Publishing, 2007), he is uniquely positioned to survey the landscape of literature (both ancient and contemporary) which seeks to identify those criteria that enable an educational discourse to qualify as philosophy of education. In 2007, Curren (2007:1) addressed the questions of "What, then, is philosophy of education? What is its object of investigation? What purposes does it bring to its investigations?"

8. *Op. cit.*:3.

9. *Op. cit.*:7.

10. Hirst and Peters, 1970; R.S. Peters, 1973; Bowen and Hobson, 1974:16; Barrow & Woods, 1975:1.

11. Siegel's (2009:1) understanding of the crucial elements to be addressed by a philosophy of education concurs with several of Curren's prerequisites; especially his inclusion of the aims of education, educational authority, the best way to carry out moral education and questions concerning the curriculum correspond to four of Curren's five areas. (Perhaps Siegel's inclusion of "the rights of students" may be identified with Curren's inclusion of the educator's responsibility, the former addressing the identical

issue from the viewpoint of the recipient with the latter focused on the responsibility of the provider.)

12. Strang, 1955:163; Barrow & Woods, 1975:181-9; Peters, 1977:viii; Burbules, 2000:5.

13. Barrow and Woods (1975:181-9) argue that the potency and significance of educational philosophy can be evidenced by its practical application to highly specific educational circumstances.

14. A secondary outcome of the process of documenting the compliance of his educational discourse with the criteria that have rendered it an educational philosophy is the clarification of whether R. Schneerson's discourse meets highly selective criteria prescribed by Rusk and Scotland (1979:4) for classification of its author as one worthy of the title "great educator." Given R. Schneerson's request (Kranzler, 1951) that focus be on his teachings and mission rather than on his personal achievements, this dissertation has been focussed on an investigation of the existence of an educational philosophy within his corpus rather than on his attainment as an educator.

15. Levy, 1973; Shaffir, 1974 & 1978; Kovacs, 1977; Shokeid, 1988; Danzger, 1989; Davidman, 1991; Kaufman, 1991; Hoffman, 1991; and Morris, 1995.

16. See Fishkoff, 2003; Kraus, 2007; and Eliezrie, 2015.

17. This is not unprecedented in Jewish history. Thus, the Talmudic and Halachic achievements of Rabbi Israel Meyer Kagan (1839-1932), more commonly known as the *Chafetz Chayim*, are often over-shadowed by the piety and saintliness which are projected as his salient features.

18. Sacks, 1980.

19. Mark, 1994; Landau, 1994; Kraus, 2007; Miller, 2014.

20. Eliezrie, 2015:353.

21. Spiegel, 1975; Lau, 1994; D'Amato, 1994; Giuliani, 1994; Kraus, 2007; Miller, 2014.

22. Bush, 1989 cited in Addenda to Shemtov (*ed.*), 1996:88-9.

23. *LS*, XXVI:132-44.

24. Address of *Nissan* 11th, 5738 [April 18th, 1978] in *SK-5738*, II:116; see also in an earlier letter (Rader & Rader [*eds.*], 1970:ix).

25. *Ibid.*

26. In 2006, "The Committee of Emissaries to the Former Soviet Union" published R. Zusia Wolf's 606-page *Diedushka: The Lubavitcher Rebbe and Russian Jewry*, which documents R. Schneerson's activities for Russian Jewry throughout his years of leadership. A historical background to Habad's engagement in this struggle is found in Brickman, 1999:9-18. For detailed documentation of Habad initiatives in the former Soviet Union, see Levin, 1989.

27. For a more detailed overview of these specific projects, see Seligson, 2005:A21-A42 and Kraus, 2007:35-176, 189-249. For a chronological

outline of R. Schneerson's calls for educational initiatives and for an overview of his formal educational initiatives see Solomon, 2000:343-9, 357-69.
28. Sacks, 1994.
29. *Ibid.*
30. On March 21st, 1972, US president Richard Nixon wrote to R. Schneerson, "Your 70th birthday gives me a welcome opportunity to applaud your
many successful years as Lubavitcher Rebbe. Your dedication to the teaching of your Faith and your emphasis on vocational training have made
the Lubavitch Movement an asset not only to the Jewish religion, but to
all citizens. Steadfastness in religious belief has been a central sustaining
force in American life and your contribution to the moral and spiritual
strength of our society has been particularly significant."
31. Ford, G., 1975.
32. R. Schneerson often expressed his gratitude to US presidents for their kind
thoughts and sentiments on his birthday, expressing his blessings that the
presidents "achieve the immense tasks and goals that await them" (Address of April 15th, 1981, in *SK-5741* [1981], III:105).
33. Bush:1989-90.
34. Concerning these Laws, President G.H.W. Bush (1989-90) wrote, "The
principles of moral and ethical conduct that have formed the basis for
all civilization come to us, in part, from the centuries-old Seven Noahide Laws. The Noahide Laws are actually seven commandments given to
man by G-d....These commandments include prohibitions against murder,
robbery, adultery, blasphemy, and greed, as well as the positive order to
establish courts of justice." (See S. Cowen, 2015.)
35. In 1978, the US Senate and House of Representatives authorized a presiden-
tial request for the establishment of an "Education Day USA" in recognition
of "the special commitment of the Lubavitch Movement to the advancement of education" and issued a Proclamation designating April 18th,
1978—the 76th birthday of R. Schneerson—as "Education Day USA." In
1982, President Ronald Reagan described R. Schneerson's Lubavitch Movement as "one shining example for peoples of all faith of what education
ought to be." Reagan referred to R. Schneerson's life-work as "a response
to that special calling [that] few are privileged to hear . . . [standing] as a
reminder to us all that knowledge is an unworthy goal unless it is accompanied by moral and spiritual wisdom and understanding." President Reagan
wrote to R. Schneerson, "Since your first moments in the United States
in 1941, you have shared your personal gift of universal understanding to
the benefit of all. Time and again, your love and spiritual guidance have
brought hope and inspiration to those confronted with despair. In bringing
solace and comfort to the human spirit, you have helped to strengthen the
foundation of faith which is mankind's most vital asset." American president Bill Clinton (1994) considered R. Schneerson's achievement to have

been "teaching the ideals of sharing and education…[and] advancing the instruction of ethics and morality to our young people."

36. For statements by Presidents Reagan, G.H.W. Bush and Clinton, see Shem-tov (*ed.*), 1994:75-90.

37. The extraordinary Congressional Gold Medal is one of the highest honors the United States bestows on outstanding citizens of the world. Awarded to those who have made significant contributions to humankind, each medal requires an Act of Congress and the president's signature. George Washington was the first recipient honored in 1776 by the Congress of a grateful new nation. Since then, fewer than 100 statespeople, military leaders, scientists and people of arts and letters have received the Congressional Gold Medal. R. Schneerson became the first religious leader to receive this award.

38. Act of [US] Congress, November 2nd, 1994, Sections 1 and 2. This same Act of Congress also stated, "Rabbi Menachem Mendel Schneerson has interpreted with keen insight the miraculous events of our time and has inspired people to a renewal of individual values of spirituality, co-operation and love of learning."

39. Shemtov (ed.), 1994:68.

40. Giuliani, R., 1994.

41. Sacks, 1994.

42. Sacks, 1994; Mark, 1994; Klein-Halevy, 1994.

43. Sacks, 2014.

44. Bagnall, 1994:26.

45. Solomon, 2000:27-34, 320-5.

46. This brings the total number of letters published in *Igrot Kodesh* to 12,220 at the time of publication of this book.

47. The entire thirty-nine-volume *Likkutei Sichot* has been published in 2004 as the forty-six-volume *Likkutei Sichot-Parshiyot* where each volume culls the addresses spread across the thirty-nine volumes of *Likkutei Sichot* and anthologizes them in such a way that exclusively devotes an entire volume to one Torah portion or double-portion (and where applicable, the festival of that time of year). *Likkutei Sichot-Parshiyot* does not include the extended addenda that are appended to volumes of the original thirty-nine-volume collection. A five-volume *Likkutei Sichot—Inyanei Ge'ula U'Mashiach* selects *sichot* that pertain to Redemption and *Mashiach*.

48. Appended to this thirty-ninth volume is a collection of R. Schneerson's elucidations of cryptic glosses on RSZ's *Tanya—Igeret HaTeshuvah* by his father RLY, as well as R. Schneerson's own commentary to *Tanya—Igeret HaTeshuvah* and addenda comprising a further anthology of personal correspondence, pastoral letters, and excerpts of transcripts of his edited addresses.

49. Also of particular significance to an assessment of R. Schneerson is Kehot's publication in 2014 of Volumes XV and XVI of correspondence

penned by RJIS between *Menachem-Av* 2nd, 5673 [Aug. 5th, 1913] and *Menachem-Av* 12th, 5689 [Aug. 18th, 1929] with his daughter, Rebbitzen Chaya Mushka Schneerson and son-in-law and future successor, R. Menachem M. Schneerson. This correspondence and his *Reshimot* [personal scholarly diaries written prior to assuming leadership of Habad] (see Solomon, 2000:34) provide an insight into the areas of his immersion in Hasidic teachings and religious thought at this time.

50. This does not include three volumes of *Torat Menachem Tiferet Levi Yitzchak*, six volumes of *Ma'amarim Melukat*, two volumes of *Ma'amarim Bati L'Gani*, *Ma'amarim Drushei Chatuna* and *Ma'amarim Drushim L'Pirkei Avot*.

51. In 1898, Habad's fifth Rebbe, Rabbi Shalom Dovber Schneersohn instructed his son and successor, RJIS, to write an educational tract for the first *Mashpi'im* [mentors] of the *Yeshivat Tomchei Temimim*. The tract was subsequently published as *Klallei HaChinuch V'HaHadracha* ["The Principles of Guidance and Instruction"] (Kehot Publication Society, New York, 1990) and is considered to be a definitive exposition of Habad educational philosophy. RJIS's *Principles of Education and Guidance* and its concluding *Chapter on Leadership* first appeared in *SH-RJIS-5703*:205-30.

52. The closest equivalent to an authoritative tract by the Rebbe as a formulation of his essential philosophy is *On the Essence of Chassidus*, which was edited and reworked by him from the transcripts of his addresses of *Kislev* 19th, 5726 [December 13th, 1965] and the last day of *Pesach, Nissan* 22nd, 5730 [April 28th, 1970].

53. In 1954, R. Schneerson wrote to Rabbi Aaron Mordechai Zilberstrom (*IK*, IX:216), "I was delighted by your proposal to compile the educational material that is currently dispersed throughout the *sichot* [addresses]...It is my hope that the resultant publication will be of benefit to diverse educational institutions." R. Aaron Mordechai Zilberstrom confirmed that he had proposed a popular distillation of complex educational concepts contained in the writings and addresses of RJIS and the early addresses of R. Menachem M. Schneerson. The proposed distillation was to have adapted lofty concepts, thereby rendering them accessible and of practical benefit to those engaged in the teaching profession. (Interview of June 19th, 2006 with R. Aaron Mordechai Zilberstrom.)

54. This approach characterized R. Schneerson's contribution to the study of Rashi's commentary to the Pentateuch. From 1964, R. Schneerson regularly devoted one *sicha* of the usual six or more *sichot* that comprised his Shabbat afternoon *farbrengen* to developing an innovative approach to interpretation of Rashi's Torah commentary. A detailed and systematic compilation of the axioms underlying Rashi's methodology as disclosed by R. Schneerson's analyses was published in 1980 by Rabbi T. Blau as *Klallei Rashi* ["Rashi's Axiomatic Principles"] by Kehot Publication Society.

The work provided an extensive compilation of 217 exegetical principles emergent from R. Schneerson's analyses of Rashi's commentary, as well as exemplification of R. Schneerson's application of these principles to his discourse. In a letter of *Adar* 11th, 5740 [February 28th, 1980], R. Schneerson expressed his appreciation to R. Blau for the first edition of this work and encouraged his publication of a more extensive edition. An expanded version of *Klallei Rashi* was published in 1991, identifying a further 182 exegetical principles and exemplifications of their application throughout R. Schneerson's discourses and thus documenting a total of 389 such underlying principles. Similarly, in 1991, R. Mordechai M. Lauffer published *Klallei Rambam* ["Maimonides' Axiomatic Principles"], which cited 268 underlying axioms of Maimonides' *Mishneh Torah* brought to light through Rabbi Schneerson's analyses of *Mishneh Torah* throughout more than forty years of his leadership.

55.   Thirty-two volumes of Rabbi Schneerson's Hebrew and Yiddish correspondence have hitherto been published as *Igrot Kodesh* by Kehot Publication Society of New York. In 1965, given the volume of correspondence received, R. Schneerson largely replaced full written responses with cryptic replies, often written in the margins of letters addressed to him. As well, Hebrew renditions of R. Schneerson's pastoral letters have been published by Kehot Publication Society as *Igrot Melech*. Some 113 of R. Schneerson's pastoral letters, authored between the years 1950 and 1978, were also published by Kehot in 1979 in their English translation, as *Letters of the Lubavitcher Rebbe*, Vol. 1, *Tishrei-Adar*. The second volume of this collection awaits publication. In 1981, the Lubavitch Women's Organization published another 25 such letters addressed to their conventions, entitled *Letters by the Lubavitcher Rebbe Shlita Rabbi Menachem Mendel Schneerson to N'shei u'Bnos Chabad 1956-1980*. Selections from R. Schneerson's extensive and highly significant English correspondence were thematically arranged and prepared for publication by his long-standing personal secretary, Rabbi Dr. Nissan Mindel. Four volumes have been published as *The Letter and the Spirit* by Nissan Mindel Publications with several further volumes awaiting publication.

56.   These are found in the following: *Likkutei Sichot Al Parshiyot HaShavuah, Chagim U'Moadim*, Vols. 1-39, Kehot Publication Society, Brooklyn, NY, 1962-1995; *Sefer HaSichot* of Rabbi Menachem M. Schneerson, 12 volumes, 5747-5752 [1986-1992], Kehot Publication Society, Brooklyn, NY, 1987-1992; *Sichot Kodesh*, 50 volumes, 5710-5741 (1950-1981), produced by groups of scholars, Brooklyn, NY, between 1950 and 1981; *Torat Menachem—Hitva'aduyot*, 62 volumes published by Kehot Publication Society, Brooklyn, New York, 1992-2018; a further 41 volumes of *Hitva'aduyot* were published by Lahak Hanachot, Brooklyn, NY, between 1982 and 1993, comprising Hebrew-language transcripts of R. Schneerson's addresses delivered between 1981 and 1992 (5742-5752).

57. In 1987, *Machon L'Hatza'ot L'Ohr*, Kollel Avreichim Habad, Nachalat Har-Habad, Kiryat Malachi, Israel published Rabbi M.M. Lauffer's *B'Tzeil HaChochmah—Reshimot V'Roshei Prakim MiDivrei Kvod Kedushat Admor Shlita MiLubavitch Im Admorim, Rabbanim, Roshei Yeshivot U'Gedolei Torah*, comprising transcripts, mostly unedited, of some 40 meetings of world Rabbinic leaders with R. Schneerson. As well, in 2009, *Machon B'Ohalei Tzadikim* of Jerusalem published *Si'ach Sarfei Kodesh: Ti'ud Pegishot Gedolei Yisrael Im HaRabbi MiLubavitch* incorporating the content of 64 extended meetings between R. Schneerson and leading Rabbinic scholars throughout the decades of his leadership.

58. By 1990, Habad educational teaching facilities numbered over 2,000 worldwide in the Diaspora. (Interview with Rabbi E. Shmotkin, February, 2000.) By 2018, given the continuing expansion of Habad institutions and the ongoing dispatching of Habad emissaries across the globe, this number has greatly increased. However, this ongoing expansion of Habad and the establishment of new institutions worldwide render problematic the accurate ascertaining of a precise contemporary quantification. In 1994, Habad emissaries numbered 1,032 whereas the current number of Habad emissaries is over 4,700 (Eliezrie, 2015:354).

59. R. Schneerson stated: "There is a special goal which takes priority over all others, and that is education." *Cabinet Communiques*, an undated report on the *Yechidut* of Representatives of the Young Leadership Cabinet of the UJA with R. Schneerson on March 4, 1973.

60. Note that more recent commentary on Multiple Intelligences prefers the term "Learning Preferences" (see H.F. Silver, R.W. Strong, & M.J. Perini, 1997).

61. For an exposition of contemplative prayer within the Habad school in particular, see N. Loewenthal (1990).

62. Tzemach Tzedek stated, "The 'ways of *Chasidut*' are that all Hasidim are to be like one family, with affection, as prescribed by the Torah…" (Tzemach Tzedek's reply to an enquiry from his son and successor, Rabbi Shmuel, *SM-RJIS*-5711:244, cited by RJIS in *HaYom Yom*, entry of *Tevet* 24th). Similarly RJIS wrote (*IK-RJIS*, IV:257, cited in *HaYom Yom*, entry of 10th of *Adar Sheini*): "Hasidim never say farewell, for they never depart from each other. Wherever they are they are one family."

63. In this context, the Yiddish term *farbrengen* refers to an informal gathering of *Hasidim* which includes a spontaneous exchange of Torah insights and Hasidic oral traditions as well as singing and refreshments, and which strives for mutual and brotherly edification. The term *farbrengen* can also refer to an assemblage addressed by a Habad Rebbe (Kaploun [*trans.*] 1987:327).

64. The demarcation of "left-brain" and "right-brain" thinking is found in Dennison & Dennison, 1985, although recently this view has received

criticism. (See https://www.psychologytoday.com/blog/the-philosophy-cognitive-modes/201401/left-brain-right-brain-wrong.)

65. See RJIS's *HaTamim*:23.

66. RJIS had related to Rabbi Mendel Feldman that upon being questioned in the course of a train ride as to his occupation, he had replied, "I am an educator." (Interview with Rabbi Mendel Feldman of Baltimore, in 2007.)

67. RJIS later reflected in an address of *Adar* 26th, 5705 [March 11th, 1945] to the Fifth Annual Commemoration of the founding of the [USA] Central Lubavitch Yeshivah (*LD-RJIS*:465b-466a), "The soul mission underlying my arrival in America [is] not 'to eat of its fruit and become sated with its bounty' but with the purpose, directed by Divine Providence, of establishing (with the Almighty's help) institutions for the dissemination of Torah study inspired by the awe of heaven and authentic Jewish education." For a detailed account of its activities and those of its sister organizations founded by RJIS, see Levin (1988:271-304) and Glitzenstein (1986, XI:67-122). See also Letter of *Tevet* 24th, 5722 [Dec. 31st, 1961] in *Letters of the Lubavitcher Rebbe*, II:259-60; *Sicha* of *Shevat* 10th, 5721 [Jan. 28th, 1961], recorded in *Letters of the Lubavitcher Rebbe*, I:263.

68. RJIS (*IK-RJIS*, IX, Letter of *Adar* 29th, 5707 [March 21st, 1947], Letter 2999), in a letter addressed to the Board of *Merkos L'Inyonei Chinuch*, suggested the speedy implementation of courses to enable *Yeshivah* heads, primary and secondary Jewish Studies teachers, to expand and develop their knowledge concerning educational methodology.

69. Dr. William Brickman (1913-1986) was an Orthodox educationalist. Between 1940 and 1942 and again from 1946 to 1962, Dr. Brickman taught the history of education and comparative education at New York University and subsequently became the Professor of Educational History and Comparative Education at the University of Pennsylvania Graduate School of Education between 1962 and 1981. He was a prolific writer on education and edited prestigious scholarly educational journals that included *School and Society*. He played a pivotal role in the accreditation for America's inaugural Orthodox Jewish day schools and *yeshivot*. He is credited with pioneering the field of comparative and international education. See Sherman-Swing, 1987:1-6; Solomon, 2010:85-101.

70. Rabenort, 1911:1-13.

71. Kleinberger, 1962.

72. See R. Schneerson's analysis of Rashi's commentary to *Bereishit*, 12:8 in his address of *Shabbat Parashat Lech L'cha, Cheshvan* 8th, 5748 [Oct. 31st, 1987] (See *TM-HIT-5748*, II:437 & 440) clarifying a difficulty with Rashi's comment raised by Rabbi Shabtai Bass (1641-1719) in his supercommentary to Rashi entitled *Siftei Chachamim*. Central to R. Schneerson's resolution of the difficulties raised by this commentary is his expectation that an educational message be communicated from father to child through expressions

of honor and respect for the child's mother, thereby conveying to the child that such behavior is the norm of the home.

73. See Rashi to *Bereishit*, 3:8; *op. cit.*, 3:24; *Ethics of the Fathers*, 5:22.

74. See for example R. Schneerson's commentary to *Ethics of the Fathers*, 4:20 in his address of *Shabbat Parashat VaEtchanan, Av* 15th, 5737 [July 30th, 1977]; See *LS*, XIX:43-4, Paragraph 7.

75. Response to *The Moshiach Times*, cited in *Dvar Melech—Likut Tshuvot M'yuchadot Me'et Kvod Kdushat Admor Shlita*:4; Archives of *Tzivot Hashem*; *SK:5741*, I:418. Besides negating the use of caricature, R. Schneerson added a general comment that the more life-like and realistic, the more effective the artistic representation as an educational tool.

76. Barrow & Woods, 1975:181-9.

77. Professor Lawrence Schiffman (2014) lists broad areas of R. Schneerson's scholarship awaiting scholarly analysis. These include R. Schneerson's commentary to the Passover *Haggadah*; his *Reshimat HaMenorah* (a treatise that deals with the *Menorah* [Candelabrum] from Halachic and Kabbalistic perspectives); *Chiddushim U'Bi'urim B'Shas* ["Novel Insights and Elucidations of the Talmud"]; comments on *Hilchot Talmud Torah* [RSZ's "The Laws of Torah Study"]; Rashi's commentary to the Penta-teuch; *Ethics of the Fathers*; Maimonides' *Mishneh Torah* (for example, his understandings of *Hilchot Beit HaBechira* ["Laws of the Jerusalem Temple"]); and innovative derivation of *hora'ot* [edifying life-lessons] from Biblical texts.

78. Bowen & Hobson, 1974:10-1.

79. "The Educational Teachings of Rabbi Menachem M. Schneerson," Jason Aronson Inc., Northvale, New Jersey and Jerusalem, 2000, based on doc-toral dissertation at La Trobe University entitled "Characteristic Themes of the Edited Addresses of Rabbi Menachem M. Schneerson and Their Relationship to his Educational Discourse" (May, 1997).

80. The previous research took the following path. Thirty randomly selected representative samples of the Rebbe's edited addresses were stratified by year of delivery, then meticulously examined and their themes identi-fied. Processes and research methodologies recommended by Lincoln and Guba (1985) which establish the reliability and validity of both data and findings were subsequently undertaken.

81. See Solomon, 2000:205-56.

82. R. Schneerson's educational discourse includes writings that address edu-cational issues in the narrower definition of the term, meaning matters of schooling in kindergartens, schools, institutes, and universities. However, in accordance with the wider understanding of education that sees educa-tion as a lifelong process, it includes writings whereby R. Schneerson's discussion has implications for the way education may shape or transform the individual and society.

83. Bowen and Hobson, 1974:10-3.

84. That there exists a correlation between R. Schneerson's general discourse and his educational recommendations is confirmed by him in *IK,* XVIII:5, Letter 6,506, penned on the day prior to *Rosh Hashanna,* 1958. At the conclusion of a correspondence of educational content addressed to Dr. Joseph Goldschmidt, Director of Jerusalem's Department of Religious Education, R. Schneerson referred to his enclosure of his pre-*Rosh Hashanna* pastoral letter of the same year. This letter spoke of empowering individuals to inspire others in matters of religious observance. R. Schneerson stated that the enclosure, while addressing wider religious issues, was of relevance to the educational matters under discussion.

85. Hebrew letter of *Tammuz* 27th, 5714 [July 28th, 1954] published in *IK,* IX:216, Letter 2,834. In this correspondence, R. Schneerson also noted, "It is understood that it of course needs to be translated into the spoken Hebrew language of Israel, while nevertheless staying as loyal as possible to the original. And perhaps the reality will be that it will be published even prior to the new school semester—may it come upon us for good—and in a way that other schools will also be able to benefit from it and there is great advantages in this as is obvious. I trust that the costs will not be exorbitant and especially as our institutions in Morocco will be able to make use of it..."

86. Rabbi Zilbershtrom's initial suggestion, which focused on anthologizing RJIS's educational writings, partially came to fruition in 2013, when R. Menachem Friedman published *Gibor BaAretz Yih'yeh Zar'o; Dor Yesharim Yevorach: Kours Iyuni U'Ma'asi L'Horim U'M'chanchim al pi Torat Hasidut Habad: Klalei HaChinuch V'Ha'Hadracha* ["An In-Depth and Practical Course for Parents and Educators according to Habad Hasidism on 'The Principles of Education and Guidance'"]. The work systematically explicates RJIS's seminal work on education.

87. The early anthologies predate R. Schneerson's written guidance on education for special children which was communicated in the 1980s.

88. Several anthologies authored in Israel do not focus on R. Schneerson's guidance for public school education in America.

89. For example, the exclusion from several anthologies of R. Schneerson's highly significant correspondence and addresses concerning educational inculcation of moral values throughout the broader community is an obvious oversight.

90. For an overview of other anthologies and adaptations of R. Schneerson's writings which are not directly related to education, see Solomon, 2000:321-5, 454-7.

91. Interviews of December 16th & 19th, 2011 with R. Naftali Roth during his visit to Sydney, Australia.

Chapter 2

THE NATURE OF EDUCATION

Most questions about education will lead one, sooner or later, to ask about the nature of education and whether there are certain aims that are somehow inherent in its nature and for some reason necessary or desirable.

— PROFESSOR RANDALL CURREN[1]

It has been argued by scholars of education that an analysis of the nature of education is a pivotal concern of educational philosophy,[2] given that understanding this is a prerequisite for addressing questions that are integral to establishing a philosophy of education. University academics Barrow and Woods[3] required that "a philosophy of education address the questions of what we mean by the terms 'education,' 'educate' and 'educated.'" English philosopher of education R.S. Peters[4] similarly argued that the term "education" itself required analysis, devoting much discussion to the processes of education, and arguing[5] "that education (as process) is a polymorphous concept and that it is a mistake to think of 'educating' as the name of one, and only one activity..."[6] This element of the philosophy of education has been aptly characterized by H.H. Horne[7] as "an interpretation of the meaning of education in the light of the general theory of the universe." Still, while Bowen[8] observed that "the study of education [had] always been important in Western thought, attracting the interest of the greatest intellects in every age," he simultaneously lamented that "yet after several thousands of years of attention, a precise definition, particularly of the more normative and ideational aspects of education, still eludes us."

We will now examine R. Schneerson's understandings of what is the nature of education.

Adopting the Broadest Understanding of Education

An expansive understanding of education was proposed by the founders of Hasidism and the spiritual leaders of its Habad school who were R. Schneerson's predecessors. His father-in-law and predecessor, the sixth Lubavitcher Rebbe, Rabbi Yosef Yitzchak Schneerson had stated:

> "Education" [*chinuch*] is a term that encompasses all, from the youngest child to the most senior adult. Education is the foundation of the "self-leadership" process [*hadracha*] where an individual provides ongoing direction for themselves. The world understands the term "education" to apply exclusively to young children, to one's sons and daughters, while "self-leadership" applies to those children who are now somewhat grown up. Habad Hasidism understands the term "education" to apply equally to adults while the concept of "self-leadership" refers specifically to a person's lifelong obligation to engage in ongoing self-direction... The education of a mature-age individual implies an individual's observing every phenomenon with the greatest attention and contemplation in order to attain a personal assessment as to how despicable one's negative character traits are, and how beautiful and pleasant are the positive character traits that one possesses.[9]

To R. Schneerson,[10] in the tradition of the Hasidic movement[11] and his predecessors,[12] life in all its manifestations offers unlimited educational possibilities to reveal the limitless learner potential, which is also a major focus of his educational discourse.[13] He therefore advocated the adoption of the broadest possible definition,[14] viewing education as an all-encompassing enterprise whereby nothing is outside its scope. Thus, his understanding of education goes beyond the account where "the term 'education' refers in its primary sense to more-or-less systematic practices of supervising and guiding the activities of persons in ways intended to promote valuable forms of learning and development."[15]

R. Schneerson distinguished "education" in its broader, all-encompassing connotation from "education" according to its narrow, legal definition. He wrote:

> "Education" *in its broader sense*... implies an obligation to apply oneself to providing the child's *every* need. It goes beyond the obligation to facilitate the child's spiritual needs as prescribed by the *literal* definition of "education." The narrow designation is but one element of the all-encompassing definition. Furthermore, education in the narrow sense is subject to time constraints, taking effect only from the time when the child reaches the formal "age of commencement of education." In contrast, education in the broader sense applies at "all times," meaning *constantly, both day and night.*[16]

While this all-encompassing definition refers to the education of children, it was also applied by R. Schneerson to adult education and self-leadership.

In pastoral letters written at the time of his formal assumption of the leadership of Habad,[17] R. Schneerson cited texts[18] that illustrate that the educational obligation extends to all children and students. In light of this adoption of the broadest possible definition, education also comprises an ongoing, lifelong process of derivation of lessons from life's phenomena and encounters,[19] going beyond the formal curriculum. He wrote, a human was given reason and intellect, so that by the powers of understanding and deduction one can see, even in the most ordinary things in life, a lesson and moral encouragement in one's duties and conduct both with regard to the Creator and to one's fellow human being.[20]

In light of this definition,[21] the educator's concern for the learner must go beyond the hours of formal instruction[22] and, indeed, defies limitations of subjects taught.[23] It follows even more strongly that if all phenomena, including seemingly neutral experiences,[24] are sources of educational instruction, then lessons in an individual's Divine service and self-edification can certainly be derived from all aspects of Torah.[25] Even seemingly peripheral information that accompanies the wisdom of the Sages, irrespective of how incidental these appear,[26] can provide individuals with opportunities for their fullest self-development.

Education as an Endeavor of Universal Significance

According to R. Schneerson, if the universe is created so that all its aspects are of potential educational significance, it follows that derivation of educational implications from worldly phenomena is of universal significance.[27] Moreover, he considers education as critical to all aspects of life, to the universe as a whole and its perfection, as well as to facilitating the individual's fullest self-realization.[28] As a universal endeavor, education becomes a highly potent process[29] whose impact is substantial.

The cosmic significance of education goes hand-in-hand with the Talmudic perception[30] whereby every individual is considered an entire universe and educating an individual is equivalent to influencing an entire universe, with even a minute improvement in just one student having cosmic ramifications.[31] To R. Schneerson, this was more than just a metaphor but an approach to education that impacts on practical educational issues.[32] In light of this understanding, a proper education can "purify" and "spiritually decontaminate" the most primitive or "spiritually insensitive" atmosphere and the individual's environment.[33] Furthermore, informal education is of no less significance than formal education.[34] Scrutinizing R. Schneerson's educational corpus in detail reveals his understanding of the cosmic significance of education and includes its impact on the individual, the community, and the universe.

Awakening the Learner's Essential Soul

To R. Schneerson, education comprises the awakening of the quintessential soul of the learner. He wrote:

> By laying a foundation in the Holy Temple in the heart of each and every one, awakening the quintessential soul which exists in every individual, regardless of his or her affiliation, because at this level, all are equal: both a person who is rich in his knowledge, and one who is poorer and more simple. And when the foundation is laid, meaning when we arouse the point of the essential soul, we can build a magnificent Holy Temple; we can see how everyone is a holy sanctuary in which G-d rests. All that is necessary is to know how to awaken this level.[35]

A further reflection of the cosmic importance of education is that education is the vessel to channel G-d's blessings[36] for both the individual student and the educator.[37] It is therapy for the student's soul, paralleling revitalization of physical health[38] and invigoration of a child, rendering the child fortunate both in this world and the afterlife.[39] Education's arousal of spiritual potential includes its facilitation of the student's simultaneous subduing of negative impulses.[40]

To R. Schneerson, education is the foundation of the entire lifetime of the learner. He believed that when one views education from an in-depth perspective, it is revealed to constitute the very foundation of the life of the learner, an idea expressed in the Biblical verse,[41] "Educate the child according to his way, so that when he grows old, he will not depart from it." Consequently, he wrote:

> The *mitzvah* of education, the guiding and training a child in the fulfillment of *mitzvot*, begins at the earliest age in the life of a Jew or Jewess. So significant is the *mitzvah* of *chinuch* that it is not merely the preparation for the child's fulfillment of *mitzvot* upon attaining the age of *Bar-* or *Bat Mitzvah* (at 13 or 12 years respectively), but rather it lays the very foundation for the entire lifetime of the child.[42]

When viewed superficially, education appears to be a means to the desired outcome whereby the child will later grow to a more advanced stage of *mitzvah* fulfillment, when obligated as an adult. R. Schneerson contended that true education is not merely acquisition of cognitive skills and internalization of information, but rather the initiation into the domain of sanctity and provision of a lifetime's foundation that ensures appropriate formation of habits of a child. As stated, education is essential for arousing the quintessential soul[43] and thereby enabling the subduing and positive transformation of negative impulses.[44]

He explained,

> when we view education from an in-depth perspective, education is revealed to constitute the very foundation of the life of the learner... Thus the true notion and concept of education is not only for the child to gain cognitive skills and to internalize information, but rather it is to familiarize and train the child, thereby initiating the child into the domain of sanctity. Through this inauguration and initiation process, the learner's very soul comes in contact with sanctity and G-d and

thereby continues to advance in the service of G-d and
the fulfillment of *mitzvot*, in the way that "also when
the child grows old, [the child] will not depart from it."[45]

R. Schneerson explained[46] that this education provides the
learner with substance and strength for his or her loyal fulfillment
of the Divine imperatives throughout his or her lifetime.

Education in Relation to the Wider Community and Nation

At a communal level, particularly when motivated by selflessness
and altruism,[47] education brings merit to the community:[48] indeed,
a positive educational influence has implications for generations
to come. Conversely, an educational problem affects not only the
contemporary generation but also future generations[49] because it
affects the essence and survival of the Jewish nation.[50] An individual student's advancement as a result of education is reflected
in his or her impact on the community, past, present and future.[51]
Moreover, a contribution to advance education serves as the spring-
board to a community's further expansion and benefits.[52]

In light of its significance, education is also the principal key
to national salvation,[53] particularly in times of crisis.[54] Education's revelation of the equal potential of self-sacrifice is seen as
overcoming enemies[55] and capable of speeding the downfall of a
contemporary Haman and his decrees,[56] serving as the antidote to
persecution[57] and bringing about the salvation of the Jewish people. Jewish education in Torah and Judaism, coupled with hope in
redemption, are antidotes to anti-Semitism and persecution, still-
ing enemies.[58] Consequently, he wrote:

In these days, which are, to borrow the wording of our
Sages (*Sanhedrin* 97b), days of harsh decrees like those of
Haman, the remedy advised by our Sages (*Bava Metzia*

85a) is to educate the son of an unlearned person [and show him his place] in our Torah heritage, and to transform a wicked person into a *baal teshuvah* [returnee], as implied by the interpretation offered by the Targum [Interpretive Aramaic translation of the Pentateuch] and Rashi [Biblical and Talmudic commentator, R. Shlomo Yitzchaki, 1040-1105] to the verse from *Jeremiah* cited in that passage. For this nullifies these harsh decrees. Everyone should picture the entire world as equally balanced between good and evil, and realize that through his good deeds he can tip the balance of the world to good and bring rescue and deliverance. (Rambam, *Mishneh Torah, Hilchot Teshuvah*, 3:4)[59]

No tactics on the part of nations, including decrees, intimidations, conspiracies, and strategies, can succeed against Jewish education.[60] Based on the vision of the Jewish people as "one body" whereby a virtuous deed performed in one location benefits individuals elsewhere, R. Schneerson saw Jewish educational activity in the US as a means to exert a positive influence on the fate of European Jewry.[61] While he was applying this metaphysical principle to his educational recommendations for the Jewish people in a spiritual or mystical context, on other occasions he spoke about the practicalities of education, and saw education as the salvation of all nations in a practical sense, explaining:

A conscious effort is called for to influence other nations, particularly developing countries and beneficiaries of American aid, to upgrade their educational systems with emphasis on those eternal moral and ethical issues which are the very foundation of a civilized society... in a concerted effort to make the world a better and safer place for all... For a human being, the material and spiritual must go hand-in-hand... Many a discreet way can be found to encourage other nations to follow the way of placing education at the top of the national priorities...[62]

R. Schneerson's perception of education as crucial to the wider community and nation is consistent with his recognition of education as an endeavor of universal significance.

Education and the Universe: Catalyst for Redemption

That education is of cosmic significance underscores its central role in the process of universal perfection and Messianic redemption, with education viewed as a central facilitator of redemption.[63] Education, which incorporates love of Torah and the embodiment of *Ahavat Yisrael* and altruism, is the antidote to exile, as caused by disregard for Torah and senseless hatred.[64] Energetic educational activity is crucial to the realization of Messianic redemption, as R. Schneerson stated:

> And in the forefront are those who kindle "the light of G-d [which] is the soul of man" (Proverbs, 20:27) in children... and they have placed them in a position of light... It is through this [uncompromised education] that the miracle will be revealed—"the publicizing of the miracle" where all will behold G-d's wonders at the redemption of His people through our righteous *Mashiach*, speedily in our days, *Amen*, so may it be His Will.[65]

Because of its potential for revealing latent good, R. Schneerson saw education as the key to both moral human beings and contributing to a better world. His anticipation of the Messianic ideal[66] and its urgent realization can be viewed from the educational perspective. In his 1991 call[67] for an education whereby the child is a living exemplification of the Messianic ideal, which focused on contributing to its realization, R. Schneerson was introducing an educational value whose outcome is that the learner must view his or her ensuing conscious thought, speech, or action as crucial factors in bringing this Messianic ideal to fruition. His call is consistent with Maimonides' requirement[68] that every individual view his or her ensuing action, speech, or thought as of crucial significance in a precariously balanced universe. His call implies an innovative application of Judaism's Messianic ideal and belief in universal redemption to the practical living of the learner. This universal view of education underscores the view of education as a priority and essential to life.

Education as the Foremost Priority

The universal significance of education is also reflected in the Talmudic rule[69] that the education of children is not to be interrupted even for construction of the Temple by the *Mashiach* himself.[70] From this educational principle and its application, R. Schneerson deduced that it is even more certainly forbidden to interrupt education for trivial reasons.[71] While it is of particular global relevance in times of crisis, education is no less the priority in times of prosperity, when children were not permitted to abandon their study even to participate in the sacred construction of the Jerusalem Temple.[72]

Given education's all-encompassing scope, its far-reaching significance, and provision of the foundation of a person's lifetime, education is a matter of life itself.[73] It is an endeavor of foremost importance demanding immediate response and an activity that may be characterized by the Talmudic application[74] of the Biblical verse,[75] "A time to act for G-d," to be addressed energetically in the context of its extraordinary urgency.[76] R. Schneerson believed passionately that every day that passes without full utilization of educational opportunities represents an irretrievable loss.[77] The vital nature of education means that it cannot be resigned to a passive role but rather it must take on an extraverted quality.[78] When seen as tantamount to awakening the quintessential soul[79] and as the antidote for the negative impulse,[80] education becomes the priority activity,[81] whereby the need for proactive and pre-emptive educational initiatives reflects this importance and urgency.[82]

Moreover, because education cuts to the very core purpose of life, R. Schneerson argued that it must address the subject of the fundamental objective of living which thinking persons frequently ask themselves. R. Schneerson noted that this was of crucial importance in the case of youth. He thus wrote,

> The question of "what is my life's purpose?" occurs more frequently and with greater force in the minds of the studying youth, who dedicate a number of their best years to study and preparation for their future life lying still fully ahead of them. Moreover, adolescents have untapped resources of energy and enthusiasm which they eagerly desire to put to good advantage. To them, the question of their life's purpose is more urgent and vital than to people of maturer years.[83]

Education as a Heavenly Endeavor

Given its impact at the individual, communal, and cosmic levels, education in R. Schneerson's discourse comprises a vital endeavor,[84] a sacred task,[85] a Heavenly assignment[86] whose value and exalted stature[87] require no explanation[88] and defy quantification.[89] In the same way that educating an individual is the equivalent of influencing an entire universe, so too, seemingly small deeds, for example, the recitation of even one extra blessing by a child as a result of Jewish education, achieve cosmic unity and enable the child who recites this blessing to attain connection within G-d's unity.[90] R. Schneerson pointed out that Abraham's activity as an inclusive educator was the culmination of his lifetime of devotion, and was considered to be even greater than his overcoming other trials. In R. Schneerson's words:

We find that the primary reason why G-d cherished
Abraham our Patriarch is, as it is written: "For he will
command—i.e., connect—his children and his household…" Despite the greatness of his Divine service
in [overcoming] the trials, [these efforts] are not at all
comparable to the importance of commanding—i.e.,
connecting others and bestowing them with merit.[91]

Metaphors That Exemplify
the Nature of Education

It should be noted that R. Schneerson often utilized metaphors to
express his understanding of the nature of education to clarify its
meaning. Metaphors are integral and legitimate to define the nature of education.[92] For example, nineteenth-century philosopher
Pestalozzi[93] and his student Froebel[94] utilized a horticultural metaphor to illustrate their understanding of education, and American
twentieth-century philosopher and educator John Dewey utilized
a biological metaphor to explain the nature of education.[95]

R. Schneerson employed a variety of metaphors to portray what
he considered to be the essence of educational endeavor. These
served as the basis of his contribution to a variety of educational
issues, with citations often serving as springboards for various
practical applications of the metaphor's consequences, succinctly
documented in Table A below.

Under R. Schneerson's exacting analysis, a metaphor would
often yield ramifications diametrically opposed to conclusions derived by other educators. Thus, while the horticultural metaphor
employed by R. Schneerson was also used by other philosophers of
education, R. Schneerson's analysis of this horticultural metaphor
sharply differentiates his usage from the wider educational literature. Pestalozzi and Froebel employ it to support their view that the
educator must stand back and simply allow natural development to
ensue based on the student's personal interests.[96] In contrast, in R.

Table A: Educational Metaphors and Their Ramifications

EDUCATIONAL METAPHOR UTILIZED	EDUCATIONAL RAMIFICATIONS WHICH FOLLOW FROM THE METAPHOR	
1. The Metaphor of Tefillin (Phylacteries)	i	Application to education is akin to the dedication and commitment of mind and heart required when donning tefillin.
2. The Home Construction Metaphor	i	The educator should strive to invest all abilities in education in the same way that people invest all their financial resources and energy in the construction of a home.
3. The Conflagration Metaphor: Education as Kindling a Candle	i	The student's potential awaits activation.
	ii	Education is recommencement of a process to which learners have an intrinsic aptitude.
	iii	Education must be proactive and extraverted, rather than awaiting learner initiative, in the same way that the candelabra must be proactively lit.
	iv	Education is about the uncompromised presentation of ideals, just as only the purest oil was to be used for the candelabra.
	v	Education is synonymous with growth and antithetical to stagnation, as the candles increase in number throughout the festival of Chanukkah.
	vi	Education confronts challenges.
	vii	Education seeks to create an independent learner.
	viii	Educator self-development is a prerequisite for learner development.
	ix	Education is about increasing and enhancing the positive, as the candle is about dispelling darkness by increasing light.

Table continued on p. 44

Table continued from p. 43

EDUCATIONAL METAPHOR UTILIZED	EDUCATIONAL RAMIFICATIONS WHICH FOLLOW FROM THE METAPHOR
4. The Horticultural Metaphor: Education as nurturing a Seedling	i Education is an endeavor that will bear fruit.
	ii Education is an awesome privilege.
	iii Education is an area where small improvements are consequential and repeated effort is worthwhile.
	iv Education means early intervention and ongoing protection.
	v Enthusiasm for education is essential.
	vi Education is an activity requiring investment of effort.
	vii Delineation of the aims of education as corresponding to the roots, trunk, and fruits of a tree: imbuing faith and values, inspiring a life of virtuous conduct, and contributing altruistically to others, to society, and to the universe.
5. The Metaphor of Life-Saving Rescue and Providing Preventative Protection	i Education must take preference over everything and education is the foremost priority not to be delayed.
	ii While education strives to "rescue" as many individuals as possible, educating (rescuing) even one individual is an outstanding achievement.
	iii An educational "call" goes forth that all must heed.
	iv Education is transformational by definition, transforming the student's family members and the very environment of the community.
	v Education (saving one's fellow's life, be it through education or physically) is the ultimate fulfillment of the Biblical command to "Love one's fellow as oneself."
	vi Education is akin to saving the student from "descending into the pit."

Table continued on p. 45

Table continued from p. 44

EDUCATIONAL METAPHOR UTILIZED		EDUCATIONAL RAMIFICATIONS WHICH FOLLOW FROM THE METAPHOR
6. The Philanthropic Metaphor	i	Education is an obligation akin to spiritual charity.
	ii	Education is one of the most refined forms of spiritual charity.
	iii	Education brings merit to the community.
	iv	Education means saving an entire world.
7. The Metaphor of Providing Guarantors	i	Education ensures Jewish continuity.
	ii	Education ensures a glorious future.
	iii	Education sets children on the path of virtue.
	iv	Education is a prerequisite for receiving the Torah.
8. The Procreation Metaphor	i	Education "creates" other individuals.
	ii	Education sets children on the path of virtue.
9. The Metaphor of Disclosure and Extrication of Hidden Treasures	i	Education clears away whatever veils the soul.
	ii	Education reveals latent spiritual potential.
10. The Prenatal Metaphor: Education Is the Reawakening of Intrinsic Awareness	i	Education re-awakens intrinsic awareness.
	ii	Education is focused on innate spiritual receptiveness.
	iii	Education facilitates the learner's truest self-fulfillment.
11. The Empathetic Metaphor: Education as Heeding the Cry of the Learner	i	Education is about sensitivity to the spiritual yearning of a student.

Table continued on p. 46

Table continued from p. 45

EDUCATIONAL METAPHOR UTILIZED	EDUCATIONAL RAMIFICATIONS WHICH FOLLOW FROM THE METAPHOR
12. The Military Metaphor	i Education seeks to achieve submission to authority.
	ii Education seeks to channel negative attributes to positive ends.
13. The Nuclear Metaphor: Education Is Ever-Increasing	i Education instigates a "chain reaction."
	ii Education inhibits negative phenomena like assimilation.
	iii Educational costs are offset by their benefits.
	iv Miniscule educational activities harness potential.
	v Education concerns realizing untapped, limitless potential.
14. Metaphor of the Electric Generator	i Education connects the student to the source of spiritual power.
15. Sundry Metaphors[97]	i Education shows concern for health of the children's soul no less than for children's physical health.
	ii Education implies concern and passion to ensure that homes are characterized by Jewish practice and custom.
	iii Education is the extrication of "the precious and honorable from the vile and corrupt."
	iv The greatness of education defies qualification.
	v Education lays the foundation of the sanctuary by awakening the quintessential soul.

Schneerson's concept, this metaphor served both as the basis for his plea for our urgent, enthusiastic, and maximum contribution to correct perceived negative influences, as well as for our application to achieving even small advancements in the education of a young child.[98] Such efforts are worthy of the educator's utmost application, given their ramifications for later life.

Having communicated R. Schneerson's understanding of the nature of education, the research will now examine the various educational writings predicated upon these axioms, the first of which is the delineation of the educational objectives that R. Schneerson considered to be the aims and goals of education.

Notes

1. Curren, 2007:7.
2. Hirst and Peters, 1970; Peters, 1973; Bowen and Hobson, 1974:16.
3. Barrow and Woods, 1975:11.
4. Cited by Burbules, 2000:7; see also Peters, 1965:87-111.
5. Peters, 1966:24-5.
6. For example, Burbules, 2000:7-8 wrote of R.S. Peters' deliberations, "The results of Peters' investigations—that the term refers to a process of 'initiation' into a form of life, and that to call something 'educational' is to valorise the means and ends of that process (as opposed to socialization into norms that may be instrumentally beneficial but not of intrinsic value)—defined an agenda of questions, and a method of inquiry, that helped shape the approach of a generation of philosophers of education throughout the English-speaking world."
7. H.H. Horne, 1932:474.
8. J. Bowen, 1972:xv.
9. Address of *Ellul* 18th, 5703 [September 18th, 1943] in *SH-RJIS-5703* [1942-3]:170-1.
10. When citing this principle, R. Schneerson would often cite the teachings of the Baal Shem Tov (see footnote below). For an example of BST's application of this principle and for R. Schneerson's explication of this example, see 1st *Farbrengen* of *Shabbat Bereishit, Tishrei* 24th, 5718 [Oct. 19th, 1957] in *TM-HIT,* XXI [5718, I]:133-7, §5-§9.
11. This idea is found in the teachings of the founder of Hasidism, R. Israel Baal Shem Tov (cited in *HaYom Yom,* entry of *Iyar* 9th and in Addenda to *Keter Shem Tov,* Paragraphs 127-9). The notion is based on Biblical

12. See RJIS's statement (*SH-RJIS-5703*:170) cited above as well as *SH-RJIS-5700*:73 & 131, *SM-RJIS-5705*:30 & *SM-RJIS-5711*:131.

13. For example, he wrote (*Letters by the Lubavitcher Rebbe*:268-9), "...G-d who is essentially good created a universe which is likewise good in essence, but... it is the purpose of man to bring forth the latent forces of good both within him and in the world that surrounds him, from the potential into the factual." See also Hebrew letter of *Shevat* 21st, 5704 [Feb. 15th, 1944] in *IK*, I:247-8, Letter 135; Addenda to *LS*, VI:308-9.

14. *LS*, VII:151, footnote 24.

15. Curren, 2007:3.

16. Edited address of Shabbat *Parashat Emor, Iyar* 20th, 5724 [May 2nd, 1964] in *LS*, VII:151, footnote 24.

17. Semi-pastoral letter of *Ellul* 18th, 5710 [Aug. 31st, 1950] published in *IK*, III:462-4, Letter 749; Hebrew (with Yiddish citation from RJIS) semi-pastoral letter of *Nissan* 11th, 5711 [April 17th, 1951] addressed to multiple recipients, published in *IK*, IV:242-3, Letter 972; see also address of *Lag B'Omer, Iyar* 18th, 5711 [May 24th, 1951] in *TM*, III [5711, II]:85-91.

18. These include Talmud, *Sanhedrin* 19b (cited in Rashi's commentary to Numbers, 3:1), *Sifri* and Rashi to Deuteronomy, 6:7, *Tanna Dvei Eliyahu Rabba*, Chapter 27, *Shir HaShirim Rabba* to Song of Songs, 1:4 and Maimonides, *Laws of Torah Study*, 1:2.

19. *Reshimot*, IV:175-81; *IK*, V:277 (footnote).

20. *Letters by the Lubavitcher Rebbe*:268-9; see also Hebrew letter of *Shevat* 1st, 5724 [Feb. 15th, 1944] *IK*, I:247-8, Letter 135; Addenda to *LS*, VI:308-9. Following his introduction, R. Schneerson continued, "Take for example the tree... What can be more common and usual a sight than an ordinary tree? There seems at first glance, nothing in it to arouse in us any special meditation...yet...we can, if we stop to ponder, learn quite a few useful lessons from it."

21. For practical ramifications of this broad understanding of the nature of education, see Chapter 8.

22. *IK*, III:344; *op. cit.*, IV:357; *op. cit.*, I:322-3.; *op. cit.*, XII:380-2; *op. cit.*, XII:445; *op. cit.*, XIII:359; *op. cit.*, XIV:16; *op. cit.*, XIV: 16, 404-6 & 409.

23. *Op. cit.*, XVII:180 where R. Schneerson urges a teacher of agriculture to exert a positive influence in the area of religious education.

24. See *Y'mei Bereishit*:337-41 for the text of R. Schneerson's address at an undated *farbrengen* of 1947-1948, where Sabbath-observant chess champion Samuel H. Reshevsky was present and R. Schneerson derived spiritual directives from chess.

25. For an example from prior to R. Schneerson's assumption of the leadership of Habad, see journal entry of *Sivan* 8th, 5702 [May 24th, 1942] in *Reshimot*, I:374-96.

26. Examples of R. Schneerson's investigation of areas considered incidental by others, include his commentary to *Ethics of the Fathers* which is replete with explorations of connections between the biography of a sage who communicated a particular moral teaching and the content of the teaching (See *TM-HIT-5742*, III: 1,454-7). He similarly repeatedly investigated the connection between a title of a Torah reading and its content (for a classic example drawn from multiple examples see *SH-5748*, II:500-6, and for multiple examples see *Chumash—The Gutnick Edition, The Name of the Parasha*:xl-lviii). He repeatedly derived instruction from the names of sages cited by Rashi in his Torah commentary. (For one of many classical examples, see *SH-5748*, II:501, Section 5, paragraph (i), f.n. 30.)

27. *SK-RJIS-5689-5710* [1929-1950]:153-4, Section 12.

28. *IK*, XXI:12-3, Letter 7,764.

29. See *Haggadah Shel Pesach Im Likkutei Ta'amim, Minhagim U'Biurim*:11 citing Talmud, *Berachot* 5b, where even a child's feigned inappropriate conduct is avoided, given its serious ramifications.

30. *Mishnah, Sanhedrin*, 4:5; Talmud, *Bava Batra*, 11a.

31. *IK*, XV:251-2, Letter 5,569; *op. cit.*, XXII:56-7, Letter 8,274; *IK*, XXVII (*ed.* S.B. Levin):34-5, Letter 10,023; *LS*, XXVI:144.

32. *IK*, IV:176-7, Letter 920; Addenda to *LS*, XXII:342-3.

33. *IK*, I:38-40, Letter 22.

34. *SK-RJIS-5689-5710* [1929-1950]:153-4, Paragraph 12.

35. *IK*, I:112-3; see Letter 66; Addenda to *LS*, XXI:495.

36. *IK*, III:254-5, Letter 572.

37. R. Schneerson believed the merit of engagement in kosher *chinuch* is capable of bringing improved health to the educator's offspring (*IK*, III:251, Letter 569*) and where every additional effort in involvement in education of youth is a rectification for the educator's former inappropriate conduct (*IK*, XXI:100, Letter 7,849 & *IK*, IV:109, Letter 853).

38. Address of *Tammuz* 22nd, 5711 [July 26th, 1951] to students departing on "*Merkos Shlichut*" [pastoral visits to isolated Jewish communities] in *TM*, III [5711, II]:224-6.

39. Yiddish letter of *Ellul* 5th, 5711 [Sept. 6th, 1951] in *IK*, IV:455-7, Letter 1,178.

40. *IK*, I:281-2, Letter 151.

41. Proverbs, 22:10.

42. Letter of *Kislev* 24th, 5735 in *IK*, XXVIII (*ed.* S.Y. Chazan):171-3, Letter 10,344.

43. *IK*, I:112-3, Letter 66; Addenda to *LS*, XXI:495.

44. *IK*, I:281-2, Letter 151.

45. *LS*, XXXV:11-2.

46. *Ibid.*
47. R. Schneerson believed that this applies particularly to the strengthening of Torah and Judaism.
48. *IK*, I:161-2, Letter 89; *op. cit.*:207-8, Letter 542.
49. *Op. cit.*, IV:121-2, Letter 865.
50. The cosmic implication of education finds expression in the understanding that the individual's joy upon becoming *Bar Mitzvah* is a collective communal joy.
51. *Reshimot*, IV:182-3.
52. *IK,* III:207-9, Letter 542. This success is contingent on a fitting individual taking responsibility for this activity.
53. *Op. cit.*, I:69-70, Letter 44.
54. *Op. cit.*, I:93-4, Letter 55.
55. *Op. cit.*, I:95-6, Letter 56; *op. cit.*, I:112-3, Letter 66.
56. *Op. cit.*, I:95-6, Letter 56; *op. cit.*, I:110-2, Letter 65.
57. *Op. cit.*, I:93-4, Letter 55; *op. cit.*, I:95-6, Letter 56 and *op. cit.*, I:112-3, Letter 66.
58. *Op. cit.*, I:78-9, Letter 49; *op. cit.*, I:93-4, Letter 55; *op. cit.*, I:102-3, Letter 60.
59. *Op. cit.*, I:69-70, Letter 44.
60. *Op. cit.*, IV:204-6, Letter 941.
61. *Op. cit.*, XXI:12-3, Letter 7,764 and *Reshimot*, III:75-7.
62. Address of *Shevat* 10th, 5739 [February 7th, 1979] cited in *Education Day U.S.A.: A Tribute and a Message*:36-7 & 42-3.
63. *IK*, I:161-2, Letter 89; Addenda to *LS*, IV:1,333 and *IK*, I:165-6, Letter 92. Education negates the causes of exile, i.e. neglect of Torah and *sinat chinam* [causeless hatred] and the resultant *Galut* [exile] and brings redemption and rebuilding of the *Beit HaMikdash* [Jerusalem Temple] by Mashiach.
64. *IK*, I:163-4, Letter 91 and *op. cit.*, I:167, Letter 93; Addenda to *LS*, XVIII:488.
65. *TM-HIT-5710* (1992 edition):7-8.
66. *LS*, XX:228-34.
67. *SH-5752* [1991-92], I:41; Address of the Eve of *Simchat Torah*, 5752 [September 20th, 1991].
68. Maimonides, *Mishneh Torah, Laws of Teshuvah*, 3:4.
69. *Shabbat*, 119b cited in RSZ, *Laws of Torah Study*, 1:10: "We don't interrupt the study of children even for the building of the Jerusalem Temple..."
70. *TM-HIT*, III [5711, II]:85-91, §19-§27 citing Talmud, *Shabbat*, 119b.
71. *Ibid.*
72. *IK*, I:102-3, Letter 60; Addenda to *LS*, XXI:494.
73. *Reshimot*, III:75-7.
74. Talmud, *Temura*, 14b.
75. Psalms, 119:126.
76. *IK*, I:38-40, Letter 22.
77. *Op. cit.*, I:110-2, Letter 65; Addenda to *LS*, XXI:492.

78. Such was the urgency for education that R. Schneerson felt there was no necessity for the educator to expend time on acquiring proficiency and formal qualifications in the English language.

79. *IK*, I:112-3, Letter 66; Addenda to *LS*, XXI:495.

80. *IK*, I:281-2, Letter 151, citing Talmud, *Bava Batra*, 16a.

81. This is further confirmed by RJIS's greatest concern being that all Jewish children should receive a proper Jewish education. ("A Message to Children on the Passing of Rabbi Joseph Isaac Schneersohn," English letter of *Shevat*, 5710 [Feb., 1950]).

82. *IK*, III:252-3, Letter 571.

83. English letter of *Adar–Rishon* 20th, 5711 [March 28th, 1951] addressed to Ms. Dena Mendelowitz, Vice-President, Jewish Culture Foundation, N.Y., electronically publicized in 2014 by chabad.org. In the same correspondence, R. Schneerson considered addressing the question of the purpose of life to be of particular urgency in the course of Jewish education as it is of even greater importance to members of "The People of the Book" for whom the Torah defines life's purpose. He argued that the epithet "The People of the Book" implied not merely that the Jewish people are a people of education and learning in general, for "The Book" refers to the Torah (Bible) with which Jews are identified. Torah means "instruction," or "guidance," for the Torah is the guiding light. The Torah makes the Jewish people constantly aware of its duties in life, giving a true definition of life's purpose, and by showing the ways and means of attaining this goal.

84. *IK*, IV:93-4, Letter 841.

85. *Op. cit.*, XXI:142, Letter 7,899.

86. *Op. cit.*, IV:371-3, Letter 1,090; *LS*, VIII:368.

87. In this correspondence, though R. Schneerson was referring to specific educational activity that would further enhance the standing of Habad, he pointed out that in general the status of educational endeavor requires no explanation. (See *IK*, III:207-8, Letter 542.)

88. *Op. cit.*, III:207-8, Letter 542.

89. *Op. cit.*, IV:425-6, Letter 1,145.

90. Addresses of *Nissan* 22rd, 5731 [April 17th, 1971], Paragraph 8 and *Nissan* 29th, 5731 [April 24th, 1971], Paragraph 3; *IK*, I:110-2, Letter 65; R. Schneerson explained, (*op. cit.*, I:114-5, Letter 68) [Addenda to *LS*, VII:251] that the blessings recited by children from booklets provide protection for those who helped produce those booklets.

91. *IK*, I:139-40, Letter 84. R. Schneerson explained that this is confirmed by *Bereishit*, 18:19 which cites Abraham's education work of "instruct[ing] his sons and his household after him to keep the way of G-d, acting with charity and justice," rather than any of his other achievements, as the justification for his being "known" [cherished] by G-d.

92. For a fuller examination of the role of metaphor in educational discourse, see I. Scheffler (1960:47-59) and W. Taylor (*ed.*), 1984.

93. See *Address on Birthday*, 1818 by Johann Heinrich Pestalozzi (1749-1827) where he wrote, "Sound education stands before me symbolized by a tree planted near fertilizing water. A little seed, which contains the design of the tree, its form and proportion, is placed in the soil. See how it germinates and expands into trunk, branches, leaves, flower, and fruit! The whole tree is an uninterrupted chain of organic parts, the plan of which existed in its seed and root. Man is similar to the tree. In the newborn child are hidden those faculties which are to unfold during life." R. Schneerson's utilization of this metaphor as a basis for his advocating early intervention was markedly different from, or perhaps antithetical to that of Pestalozzi and Froebel. As Cole (1931:257) has noted, "Pestalozzi would do nothing without the co-operation of the child"...[and as Pestalozzi wrote] 'Let the child use his chalk or pencil freely, assisted occasionally by his teacher, but do not force him into directions that do not appeal to him...Only when the child feels the need of assistance should assistance be extended to him.'" The conclusions derived by Pestalozzi and Froebel from the horticultural metaphor are at odds with the implications derived by R. Schneerson from the horticultural metaphor.

94. Similarly, German educationalist Friedrich Froebel (1782-1857), a loyal disciple of Pestalozzi, wrote: "So the man must be viewed not as already become perfect, not as fixed and stationary, but as constant yet always progressively developing...always advancing from one stage of development to another." See Froebel, *On the Education of Man [Die Menschenerziehung]*, Vienna, 1826:Section 16.

95. Dewey (1934:4-5) argued that "...just as growth does not have an end but is an end, so too, education is not necessarily a matter of age; for education means the enterprise of supplying the conditions which ensure growth, or adequacy of life, irrespective of age." Dewey maintained that "as living has its own intrinsic quality, whether in youth or in maturity, so too the business of education is in keeping with that quality." Much has been written (I. Scheffler, 1960:53*ff*; R.S. Peters, 1977:104-5) about the unsatisfactoriness of the biological metaphor employed by Dewey to impose unity on his theorizing. In light of his biological metaphor, Dewey was constrained to write an entire book entitled *Experience and Education* (New York: Macmillan, 1938) "in order to disclaim responsibility for some of the doctrines and practices of the Progressive Education Movement and to rectify misunderstandings of his more moderate position" (Peters, 1965:94).

96. Froebel required that the teacher have minimal input so as not to distract from the student's intuition when he wrote: "Therefore education, instruction and teaching should in the first characteristic necessarily be passive, watchfully and protectively following, not dictatorial not invariable, not

visibly, interfering... The still young being, even though as yet uncon-
sciously, like a product of nature, precisely and surely wills that which is
best for himself, and moreover, in a form which is quite suitable to him,
and which he feels within himself the disposition, power and means to
represent." (See Froebel, *op. cit.*, section 7.)

97. A variety of further metaphors are periodically found within R. Schneerson's corpus, though being that they do not appear in an educational
context with the same regularity or with an extended educational exposition that accompanies the metaphors listed above, they are cited only
where of relevance to the elements of R. Schneerson's educational discourse. These include metaphors that liken education to the construction
of the Biblical sanctuary to parenting (according to which, concern for
children's physical health must be matched by concern for health of the
children's soul and a passion to ensure homes are characterized by Jewish
practice and custom, see *IK*, IV:434, Letter 1,155; *op. cit.*, V:56-7, Letter
1,272) as well as an extrication metaphor (where education is likened to
the extrication of "the precious and honorable from the vile and corrupt")
(see *IK*, V:114, Letter 1,324) and is therefore an act whose greatness defies
qualification (*op. cit.*, XXI:81, Letter 7,828), a dietary metaphor (*op. cit.*,
IV:227-8, Letter 958) and a pharmaceutical metaphor (*Op. cit.*, III:144-7,
Letter 505).

98. In an English-language letter of *Ellul* 28th, 5730 [September 29th, 1970]
published in *Return to Roots*:222, R. Schneerson stated, "...As has been
often mentioned before, every activity in education should be carried out
with particular enthusiasm, inasmuch as it is like planting a seed, or taking care of a seedling, where every additional effort, however small, will
eventually be translated into extraordinary benefits when the said seed or
seedling becomes a mature fruit-bearing tree. The same is true of the care
taken to shield the seed or seedling from harmful effects..."

CHAPTER 3

THE AIMS OF EDUCATION

Education has two basic purposes: a) to impart a quantity of knowledge to the student; b) to educate the student toward proper conduct in his future life. Each of these areas is obviously comprised of many fields; regarding the behavioral aspect of education, there is the field of interpersonal relations, and the field of the student's individual personality development—the manner in which he will regard his own drives and desires.

—Rabbi Menachem M. Schneerson[1]

The area of the aims of education is an integral element of a comprehensive educational philosophy, as educational aims are both conceptually connected to understanding the essential meaning of education, and central to what it means to be educated,[2] as opposed to being trained or indoctrinated. For this reason, clarification of the aims of education has clear implications for all other elements of systematic educational philosophy. Educational philosopher R.S. Peters confirmed the "particular interrelatedness" of education and aims, noting that education in particular is associated with aims and arguing that "education...has norms built into it, which generate the aims which educators strive to develop or attain."[3] He explained the term "aims" as referring to a suggestion "that is not too near at hand or too easy to attain" and suggested "that the action or activity in question is not obviously structured in relation to such an objective, however important." This is because aims (in both educational and other contexts) motivate people "to specify more precisely what they are trying to do." As well, aims enable "concentration and the direction of effort towards an objective that is not too palpable or close at hand," and they also suggest the "possibility of failure or falling short,"[4] thereby encouraging further educational efforts toward their greater realization.

Furthermore, the aims of education are also intertwined with the content and methodologies for education, and R.S. Peters argued that an educational aim is actually a fusion of content and procedure.[5] Given this understanding, this section will outline what R. Schneerson contributes to this discussion with emphasis on what may be uniquely different.

A discussion of the aims, goals, and objectives of education pervades R. Schneerson's educational discourse, and is especially pertinent in light of his view that in all areas of human endeavor, "every action must have an aim and an appropriate outcome."[6] It is apparent from R. Schneerson's writings that his representation of the aims of education is predicated on ideals established in Kabbalistic as well as the Habad-Hasidic literature. According to R. Schneerson, the aims of education encompass a vast area that includes the individual student, society, and even the universe as a whole. Before exploring his understanding of the aims of education for society and the universe, the aims of education for the individual student are examined.

R. Schneerson considered the foremost aim of education to be the imbuing of belief in a Higher Authority and an awareness of a supernatural dimension to life, whose acquisition is the prerequisite for internalization of values that include self-discipline and selfless idealism. R. Schneerson considered this belief to be a vital precondition for inspiring the learner to opt for a life of virtuous deeds and live life by a higher moral code. Such living, characterized by appropriate conduct and continuing engagement in lifelong character development and self-refinement, was also, in R. Schneerson's view, a pivotal aim of the education process. A parallel aim advocated by R. Schneerson was the student's maximum realization of his or her potential, with ongoing student advancement and self-transformation, thereby ensuring that the learner will ultimately become independent of the teacher's input.

Awareness of a Higher Authority

R. Schneerson employed the horticultural metaphor to both encapsulate the concept of education and delineate its goals and outcomes.[7] He subdivided the aims of education into three broad domains corresponding to the roots, trunk, and fruits of the tree. The first goal, symbolized by the roots, concerns imbuing belief in a Higher Authority and instilling piety and values. He wrote:

> Corresponding to nurturing the roots of the tree is the inculcation of a belief system and values. Just as the roots, hidden from view, link the tree to the soil, allowing and facilitating absorption of vital nutrients from the soil, so too, education must nurture values and beliefs which underlie and motivate a life of purpose and virtue. These are the ethical principles and ideals that underlie our lives.[8]

It is important to note that the Hebrew term employed for piety, *yirat shamayim* [lit. "fear of Heaven"] is misleading when literally translated, given a possible association of fear with "fear of darkness." Due to this association, "awe" is a more accurate translation and "respect" is a more appropriate approximation to the term's inner content. In the context of the husband-wife relationship, the term *yira* refers to the dimension of paying respect and creating boundaries for one's partner, as distinct from an affinity exemplified by closeness. Similarly, the notion of "a Higher Authority," in light of contemporary discomfort with authority, is best understood as being akin to standing in awe, or deferring to the will of one whose ability is incomparably superior to one's own.[9] To

R. Schneerson, the student's awareness of a Higher Authority and the acquisition of piety and values that follow are considered essential prerequisites if education is to perform its broader aims of transforming society's wilderness and rendering it civilization. In a letter written in 1982 in connection with his establishing the *Tzivot Hashem* initiative for children, R. Schneerson wrote:

> Such an acknowledgment [of G-d] is necessary in order to impress upon the minds of the developing child that the world in which he or she lives is not a jungle, where brute force, cunning and unbridled passion rule supreme, but that it has a Master who is not an abstraction, but a personal G-d.[10]

While this letter clearly enunciates the educational aim of imbuing faith, this goal was repeatedly expressed by R. Schneerson. Educating with the aim that the belief and ideals be uncompromised is of such importance in R. Schneerson's discourse that a slight deviation from an ideal in the educational context is seen as threatening to the integrity of the human being and his or her fullest self-realization.[11] To R. Schneerson, such deprivation is analogous to its horticultural equivalent, where, without subterranean roots, a tree is unable to receive its vital nurture and its very integrity is thus jeopardized.[12] R. Schneerson was therefore insistent that education be *al taharat hakodesh*, meaning "of untainted holiness," so that ideals of sanctity and belief are uncompromised.[13] As confirmation of this view, R. Schneerson cited the dismissal by Rabbi Shalom DovBer Schneersohn (the fifth Lubavitcher Rebbe) of his daughters' teacher who had objected to communicating to them anything outside the purely rational, lest teaching about the supernatural might confound the children's intellects. R. Schneerson believed that to instill belief, education should include miracle stories, however astonishing they may be.[14] By introducing belief in the supernatural as a vital component of education, R. Schneerson contended that the student is thereby empowered to rise above and overcome obstacles to his or her fullest realization of spiritual ideals, the obstacle most often resulting from living in a material world whose appealing materialism deflects from or even obscures the individual's desire to pursue pleasures of a spiritual nature.[15]

Therefore, R. Schneerson was insistent that education not be confined to understanding the purely rational and natural world,[16] urging that faith and living by higher principles take priority over the empirical and practical.[17] This is also because he believed that a life based exclusively on human logic and rational deduction without reference to a Higher Power can lead to self-deception where people rationalize the unethical and the immoral.[18] R. Schneerson cited the barbaric acts perpetrated by the Nazis as a timely reminder that without belief in a Divine power, human intellect alone can lead to self-deception. He wrote:

> In our generation we have seen, to our great distress, the ineffectuality of relying on the sense of justice and righteousness imparted by the teacher, or on the influence of the student's elder brother, or even on his fear of the policeman...As for the civilizing influence of the "humanities," we have seen what has transpired in Germany, whose superiority in philosophy, and even "moral philosophy," was world-renowned, but in actuality, that country produced generations of beasts in the form of men.[19]

Thus, education must imbue a faith that transcends both an exclusively rational approach to morality, so that it encompasses supernatural faith as the foundation for the subsequent introduction of reason, and intellectual engagement in the process of spiritual self-realization.

R. Schneerson also advocated a healthy alignment of body and soul,[20] where physical power is based on spiritual foundations, functioning side-by-side with the health of the soul, and integrated with faith and devotion to spiritual and G-dly ideals.[21] This faith includes realization by the learner that Divinity is the animating force and true essence of material physicality.[22] The educator's application of this understanding of education where everything is educational and nothing is outside the domain of education is a direct outcome of belief in a Higher Power, because belief in G-d's unity implies "there is nothing besides Him."[23] From this, R. Schneerson[24] derived the principle whereby everything in the universe is ultimately created for its application for Divine service. Moreover, drawing on the same principle, R. Schneerson argued[25] that there follows the imperative for the student's harnessing of even negative energies for Divine service, given that the negative impulse is also ultimately created for Divine ends. Instilling belief is thus a crucial objective of education, because through it, the student is inspired and empowered to perceive spirituality as the animation of coarse physicality and recognize the pre-eminence of Divinity as the true essence of the material world.[26] He wrote:

> ...among the most primary functions of the school [is] to educate the student to be a human being worthy of his name—as distinguished from a mere beast. And the primary difference between man and beast is that the human being is not subservient to his natural instincts, desires and tendencies, and, at the very least, endeavors to restrain them and control them.[27]

R. Schneerson observed that though the roots of a plant are concealed from sight, they are still the primary facilitators of the life-force of the tree, providing unyielding support so that it is not uprooted by winds. He argued that, in the same way, belief and values nurtured through education connect the student to the Creator and thus to the very source of his or her existence.[28] Faith imbued when young is of importance for later life, as even when a person matures and advances in wisdom, his or her vitality for Torah and *mitzvot* is drawn from faith in G-d and Torah that were nurtured from the earliest years.[29] Education that aims to introduce the learner to the supernatural aspires thereby to elevate him or her from the lowest depths to the highest heights, and to perceive light in the midst of darkness that might otherwise engulf the individual. He wrote:

> It is clear that there exists no other way to implant in the hearts of children and youth a true and functional self-discipline except through the fear or love of a force greater than man. Only in this way can they be truly trained to exercise control over their will and desires. And this is something that cannot be postponed until the child reaches the age of 18, or even the age of 13, while allowing him until then to follow his heart's vagaries, in the hope that the fear of human institutions will direct him along a good and righteous path. One sees no other way than to instil in the hearts of the children, from their earliest years, a strong belief in Him Who created the world and continues to rule it and direct it. In the words of our sages, there is "an eye that sees, an ear that hears, and that all one's deeds are recorded in a book"—a book that cannot be forged, an eye and an ear that cannot be bribed or out-smarted by any schemes or deceptions.[30]

In the same way that the roots draw nurture from the soil and through the roots the branches and leaves gain their vitality, so too, from nurturing belief together with energizing the latent power of *mesirat nefesh* (literally, "self-sacrifice") or selfless idealism and dedication in the learner, the learner derives vitality, because these two phenomena inspire all of a person's Torah and *mitzvot*, symbolized by the trunk of the tree.[31]

A Life of Virtue and Goodness

To R. Schneerson, the second aim of education is to impact on the realm of the learner's deeds and actions and not remain theoretical.[32] Indeed, anything without a practical application was antithetical to

R. Schneerson's educational thinking[33] and he frequently cited Judaism's prioritization of the practical[34] as confirmation of this principle. Therefore, after imbuing the student with an awareness of G-d, the encouraging of a life of virtuous deeds is a priority outcome of the education process.[35] That this virtuous activity be inspired and accompanied by piety[36] was also a major outcome of education in R. Schneerson's discourse. Thus, the second central educational goal in R. Schneerson's educational discourse is to raise a learner who lives a life of virtue, corresponding to the second feature of the tree, namely, the trunk, which is considered indicative of a life of substantial virtuous accomplishment and plentiful good deeds. In R. Schneerson's discourse, such virtuous deeds are the fulfillment of the *mitzvot* (Biblical commandments including the Noahide Laws for humanity), their ramifications for moral behavior, acts of altruism, and benevolence. R. Schneerson's emphasis on virtue in education is compatible with the twenty-first century's increased interest in values education and social or emotional learning in order to facilitate more internalizing and less off-task behavior, both of which are of particular benefit to secondary school students.[37] It is also consistent with capacity-building approaches to education that seek to contribute to healthy interpersonal and intrapersonal functioning by students.

R. Schneerson argued[38] that like an undeveloped seedling, without education, a "seed" with great potential may fail to flourish and develop into a "fully grown tree." He thereby explained that the extent to which we realize our potential will determine just how spiritually significant our lives will be. Education must concern itself with ensuring that students lead spiritually substantial lives characterized by many acts of meaning and positivity. Just as a tree can remain stunted in its growth, staying little more than a sapling, so too, without education, a "seed-like" child with great potential may, in an educational sense, not become "a fully grown tree." From the application of the horticultural metaphor, R. Schneerson derived confirmation for the notion that a principal goal of education is to set the child on the path of appropriate conduct[39] and lead the student in ways of goodness and virtue.[40] In the context of general education, R. Schneerson wrote that "Education...should not be limited to the acquisition of knowledge and preparation for a career."[41] The education system must primarily devote its attention to developing the character of the learner while attaching great importance to moral and principled values. He maintained[42] that "the public schools have *not* succeeded in the area of the student's character development and in training him to curb his desires." He therefore believed that the aims of education must:

> [focus] attention on the ancient ethical principles and moral values which are the foundation of our character as a nation and on the time-honored truth that education must be more than factual enlightenment—it must enrich the character as well as the mind.[43]

He also wrote[44] that "the educational system must...pay more attention, indeed, the main attention, to the building of character, with emphasis on moral and ethical values." A life of fulfillment is one lived with wisdom and virtuous deeds and where an individual's primary, significant preoccupation is with ever-increasing fulfillment of virtuous deeds.[45] While the deeds referred to here include Biblical commands and acts of altruism, even neutral actions that are prerequisites for fulfillment of those deeds, such as eating and sleeping, take on sanctity of their own, as without them the fulfillment of *mitzvot* cannot take place. The healthy alignment of body and soul was an educational aim advanced by R. Schneerson. The aim of education must not be bodily health and physical prowess alone, nor the prioritization of physical strength[46] that sanctifies the animalistic, which may lead to rejecting the spiritual and eventually to adopting inappropriate conduct.[47] Rather, education must aim to produce students whose primary preoccupation is with fulfillment of virtuous deeds. Indeed, education's aim of inspiring a life of wisdom and virtuous deeds is symbolized by the tree trunk whose girth, branches, and leaves must periodically increase, and through which the tree's maturity is ascertained.[48]

Education must strive to enable the learner to find the upright path that provides material and spiritual fulfillment.[49] Educators should therefore aim to raise an individual who aspires to become the most elevated dimension of the human being,[50] being a learner who seeks a daily enhancement of his or her ethical conduct, in the same way that a tree constantly grows in its quality and essence.[51] Furthermore, because "The primary aspect of education and especially the beginning of education is the concept of piety (literally, 'awe of Heaven'),"[52] in the hierarchy of aims of an educational institution, proficiency in language is secondary to instilling piety.[53] Indeed, all other considerations are less important because piety and "awe of Heaven" are prerequisites for a learner who is mindful of G-d and imbued with an attitude of idealism and integrity.[54]

The ideal of virtue accompanied by piety which is the aim of education also expresses itself in the value of modesty.[55] This principle refers not only to physical modesty in a person's attire but also to the ideal of intellectual humility[56] and self-discipline where the learner engages in self-cultivation to curb excessive ego, and takes control of any self-centered perception of the superior status of his or her intellect. If left uncontrolled, intellectual arrogance can lead the individual to determining moral issues independent of Divine imperatives.[57] Moreover, student idealism, devotion and self-sacrifice are expectations which R. Schneerson contends should be inspired by an education that aims for virtue and goodness.[58] Educational goals that R. Schneerson believed to be within the grasp of every learner included the overcoming of all trials and temptations that could deflect from a virtuous life, thus producing a learner who is guided by a high moral code.[59]

R. Schneerson believed that awareness of a Higher Authority was integral to education, encouraging children to live accordingly. R. Schneerson wrote:

> Children have to be trained from their earliest youth to be constantly aware of "the Eye that sees and the Ear that hears." We cannot leave it to the law-enforcing agencies

to be the keepers of the ethics and morals of our young generation. The boy or girl who has embarked upon a course of truancy will not be intimidated by the policeman, teacher or parent, whom he or she thinks fair game to outsmart. Furthermore, the crux of the problem lies in the success or failure of bringing up the children to an awareness of a Supreme Authority, Who is not only to be feared, but also loved.[60]

In the context of Jewish education, nurturing faith is the first educational goal, and even when still not developed to its maximum capacity, it remains vital. Nevertheless, education must include an aim for there to follow an imperative daily advancement by the learner in areas of Torah study and *mitzvah* fulfillment. Imbuing faith must inspire a learner to live a lifestyle in accordance with that faith. This is essential, for otherwise there is no overriding reason for a student not to merely pursue a life of luxury and indulgence.[61] Jewish education must therefore aim to inspire a life of Torah study and *mitzvah* fulfillment on the part of the learner, which must be the substantive focus of their deeds. In this context, Torah study[62] is an act whereby the learner becomes one with Torah teachings in a process for which prayer is also a prerequisite.[63] This second aim of education stresses that a student should not merely attain the necessary knowledge, but that he or she must also acquire the enthusiasm, eagerness, and love for the study of Torah,[64] as well as the fulfillment of its commandments which are vital for Jewish existence.[65]

To R. Schneerson, "Piety is everything,"[66] and Jewish education must aim for the learner to be mindful that life is for action and therefore engage in Divine service and self-cultivation rather than in physical indulgence,[67] with education seeking to draw young people close to the awe of Heaven, to Torah and its *mitzvot*.[68] R. Schneerson insisted that Jewish education does not aim to produce rabbis and *rebbitzens* (wives of rabbis) but rather to raise moral and exemplary individuals, both male and female, upon whose hearts are engraved a religious identity and who are fully aware of the sanctity and purity of Jewish living, even when holding no formal positions as religious functionaries.[69]

Similarly, the primary aim of the *Yeshivah* (Talmudic academy) or *Talmud Torah* (after-school religious instruction) is not the student's acquisition of Torah knowledge, but rather the imbuing of piety, engendering genuine religiosity, and enhancing the practice of *mitzvot*.[70] Jewish education must therefore not aim to merely communicate knowledge but rather produce complete, fulfilled individuals in all areas of their lives.[71] Thus, the aspiration to produce a student who leads a life of virtue and *yirat shamayim* or awe (literally, "Fear of Heaven") is a priority outcome of the education process.[72] R. Schneerson argued that education aims to influence Jewish children and draw them close to piety, love of G-d and His Torah, and to their fellow, conscious that each individual is "a child of G-d,"[73] as well as the fulfillment of *mitzvot*.[74] Not surprisingly, the ideal student will be appropriately focused on the fulfillment of six constant *mitzvot*. R. Schneerson wrote:

> Let each one be engaged with the appropriate attention to the Torah domain of "Duties of the Heart." As is well-known, there are six *mitzvot* whose obligation applies to everyone, at all times and in every location and they are all "Duties of the Heart." They are:
> - To believe in G-d
> - Not to believe in anything besides G-d
> - To believe in G-d's unity
> - To love G-d
> - To be in awe of G-d
> - Not to diverge from G-d's directives by following thoughts of one's heart and visual stimuli.[75]

Such a student will be mindful of the objective to return his or her soul to the Creator in an unblemished state after a life of meaning[76] and actualize his or her potential for *teshuvah* [return to religious observance] to its most sublime level,[77] where "the soul returns to G-d

Who gave it."[78] Not surprisingly, R. Schneerson also reiterated[79] ideals of his predecessors that included the *pnimi*,[80] meaning, one who is concerned for inner integrity and the innermost dimension of a person or thing, and the *atzmi,* meaning, one who is true to oneself.

While the production of a virtuous student follows from belief in G-d, living a virtuous life with only minimal impact on the community is not the final goal of education.[81] Rather, educating a student who inspires virtue and goodness in others, by example or by education, is the third goal of education.

Maximum Realization of Learner Potential

Commenting on the words "A bright flame" in reference to the lighting of the candelabrum in the Sanctuary,[82] R. Schneerson wrote:

> The *menorah* may be ready, its oil and wick may be present in the appropriate vessel, yet this is not enough. It is our task to actually light the *menorah*. This means that we may have unlimited spiritual potential but this potential is not enough. We must activate our soul's fullest potential, so that it grows from being merely a tiny flame to a burning bright flame whose powerful light shines brightly far beyond its immediate environment.[83]

R. Schneerson viewed education as the key to activation of learner potential where a learner engages in both the process of constant self-refinement and spiritual advancement.[84] Such a student replenishes his or her aspirations and engages in self-transformation to the point that Torah permeates his or her whole being and utterly uproots former negative inclinations.[85] This student is capable of changing the past and eradicating former misdemeanors so that no blemish remains.[86] The student is then able to utilize all talents for sacred purposes,[87] striving for maximum application of abilities, so that when capable of elevated Divine service, the individual will not be satisfied with mere menial tasks.[88] Commenting on the words "that rises" in relation to the flame of the *menorah*, R. Schneerson wrote:

> Just as a flame starts out small but grows to be a great flame, so too each of us must never stand still in our *Yiddishkeit*. We must always follow the rule of *ma'alin bakodesh*, meaning to constantly ascend to a higher level in all matters of Torah and *mitzvot*.[89]

Engagement in Self-Transformation

A consequence of the belief in the unity of G-d inspired by education is the realization that "there is nothing besides Him."[90] Given that nothing is independent of G-d, it follows that all phenomena, however negative, can serve a positive role in the Divine plan, which in turn implies the imperative for harnessing a person's negative impulse for Divine service.[91] Education is thus inextricably intertwined with self-transformation because, while teachers initiate the transformative process that is education, the student is thereby inspired to continue this process through engaging personally in an ongoing process of self-transformation. Self-transformation means extricating oneself from negative impulses[92] and particularly from a preoccupation with material concerns.[93] However, for the student to engage in this process of self-transformation, education must provide the knowledge that enables fulfillment of this aim.[94] Education is also of critical importance because each individual is obligated to seek guidance regarding the appropriate path of self-transformation, both in regard to one's own service and even of our neighbors.[95] This process requires clarification of the spiritual standing of the learner, identifying his or her path of service and the learner's connection to a spiritual mentor.[96] Education must also work to extricate the student from the potential danger of enslavement of his or her soul to materialism,[97] until the shackles of its slavery are completely broken. Like Joseph in Egypt who emerged from slavery to become viceroy of Egypt, the G-dly soul can extricate itself to attain the domination of the bodily and material dimensions, thereby enabling the full attainment of its Divinely assigned goal.[98]

The learner can approach self-transformation with confidence,[99] knowing that Divine assistance ensures victory in this task of controlling the body and material world.[100] The process[101] involves probing the innermost recesses of self[102] and transforming even inner forces of darkness.[103] In harmony with Habad-Hasidic philosophy,[104] R. Schneerson cited[105] the idea that the purpose of the descent of the soul into the world is to achieve an ascent, which occurs when the soul transforms the body and its bodily drives and even elevates the physical environment.[106] The ideal student will continually derive life-lessons for Divine service and for the process of self-transformation from all matters, even from worldly phenomena and certainly from matters pertaining to Torah and *mitzvot*.[107] The outcome of this process will be a fusion of body and soul in the service of G-d.[108] For example, harnessing the individual's natural talents and physical aspirations for G-dly purposes can harmonize the physical with the spiritual. When others living a more G-dly life are inspired by a person's musical[109] or artistic[110] expression, this synthesis of natural talent and G-dly causes occurs. Likewise, channeling physical or sporting abilities for spiritual ends elevates these talents and allows individuals in possession of such abilities to find their truest self-fulfillment.[111]

Self-transformation occurs through self-discipline and a comprehension of the greatness of Divine service,[112] characterized by the harmonious utilization of even contradictory emotions for Divine ends.[113] In terms of the flame metaphor cited by R. Schneerson,[114] just as oil combines with the wick of a candle, so too, the body and G-dly soul must work together to illuminate the animal soul so that these unite in harmony to serve G-d.

At its deepest, most mystical dimension, education aims to awaken the quintessential soul of the learner[115] and achieve his

or her transformation,[116] seeking to accomplish a turnaround in
the mind and heart of the student.[117] In the context of the Habad-
Hasidic psychological system,[118] life involves a war between our
G-dly soul and our body with its animal soul, where the body and
animal soul have a prior claim over the G-dly soul as the animal
soul occupied the body first.[119] Learners must wean themselves off
their negative impulses and achieve mastery of their bodily and
animalistic impulses.[120] Such a learner will not make the animalistic or the materialistic *per se* the focus of life, as these consequently
become the means to ends of spirituality and sanctity.[121]

It is important that this ideal is not confused with asceticism, as
Hasidic philosophy believes that engagement in material and bodily
activity is an essential aspect of the totality of our spiritual service.
This process implies conquest of the body and all negative impulses[122]
because people are mindful of the objective to return their soul unblemished[123] after its earthly sojourn. This raises the potential for
teshuvah to its most sublime level, as represented by the Biblical
verse,[124] "the soul returns to G-d Who gave it." Self-transformation
includes breaking an inappropriate character trait by devoted application to its corresponding positive attribute, leading to refinement
of our desires by utilizing them for exclusively positive ends.[125] Trials and temptations are overcome by being guided by the higher
moral code that accompanies us, starting from the time a child first
received education in matters of morality and spiritual accountability.[126] This is an ongoing process because the individual must
continually increase in spiritual light and sanctity,[127] constantly
seeking mastery of thought, speech and action, with the heart
prompting the head to inspire appropriate conduct.[128]

Independence from Teachers

R. Schneerson believed education should produce students capable
of independence,[129] as encountered in the metaphor of "kindling
the 'light of the soul'" until it lights by itself for a lifetime.[130] He

cited his predecessor, RJIS, as striving to produce a learner whose study is eventually independent of external motivation from the educator.[131] Utilizing the conflagration metaphor and obligation to kindle the candelabra until its flame lights independent of this combustion, R. Schneerson wrote:

> *On its own:* This means that like the flame burning bright, without continued input from the source of its initial ignition, so too must we grow to stand on our own, independent of outside help. We must learn Torah of our own desire and perform *mitzvot* without being told [to do so] by parents and teachers…[132]

R. Schneerson further applied this metaphor in support of three ideals central to his educational agenda, namely:

(i)   the maximal realization of learner potential;

(ii) the utmost *tangible* expression of the learner's potential; and

(iii) the ongoing nature of educational endeavor which empowers the student to, of their own accord, continue the process independently. While sparked by the educator, education must continue independent of the educator.

He thus wrote:

> *Parashat Beha'alotecha* begins with the *mitzvah* of the lighting of the *menorah*. Commenting on the words "when you light the candles," Rashi points out that instead of the usual word for lighting, *l'hadlik*, the Torah uses the word *Beha'alotecha* which means "to raise up" (its root is the same as that of the word *aliyah* meaning "rising up"). Rashi explains that this word is used as it signifies that there is a *mitzvah* for the person lighting

the *menorah* not merely to kindle the *menorah* but to ensure that its flame becomes a *shalhevet ha'olah me'aleha*,
[a bright burning flame that rises on its own]...[133]

Undaunted by Derision

In light of the sometimes antagonistic attitude of society to values considered vital in the Jewish tradition, an educational aim articulated by
R. Schneerson was that of raising a learner who is undaunted by derision but capable of withstanding even opposition to his or her ideals
or values. Such a learner, notwithstanding the secular sentiment of
his or her environment, ignores ridicule and proactively declares spiritual values to others, irrespective of their popularity.[134] Such a learner
is unshaken by the challenges of being part of a spiritual minority[135]
and is filled with the strength to live a life of self-sacrifice and selfless devotion, defying peer pressure that opposes acting morally and
maintaining idealistic principles, irrespective of their lack of popularity.[136] This student is self-confident and unembarrassed, proceeding
undeterred by the challenges of the physical power of others because
he or she has the courage to withstand such opposition.[137]

When a student is at one with the ideals he or she exemplifies
for others[138] and undeterred by offensiveness and opposition, he or
she exhibits a level of great commitment and idealism, inspired to
being a motivation to others,[139] becoming ready to transform his
or her colleague.

A Life of Altruism and Influencing Society

As a corollary of this all-encompassing educational goal, besides inspiring a learner to be engaged in his or her own virtuous conduct,
according to R. Schneerson, education aims to empower students
to transform others in a way that these others serve as exemplars
and models of changed behavior.[140] Thus, to R. Schneerson, the

third aim of education, symbolized in the horticultural metaphor by the fruits of the tree, is producing a learner who has been empowered to engage in selfless, altruistic endeavor and thus strives to exert a positive influence on others. R. Schneerson wrote:

> It is, however, *the fruits,* which represent the ultimate "achievement" and the peak of growth and perfection of the tree—especially since the seeds in the fruit are the means by which the tree produces more of its own kind, bringing about the growth of generation after generation of new trees. From *the fruits,* we learn that we too reach the peak of our perfection and growth when—in addition to fulfilling all those duties that are *our own* responsibility—we also exert a positive influence on our friends and all people in our environment so that they too become "trees" possessing strong "roots," a trunk and branches and come to bear fruit. In other words, the people with whom we come in contact should as a result of our influence also possess basic tenets of faith, Torah, and good deeds, as well as exerting further positive influence on many others. By influencing others, we fulfill the goal and purpose of our creation. When we act in this way, our action bears fruits and fruits of fruits, generation after generation, and all the immense merit of this ever-spreading process is attributable to us![141]

Developing the horticultural metaphor to further clarify the aims of education, R. Schneerson observed that just as the tree's contribution is ongoing from generation to generation, so too, the tree continually bears fruit[142] and becomes the measure in which a person's life has exerted a transforming effect on others.

Inspiring altruism where the learner aspires to transform others is also crucial to learner self-fulfillment. Human perfection and truest self-realization are attained precisely by exerting a transformational influence on others so that they realize the purpose of their creation.[143]

Altruism is a vital aim of education because a person achieves self-fulfillment when, besides his or her own appropriate behavior, that person exerts a positive influence on others and the environment, so that these too act and react appropriately. This is akin to a "seed" that gives forth roots, a stem and branches and fruits, which bear the seeds of more fruits. Indeed, this is one of the purposes of creation, that people's virtuous deeds should be cumulative, like the fruits that represent the tree's fulfillment and self-realization.[144]

The goal and desired outcome of education and its fundamental purpose is to "enliven the dead" by educating others and adding a dimension of "essential life" to the living person who is otherwise oblivious to the vital aspects of life.[145] This aim of education also includes a goal to influence society in general by producing students who will make a productive contribution to society as a whole. As R. Schneerson wrote:

> And because every student grows up to be an educator, whether as a parent or a teacher, or even simply as a member of society in which he or she lives, Jews have been inspired in their educational efforts by an unshakeable belief that the effects of education are lasting and cumulative and reproduce from generation to generation.[146]

Whereas many other educational thinkers[147] are focused on the learner's own development and pay little attention to the need for the learner to enlighten others,[148] R. Schneerson was insistent that a crucial component of education was agency and empowerment of the learner, so that the learner becomes an agent of change. Examination of R. Schneerson's utilization of both the horticultural metaphor and the conflagration metaphor, where lighting the *menorah* is viewed as indicative of the educational process,[149] reveals his conviction that the learner's positive impact on other learners is an essential prerequisite for the learner's own successful educational achievement.

The ideal student is committed to educating the child of the unlearned.[150] A corollary of this aim is the production of a student who is inspired to transform his or her fellow human being[151] in fulfillment of the ideals[152] of transforming the wicked into a repentant person and "extracting the precious from the corrupt,"[153] which R. Schneerson saw as the highest good.[154] Such a student will seek to transform and actualize the potential of his or her fellow for *teshuvah* to its most sublime level[155] where "the soul returns to G-d Who gave it."[156]

Furthermore, education aims to produce students who are prepared to set themselves aside to lead and educate others,[157] thereby making an impact on them.[158] To R. Schneerson, education thus aims to educate a student with the determination to at least exert an influence on his or her immediate environment,[159] to take youth in hand and capture their hearts.[160] Education must aim to cultivate an attitude of selfless devotion in the altruism displayed by the student[161] who is not only preoccupied with his or her self, but whose concern for others, characterized by self-sacrifice, is a pivotal aspect of his or her own self-fulfillment.[162] Such a student must acquire a feeling of responsibility for the welfare of his or her fellow humans. This feeling of responsibility must be especially robust among youth, because they are recipients of G-d's generous blessing of enormous powers of enthusiasm, strength, and excitement.[163] R. Schneerson aimed for education to raise a student who influences the environment[164] and disseminates belief in G-d and spiritual values in his or her environment.[165] In summary, to R. Schneerson, education is by very definition transformational,[166] aiming to achieve "the correction and transformation of one's self, one's body and vital soul"[167] as well as "one's fellow and one's portion in the world,"[168] emphasizing his cosmic view of the outcomes of education.

Empowering the student was a crucial element of R. Schneerson's view of the aims of education. By producing a learner who is an exemplary role-model of virtue[169] and raising students who are "shining lights"[170] who exemplify ideals,[171] then these exemplary youth[172] (who are described as "signs and wonders") can even influence and illuminate their own parents' homes.[173] This ideal has been a central aspect of Habad education, since the foundation of the Habad *Tomchei Temimim Yeshivah* by RSB, who wanted *Tomchei Temimim* students to be *nerot l'ha'ir* ["lamps to diffuse light"],[174] or exemplars whose behavior replicates time-honored Habad ideals,[175] such as engaging in lengthy, contemplative prayer.[176] While the learner's exerting an impact on his or her contemporaries is an aim deserving of significant educator effort, the extent of the learner's influence extends even to future generations, with this educational aim including the creation of a learner who perpetuates his or her spiritual heritage to their offspring.

Perpetuation of Spiritual Heritage and Values

To R. Schneerson, a pivotal objective of education is to raise an upright generation in all aspects, despite unfavorable environmental and temporal conditions,[177] by protecting them from "dangerous gusts."[178] A clear ideal that emerges from R. Schneerson's discourse is transmission of a person's spiritual heritage and faith to future generations, especially to youth,[179] with a view to raising a new upright generation with pride and honor in their Jewish heritage.[180]

For example, R. Schneerson saw the role of educating girls at Beth Rivkah schools as one of producing students loyal to Torah who will be sisters, wives, and the mothers of the next generation, upholding the faith of the Jewish people.[181] These graduates would be people in whom the entire Jewish people can take pride.[182]

According to R. Schneerson, acting to perpetuate the Torah among the young generation in particular contributes toward the enlightenment of the world universally and brings real happiness to those engaged in this task, the Jewish people, and humanity in general.[183] Because perpetuation of a person's heritage for three generations represents the truest self-fulfillment,[184] in order to achieve this, education must seek to raise a student who himself aims to raise his or her children in the path of that education, and will in turn educate their children to aspire to study Torah.[185]

A Learner's Transformation of the Universe

Education does not merely seek to impact on the learner alone or on the broader society, but is of cosmic significance, exerting an impact on the universe. The ultimate aims of education include revealing the Divine presence in the material world, the subjugation of evil, and transformation of darkness into light so that the infinite light of the Divine will shine forth.[186] Education is crucial to the fulfillment of this goal because it produces a human being who contributes through his or her engagement in Divine service, to bringing the universe closer to its ultimate perfection.[187]

R. Schneerson believed[188] that education must aim to produce a learner who is mindful of the principle enunciated by Maimonides that one's every thought, speech, or action is of cosmic significance.[189] Such a learner sees the world as precariously balanced, where one good thought, speech, or deed can "tip the balance of the world to good and bring rescue and deliverance."[190] Universal transformation also occurs because of the educational ideal whereby Torah absorbed by the student influences and permeates the mundane world,[191] for example, when Torah ideals define and prescribe ethical conduct in the world of commerce.[192] Similarly, the utilization of material substance for the performance of a *mitzvah* achieves this transformation because the *mitzvah*'s fulfillment draws G-d's infinite light into the body and animal soul of the individual and into the material substance through which the *mitzvah* is accomplished.[193] Consequently, this ideal of transforming the universe is realized when the Torah enlightens a person's most external affairs and illuminates even forces antithetical to holiness.[194]

R. Schneerson's understandings of the concept of education have led directly to his delineation of educational aims. His educational thinking is focused on action, with a Habad imperative that abstract deliberations about education inspire tangible initiatives.[195] At a global level, education aims to inspire the learner to make a contribution that will significantly play a part in repairing and healing the universe, through the learner's exemplary conduct which has a broad impact. The nature of the authority for the intervention required for fulfillment of these goals needs to be clarified.

Notes

1. *Op. cit.*, XXII:494-7, Letter 8,664.
2. R.S. Peters, 1973,11-29.
3. *Op. cit.*, 17.
4. *Op. cit.*, 14.
5. *Op. cit.*, 24-7.
6. *IK*, IV:454-5; Letter 1,177 [Addenda to *LS*, IX:306-7].
7. R. Schneerson qualified this delineation by explaining that the three broad aims of education derived from the horticultural metaphor are to be attained in a genuine way and not merely superficially (*IK*, II:314-6, Letter 343).
8. *LS*, VI:308-9; *IK*, I:247-50, Letter 135 and its variant version in Letter 136.
9. Address of Rabbi Simon Jacobson to the Habad fraternity of Sydney, Australia, on September 21st, 2014 at Chabad of Double Bay.
10. R. Schneerson cited insubordination and lack of subordination to authority as motivations for his founding *Tzivot Hashem* for children in 1981. See letter of *Tevet* 26th, 5742 [Jan. 21st, 1982] (published in *Letters from the Rebbe*, VI: 190-4, Letter 133) in response to reservations that the *Tzivot Hashem* Campaign was based on "the glorification of the military and aggrandisement of arms, wars and battlefields."
11. *IK*, I:249-50, Letter 136; *TM-5710* (1992 edition):7-8.
12. *IK*, I:247-8, Letter 135.
13. *Op. cit.*, I:56-7, Letter 34.
14. *LS*, XIX:91-3, §5-§6.
15. *Reshimot*, II:114-22 [*Reshima* No. 19] and *op. cit.*, IV:254-62 [*Reshima* No. 138].
16. *IK*, I:249-50, Letter 136.
17. *Reshimot*, II:114-22 [*Reshima* No. 19].
18. *Op. cit.*, II:95-101 [*Reshima* No. 17].
19. *IK*, XXII:494-7, Letter 8,664.
20. *Op. cit.*, IV:328-9, Letter 1,051.
21. *Reshimot*, II:100 [*Reshima* No. 17].
22. *Op. cit.*, IV:254-62 [*Reshima* No. 138].
23. Deuteronomy, 4:39 as elucidated in *Tanya*, Section 2:Ch. 6.
24. *Reshimot*, IV:175-81 [*Reshima* No. 130].
25. *IK*, I:154-7, Letter 86.
26. *Reshimot*, IV:254-62 [*Reshima* No. 138].

27. *IK*, XXII:494-7, Letter 8,664.

28. *Op. cit.*, I:247-8, Letter 135. To ensure the nurture of pristine, untainted belief, the educator must ensure that no negative influences corrupt the communication of ideals.

29. *Op. cit.*, I:249-50, Letter 136.

30. *Op. cit.*, XXII:496.

31. *Op. cit.*, I:249-50, Letter 136.

32. *SH-5749* [1988-89], I:415.

33. *LS*, VIII:110.

34. *Avot* 1:17.

35. *IK*, IV:213-5, Letter 949.

36. The Hebrew term is *yirat shamayim*, literally translated as "fear of Heaven."

37. See M.E. Elias and H. Arnold (*eds.*), 2006; Merrell and Gueldner, 2010.

38. *IK*, I:247-50, Letters 138 and 139; *LS*, VI:308-9.

39. Addenda to *LS*, X:210-1 (Undated letter of 5704 [1943-4]).

40. *IK*, XXI:45-6, Letter 7,795.

41. Address of *Nissan* 11th, 5738 [April 18th, 1978] in *SK-5738*, II:116-35, §7-§51.

42. *Ibid.*

43. English letter of *Nissan* 25th, 5742 [April 18th, 1982] addressed to US president Ronald Reagan.

44. English letter of *Shevat* 29th, 5739 [February 26, 1979] addressed to US vice-president William F. Mondale in *Letters from the Rebbe*, II:204-5, Letter 96.

45. *IK*, I:249-50, Letter 136.

46. *Reshimot*, II:95-101 [*Reshima* No. 17].

47. *Op. cit.*, II:95-101, [*Reshima* No. 7].

48. *IK*, I:247-8, Letter 135 and *op. cit.*, I:247-8, Letter 135.

49. *Op. cit.*, I:183-4, Letter 100.

50. *Op. cit.*, III:350, Letter 652.

51. *Op. cit.*, I:249-50, Letter 136.

52. *Op. cit.*, IV:447, Letter 1,169.

53. English letter of 4th Day *Chanukkah*, *Kislev* 28th, 5715 [Dec. 23rd, 1954] *Letters from the Rebbe*, II:41-5, Letter 15.

54. *IK*, IV:447, Letter 1,169.

55. *Op. cit.*, IV:67-8, Letter 821.

56. *TM-HIT* [5711, I], II:91-2 & 94-5, §13-§14 & §17.

57. *IK*, IV:216, Letter 950.

58. *Op. cit.*, IV:14-6, Letter 780.

59. *Letters of the Rebbe*, III:17-8, Letter 11.

60. *Op. cit.*, IV:64-74, Letter 38.

61. *Reshimot*, II:95-101 [*Reshima* No. 17].

62. Here there are dual components of Torah study, namely, the acquisition of Torah knowledge and constant application to study. (See *Reshimot*, II:260-8 [*Reshima* No. 30].)

63. *IK*, I:42-4, Letter 25.

64. This ideal of devotion to Torah study is symbolized by Jacob's prioritization of interaction with the elderly sages of his time (Shem and Eber) over socializing with the contemporaries of Esau (*Reshimot*, II:114-22 [*Reshima* No. 19]). Engaging in the study of both Talmud and Hasidic philosophy was to be with vitality, enthusiasm, and excitement (*IK*, V:26-7, Letter 1,246).

65. *Letters from the Rebbe*, III:6-7, Letter 5.

66. *TM-HIT*, III [5711, II]:85-92, §19-§27 & §29.

67. *Reshimot*, III:145-50 [*Reshima* No. 59].

68. *IK*, IV:109-10, Letter 854.

69. *Reshimot*, II:60-8 [*Reshima* No. 30]; *IK*, III:435-6, Letter 730.

70. *IK*, IV:113-4, Letter 858 and *op. cit.*, 213-5, Letter 949.

71. *Op. cit.*, IV:469-70, Letter 1,188.

72. *Op. cit.*, IV:213-5, Letter 949.

73. *Op. cit.*, IV:109. Letter 853.

74. *Op. cit.*, IV:109-10, Letter 854.

75. *Op. cit.*, XXI:12-3, Letter 7,764.

76. *Reshimot*, IV:175-81 [*Reshima* No. 130].

77. *IK*, I:186-7, Letter 102.

78. Ecclesiastes, 12:7.

79. *IK*, III:472-4, Letter 755.

80. RSB, *Torat Shalom*, 39*ff.*

81. See *LS*, III:880-1.

82. Numbers, 8:2.

83. Address of *Sivan* 19th, 5751 [June 1st, 1991] (see *SH-5751*, II:601ff.).

84. *IK*, XXI:12-3, Letter 7,764.

85. *Op. cit.*, I:122-4, Letter 74.

86. *Op. cit.*, I:42-4, Letter 25.

87. *Op. cit.*, I:250-1, Letter 137; see also *IK-RJIS*, VIII:136.

88. *Op. cit.*, II:314-6, Letter 343.

89. Address of *Sivan* 19th, 5751 [June 1st, 1991] in *SK-5751*, II:601*ff.*

90. See Deuteronomy, 4:39 as explained in *Tanya, Shaar HaYichud V'HaEmunah*:Chapters 1-4.

91. *IK*, I:154-7, Letter 86.

92. *Reshimot*, II:95-101 [*Reshima* No. 17].

93. *Op. cit.*, IV:254-62 [*Reshima* No. 138].

94. *IK*, I:183-4, Letter 100.

95. *Op. cit.*, II:314-6, Letter 343.

96. *Ibid.*

97. *IK*, IV:245-6, Letter 975.
98. *Letters of the Rebbe*, III:17-8, Letter 11; *IK*, II:314-6, Letter 343.
99. *TM*, II [5711:I]:311-23.
100. *IK*, II:168-9, Letter 246.
101. The Biblical obligation to remember the Exodus from Egypt (Deuteronomy, 16:3) is symbolic of this self-transformation. (See *IK*, IV:14-6, Letter 780.)
102. English letter of *Adar–Rishon* 20th, 5711 [March 28th, 1951] Addressee: Ms. Dena Mendelowitz, Vice-President, Jewish Culture Foundation, N.Y. (Electronically publicized in 2014 by chabad.org.)
103. *IK*, I:62-3, Letter 39; *op. cit*, I:63-4, Letter 40.
104. *Tanya*, Section I:Chapter 31 and *Iggeret HaKodesh*, Chapter 23; *Likkutei Torah, Vayikra*:41a.
105. *IK*, II:159-61, Letter 241*; *Yemei Bereishit*:337-41.
106. *IK*, I:211-3, Letter 118.
107. *Reshimot*, I:374-96 [*Reshima* No. 13] (Based on Ecclesiastes, 12:13 and Deuteronomy, 6:24).
108. *IK*, I:194-6, Letter 108.
109. Unpublished English letter of *Av* 15th, 5738 [Aug. 18th, 1978] addressed to "All Participants in the Chasidic Song Festival, Sydney, Australia"; see also *Letters from the Rebbe*, VI:95-6, Letter 67.
110. *IK*, XXIX (*ed*. S.B. Levin):108, Letter 11,082; See *Letters From the Rebbe*, I:2 & *op. cit*., V:91-2, Letter 66.
111. *Reshimot*, IV:175-81 [*Reshima* No. 130]; *SK-5740*, II:810-20, §28-§39.
112. *IK*, I:75-8, Letter 48.
113. *Op. cit*., II:159-61, Letter 241*.
114. *Op. cit*., IV:228-9, Letter 959.
115. *IK*, I:112-3, Letter 66. Here, R. Schneerson noted that it is precisely such an education that is the salvation of our nation and the antidote to Haman.
116. *Op. cit*., I:214-5, Letter 120.
117. *Op. cit*., IV:56-7, Letter 812.
118. See *Tanya*, Section 1.
119. *IK*, II:168-9, Letter 246.
120. *Reshimot*, IV:175-81 [*Reshima* No. 130].
121. *Op. cit*., II:114-22 [*Reshima* No. 19].
122. *IK*, I:281-2, Letter 151.
123. *Reshimot*, IV:175-81 [*Reshima* No. 130].
124. *IK*, I:186-7, Letter 102.
125. *Op. cit*., II:314-6, Letter 343.
126. *Letters of the Rebbe*, III:17-8, Letter 11.
127. *IK*, IV:94-6, Letter 842.
128. *Op. cit*., III:239-41, Letter 560.
129. R. Schneerson himself applied this principle, as indicated by his expectation that his devotees in Canada act independently to decide how to best

implement four education suggestions. He thus wrote (*I.K.*, I:38-40, Letter 22), "I rely on your understanding."

130. *Op. cit.,* I:83-4, Letter 53.

131. *Op. cit.,* IV:53-4, Letter 810.

132. *SH-5749* [1989], II:526-7.

133. *Ibid.* He pointed out, "If we analyze each of the three words used by Rashi in the phrase *shalhevet ha'olah me'aleha* (meaning 'a bright flame,' 'that rises,' 'on its own') we see that each conveys a potent directive for just how we can best serve G-d."

134. *Reshimot,* III:145-50 [*Reshima* No. 59].

135. *Ibid.*

136. *IK.,* IV:175-81 [*Reshima* No. 130]; *IK,* IV:328-9, Letter 1,051.

137. *IK,* IV:342-3, Letter 1,062.

138. *Op. cit.,* III:246-8, Letter 566.

139. For an understanding of this concept, R. Schneerson would cite the frequently used Jewish legal term of *Tofe'ach Al M'nat L'Hatfi'ach,* meaning, "a state of saturation to the extent whereby this item dampens other items with which it comes in contact."

140. *IK,* I:110-2, Letter 65.

141. *Op. cit.,* I:247-8, Letter 135.

142. *Ibid.*

143. R. Schneerson argued (*IK,* I:249-50, Letter 136) that the notion of the student exerting an influence on others, represented by the fruits of the tree, is in harmony with the plan of creation and its ultimate goal, as evidenced by the belief that prior to the sin of the Tree of Knowledge all trees bore fruit as will all barren trees in the Time to Come.

144. *Op. cit.,* I:247-8, Letter 135; *op. cit.,* I:249-50, Letter 136.

145. *Op. cit.,* III:265-6, Letter 579.

146. Unpublished letter of *Iyar* 1st, 5740 [April 17th, 1980] addressed to all participants in the dedication of the new building of Yeshiva College, Sydney, Australia. See also *IK,* V:67.

147. For example, Pestalozzi and Froebel focus on the development of the learner as an individual rather than on the learner's obligations to enlighten others.

148. At the time of R. Schneerson's assumption of leadership of Habad, this attitude was prevalent among Jewish educators to the point that R. Schneerson dedicated a large number of his early addresses and pastoral letters to identifying the fallacy of this approach. (See *LS,* III:880.) Interview of November 29th, 1981 with Rabbi Yosef Wineberg.

149. *SH-5750,* II:504*ff*; *IK,* XXIII:403-4, Letter 8,990.

150. In the context of Jewish education, this phrase refers to a person from a family devoid of Torah knowledge and the obligation to show that

individual "his or her place in Torah" (*IK*, I:62-3, Letter 39; *op. cit.*, I:63-4, Letter 40).

151. *IK*, I:75-8, Letter 48.
152. Talmud, *Bava Metzia*, 85a; *Targum* & *Rashi* to Jeremiah, 15:19.
153. *IK*, V:114, Letter 1,324.
154. *Op. cit.*, I:62-3, Letter 39; *op. cit.*, I:63-4, Letter 40; *op. cit.*, I:69-70, Letter 44; *op. cit.*, I:78-9, Letter 49.
155. *Op. cit.*, I:186-7, Letter 102.
156. Ecclesiastes, 12:7.
157. *LS*, I:63-5.
158. *TM*, IV [*HIT-TM -5712*:I]:227-31.
159. *IK*, V:107-8, Letter 1,317.
160. *Op. cit.*, IV:242-3, Letter 972.
161. *Reshimot*, IV:175-81 [*Reshima* No. 130].
162. *Op. cit.*, IV:182-3 [*Reshima* No. 130].
163. *TM*, III [5711, II]:333-5.
164. *IK*, IV:342-3, Letter 1,062.
165. *Ibid*.
166. *IK*, I:61-2, Letter 38; *op. cit.*, I:62-3, Letter 39; *op. cit.*, I:63-4, Letter 40.
167. *Op. cit.*, II:159-61, Letter 241*.
168. *Op. cit.*, I:211-3, Letter 118; *op. cit*, I:213-4, Letter 119. According to Hasidic philosophy, fulfillment of these transformational tasks are the purpose of the soul's descent to the body.
169. *Reshimot*, III:145-50 [*Reshima* No. 59].
170. *IK*, IV:228-9, Letter 959.
171. *Op. cit.*, III:251-2, Letter 570.
172. *Op. cit.*, IV:202-4, Letter 940
173. *Op. cit.*, IV:170-1, Letter 914.
174. *HIT-TM*, IV [*HIT-TM-5712*:I]:227-31.
175. *IK*, V:26-7, Letter 1,246. The *yeshivah* was to replicate *Tomchei Temimim* but would incorporate essential changes appropriate to the contemporary environment.
176. R. Schneerson directed (*op. cit*, XXI:141-2, Letter 7,898) that if praying at length was to cause one to miss part of the *yeshivah* schedule, it was to be rectified with additional hours of Torah study after formal conclusion of the daily *yeshivah* program.
177. *Op. cit.*, I:284-6, Letter 153.
178. *Op. cit.*, IV:469-70, Letter 1,188.
179. *Reshimot*, II:95-101 [*Reshima* No. 17]; *op. cit*, II:114-22 [*Reshima* No. 19].
180. *IK*, I:56-7, Letter 34.
181. *Op. cit.*, I:95-6, Letter 56.
182. *Op. cit.*, I:183-4, Letter 100; *IK*, XXI:45-6, Letter 7,795.
183. English letter of *Adar-Sheni* 19th, 5711 [March 27th, 1951].

184. Talmud, *Bava Metzia*, 85a.

185. *IK*, IV:84-5, Letter 833.

186. *Op. cit.*, IV:213-5, Letter 949; *op. cit*, IV:216, Letter 950.

187. *Reshimot*, IV:175-81 [*Reshima* No. 130].

188. *IK*, I:69-70, Letter 44.

189. *Op. cit.*, XXI:38-9, Letter 7,787.

190. Maimonides, *Mishneh Torah, Laws of Teshuvah*, 3:4.

191. The notion of purification of the environment through recitation of Torah (*IK*, I:38-40, Letter 22) further highlights this ideal.

192. *LS*, III:792-4.

193. *IK*, II:168-9, Letter 246.

194. This ideal is symbolized by the lighting of the *menorah* after dark at the doorway of the home leading to the public thoroughfare, meaning that the "light" must impact "outside," namely in the world of practical application, where darkness has previously been present. (See *TM*, IV [*HIT-TM-5712*:I]:227-31.)

195. *LS*, XXIX:9-17.

Chapter 4

EDUCATIONAL AUTHORITY

> The education of children is an enterprise predicated on
> some authority or right to determine within limits the
> aims to be achieved, the content to be taught, and the
> manner in which the enterprise is carried out. This au-
> thority is, in the first place, a right to limit the freedom of
> children pursuant to certain goals and subject to certain
> constraints.
>
> —Randall Curren[1]

This chapter investigates whether the third element of comprehensive educational thought, namely, educational authority, is found
in R. Schneerson's educational writings. The question of upon
whose authority these aims may be implemented and upon whose
jurisdiction the responsibility rests is explored. Thus, analysis of
R. Schneerson's educational thinking will determine elements that
align with the question, "On what authority does education rest?"

It is apparent from the list of samples of individual entries of R.
Schneerson's educational corpus compiled in chronological order that
significantly less volume is devoted to the question of authority for
education than to other prerequisite elements of educational philosophy.[2] This relative brevity is not unexpected, given that R. Schneerson
communicated his educational thinking within the parameters of
Jewish thought and its mystical teachings, which are dependent on
the axioms of Biblical and Rabbinic perspectives of authority. The

contribution of Emeritus Chief Rabbi Professor Jonathan Sacks, who has authored several texts on this topic, is a particular focus.

Judaic Perspective on Authority

Rabbi Professor Jonathan Sacks[3] has argued that from Ancient Greek times of Plato and Aristotle until the contemporary era, there has existed a questioning and discussion of rights to authority and government in general and on the contractual nature of the relationship between "ruler" and "ruled," as evident from discussion in Plato's *The Republic*. He[4] has also noted that this discussion about political philosophy is also relevant to the question of the educator's right to exert authority over the student.

After observing that "the human condition is fraught with the tension of clashing interests, desires, passions and pursuits," Rabbi Sacks differentiates two approaches to "the problem of freedom" and the question of prevailing wills. The first contractual approach uses "force, centralized in the form of the state" as a means "to preventing one person robbing or injuring another." He notes that Ancient Greece was preoccupied with distinguishing different forms of government and the issue of what constitutes the state. The question of the intrusiveness of the state also concerned "figures like John Stuart Mill, who argued that the state should never interfere with people's lives unless they were harming others."[5]

After portraying the contractual approach, Rabbi Sacks defined the covenantal approach to broader issues of freedom and authority, which is distinctive to Judaic thinking and which sharply contrasts with Western philosophy:

> Imagine that you and I, different in our interests and strengths, realize that we would both gain if we were to work together. Neither of us wants to use force. That would be an assault on the other's integrity. But neither of us wants to risk betrayal by the other. The alternative

to the use of force is trust. Trust is created by the use of language. We talk, communicate, and share our dreams; we begin to understand one another and realize that we can work together. We can then go further and make a promise to one another. We can enter into a mutual pledge. This is a highly specialized use of language known as performative utterance. It means, the use of words to create facts, in this case, mutually binding obligations. What then has to happen for trust to be effective is that I must keep my word, and you, yours. The Torah has a special word for a mutual pledge of this kind. It calls it a *brit*, a covenant.[6]

In describing the Judaic notion of covenantal society,[7] Rabbi Sacks[8] cited marriage as the most basic form of this covenant[9] and asked, "What if covenant might be the basis not only of marriage but of a society as a whole?" He explained that this notion of a covenantal rather than a contractual society is one where a nation is united by the force of verbal communication rather than through coercion by sovereigns, the military, law enforcers, and legal systems. The Israelites pioneered the adoption of this type of society where, because of the centrality of verbal communication, the Torah was its charter. While the Torah's words were holy as well as committing, compelling, restricting, and obligating to its followers, it simultaneously inspired allegiance and mutual devotion. The Jewish system of religious belief is thus based on the word of G-d, where G-d forms a marriage-like covenant, whereby devotion is expressed in regulations and rules that are indicative of affection.[10]

Rabbi Sacks pointed to a common ethical value system and the education of future generations so that they absorb the Torah's ideals, as central to covenantal authority and the path to achieving true freedom. He further explained that the values of the Torah, while both exalted and realistic, require some government synchronicity with the individual's self-discipline, with the external rule of the body-politic subsidiary to the citizen's self-regulation of desires. Sacks observed that covenantal society has a unique ability to be self-restraining in order to keep alive an enduring governmental structure of freedom. Rabbi Sacks contends that this is because without ethical self-limitation, the community is forced to fluctuate between lawlessness and enslavement and between insufficient regulation and excessive control, with both extremes even sometimes occurring simultaneously.

Judaic Perspective on Authority for Education

It follows from Rabbi Sacks' distinction that in contrast to those who considered the authority to educate as part of a contractual relationship, Judaism identifies the relationship between educator and student to be covenantal. Thus, the Judaic tradition is primarily focused on the covenantal aspect of authority, whereby a mutual relationship between G-d and the individual exists, meaning that there are rights whereby the educator exerts authority over the student, and a general willingness by the student to be inspired and guided by the educator.

Describing the educational consequences of a covenantal approach to educational authority, Rabbi Sacks[11] noted that this model imposes a more substantial responsibility on the learner's acquisition of a sense of right or wrong than in other governmental structures. Therefore, it needs unique educational institutions and requires continuous teaching and guidance. Individuals need to be aware of the commandments, which in turn need to be communicated to their offspring. These guiding principles and regulations must also be discussed constantly until they become an integral dimension of their children's essential being. Systematic reiteration through graphic confirmation on special days of remembrance is also useful and required, so that the Jewish people refresh their memory of their historic mission and its origins.[12] Furthermore, in Judaism, the authority for education is considered to be Divinely invested, meaning that educators and parents are Divinely empowered to influence students to achieve the aims of education.

Discussion that characterizes the contractual dimension of education in wider educational literature does not concern R. Schneerson's educational discourse. Rather, it is the Divinely empowered aspect of education and the reciprocal or covenantal aspect of the authority for education that feature in his writings.

R. Schneerson's Perspective on Authority for Education

In his exploration of the parameters of the authority for education, R. Schneerson explained[13] that notwithstanding the absence of an explicitly-stated Biblical command[14] obligating parents and educators to engage in training young children for virtuous living and for their practice of *mitzvot* as adults, the Divinely-bestowed authority for education was undiminished. When addressing this anomaly he stated that "...it is astounding that given that education is the foundation of all the Divine commands that one fulfils as an adult, there is no Biblical imperative to educate...."[15] In addressing why the authority for education is rabbinic, rather than a Biblical obligation, he suggested explanations which view the absence of a Biblical command as indicative of the vital importance, unique character and preeminence of educational authority.

(i) In Judaism, the self-understood requires no formal Biblical commandment.

R. Schneerson argued that the absence of a Biblical command served to underscore the vital importance of educating a child for both a life of civilized, ethical conduct and fulfilment of *mitzvot*. He stated:

> ...Such an education is an imperative that follows inexorably from common-sense and from the perspective of fostering a civilized society. It is no less imperative than

the obligation for the parent to provide physical sustenance for children, an attitude that humans share with
the birds of the heavens. So too, in regard to education
and training in the performance of *mitzvot*, our intellect
and basic logic dictate that it is imperative that we do
all within our power and even more so to educate our
children in the paths of Torah...[16]

It is thus apparent that R. Schneerson considered education to be
a self-evident imperative, no less essential than providing physical
nurture for a human being's own offspring or for children under
their jurisdiction. So axiomatic is the preparatory educational process on which the Biblically-legislated outcome is dependent and
so central is it to ensuring a desired lifestyle upon reaching *Bar-
Mitzvah* or *Bat-Mitzvah*, that its imperative is self-evident, even
not needing a formal command.[17] Thus he wrote, "Because education is of such vital necessity, people will naturally engage in this
activity of their own initiative and a specific Biblical obligation is
therefore unnecessary."[18] To R. Schneerson, education is essential
to ensuring that a virtuous lifestyle comes about and the authority to educate is an obvious prerequisite for the fulfilment of life's
meaningful realization.

(ii) Biblical educational authority takes effect empathetically
    and realistically at adulthood.

In searching for further factors that might render unnecessary a
specific Torah commandment for *chinuch*, R. Schneerson explored
the hypothesis that as a prerequisite act for a *mitzvah* upon attaining maturity, education might automatically attain the Torah
status of the *mitzvot* for which it serves as preparation. This provisional assertion suggests that because education is the preparation
and training of a minor for fulfilment of the Biblical *mitzvot* upon
attaining adulthood, it might automatically adopt a status equivalent to the Biblical commands for which it prepares.[19] Because no

Halachic codifier considers the education of a minor to be a Torah obligation and RSZ[20] rules definitively that *chinuch* is a Rabbinic *mitzvah*, R. Schneerson[21] rejected this provisional assertion.

R. Schneerson suggested[22] that the absence of a Biblical command to educate young children is due to a pre-*Bar-Mitzvah* boy or pre-*Bat-Mitzvah* girl being a minor whose performance of precepts while they are "being trained", however essential, cannot be accorded the status of the full Biblical obligation of an adult. He likened this to the inability of a Torah obligation to apply to the pre-conversion preparatory practice for subsequent Jewish living by a candidate for conversion to Judaism, as it is only after conversion and acceptance of the authority of the commandment that it can take effect.

Because the Torah obligation for *mitzvot* can only begin at *Bar-* or *Bat-Mitzvah*, R. Schneerson therefore introduced a novel understanding where Torah educational authority empathetically accommodates practical reality by making allowance for the imperfections in *mitzvah* fulfilment during the initial period of familiarization. It allows for inaccurate fulfilment of *mitzvot* by youth who have just attained *Bar-* or *Bat-Mitzvah* until mastery has been attained.[23]

Interestingly, the rabbinic authority to train a minor in fulfilment of *mitzvot* prior to *Bar-* or *Bat-Mitzvah* requires the child's proper *mitzvah*-fulfilment like that of an adult at that time and demands far more than mere symbolic acclimatization.

(iii) Education is of such an exalted status that it defies formal categorization as a *mitzvah*.

R. Schneerson argued that because education is of an exalted status, it transcends formal categorization as a command. He considered educational authority to be a Divinely-mandated imperative of such lofty significance that without it, a virtuous life could simply not be attained. He considered it to be in a category of those central imperatives that are even more important than those specific

obligations requiring a Biblical command. He explained that because education seeks to imbue in a child the ideal of *kabbalat ol*
[acceptance of Divine authority], it was in the same category as
kabbalat ol, a prerequisite of such importance that fulfilment of
every *mitzvah* is predicated upon it and it is therefore not listed as
a *mitzvah*. He wrote:

> The fulfilment of Torah and *mitzvot* by young children
> transcends and defies categorisation as a Biblical com-
> mand. Just as acceptance of Divine authority is not
> legislated as one of the 613 Biblical commands, it is
> nevertheless obvious that it is an attainment in its own
> right and not merely a prerequisite for fulfilment of a
> Divine precept [*mitzvah*], because a *mitzvah* can only
> be meaningful after one accepts G-d's authority to obey
> the command. Willingness to accept G-d's authority
> cannot be legislated as an independent activity before
> the utterance of a specific command, because it is the
> very meaning of the command....[24]

Thus, in R. Schneerson's view, the authority for educational training of young children upon which the outcome of a virtuous adult
is predicated, is so imperative and self-evident, that it does not
require a formal Biblical command. Also, this educational prerequisite is so exalted that no special Biblical authority needs to be
applied to it. The Biblical authority to educate applies to those who
have attained adulthood and a rabbinic obligation mandates thorough training of children from an early age in virtuous living and
the detailed practice of *mitzvot*. The Biblical authority still makes
allowance for an inaugural period of familarization and practice
that takes account of the realities of this task.

The absence of prolonged discussion of the issues of "rights" of
the learner by R. Schneerson can be understood in light of his perceptions of the authority for education.

A Reciprocal Arrangement

In Jewish thinking generally, and R. Schneerson's writings in particular, education and the communication of intellectual ideas entail a mutual arrangement where the educator primarily operates with involvement inspired by altruistic motivations toward the learner. At the same time, in the cognitive domain of education, according to R. Schneerson,[25] the learner willingly responds to the educator's altruism by:

(i)   adopting a position of submitting before the educator's authority as the educator endeavors to communicate a concept;

(ii) applying thereafter his or her unique individual intellectual abilities to the comprehension of the concept that was communicated; and

(iii) attaining ultimately a mastery of the discipline under study identical to that of the teacher and pursuing self-development so that the learner can equal or even surpass the educator's level of understanding.

It was not only in the area of cognitive education that self-abnegation before the teacher was seen as vital, but also in the field of spiritual enlightenment before the mentor. Indeed, R. Schneerson viewed[26] the absence of student humility to be "a tragic symptom of contemporary education" and urged teachers to implement educational activities that introduce and enhance educator humility, pleading for them to be included in the curriculum of public school education.[27] When it comes to internalization and adoption of values from a mentor, as distinct from communication of cognitive skills, the willing acknowledgment by the mentee of the mentor's authoritative pre-eminence is fundamental in Jewish thinking. This is evident in the directive of *Ethics of the Fathers* 1:6, "appoint a teacher for yourself," and in commentaries on this text. Indeed, R. Schneerson campaigned[28] that every person must have a mentor to whom they turn for guidance in the path of spiritual upliftment, urging choosing a personal teacher or *mashpi'a* [spiritual mentor] to whom one is accountable.[29]

Implications for Education

Some examples of interrelatedness of elements that emerge from R. Schneerson's view of the authority of education are apparent. The understanding of the authority for education has implications for the nature, aims, methodology, and content of education, as well as for the responsibility for education.

Education as an Attainable Goal

To R. Schneerson, education was a Divine imperative, even though a specific Biblical commandment is not obvious; indeed, he considered the Divine imperative to be even underscored by this absence. As a corollary of the Divine imperative that all abide by the Biblical code of virtuous conduct and predicated on the Rabbinic principle[30] that "G-d only demands of a human being that which is attainable" and that "G-d does not demand unattainable objectives of his creatures,"[31] R. Schneerson deduced the following observations on the nature of education which became central to his educational philosophy:[32]

  (i)   Education is an attainable process. Given the Divine imperative and Biblical obligation that the individual lead a virtuous life, it follows that the individual is capable of, and Divinely empowered to meet this expectation;

  (ii) R. Schneerson considered the student to be Divinely empowered to rule over bodily and inferior impulses[33] and to achieve self-mastery, thereby realizing his or her Divinely imbued, unlimited potential; and,

  (iii) The educator is Divinely empowered to succeed in attaining educational goals, even in situations that appear exceptionally challenging, both physically and spiritually.

Given the Judaic axiom[34] that G-d only requires what the individual is capable of, to R. Schneerson it follows that the educator is capable of influencing and transforming the most challenging types of students.[35] R. Schneerson figuratively interpreted[36] the Biblical command that adults caution their children regarding three specific matters (consumption of blood, consumption of insects, and avoidance of impurity by priests) to parallel three circumstances of opposition that confront educators who seek to influence young children.[37] These daunting challenges include:[38]

(a) Entrenched student degeneracy and adoption of a hedonistic lifestyle by a student submerged in pleasure-seeking and primitive conduct, as symbolized by consumption of blood;

(b) Defiance as symbolized by consumption of forbidden insects, on the part of the antagonistic student; and

(c) Disbelief in, and cynicism regarding the transcendent dimension and an apathetic, assimilationist approach, as symbolized by apathy by priests toward ensuring avoidance of impurity and an unwillingness to maintain special responsibilities that are supra-rational commands.

R. Schneerson argued[39] that each individual learner essentially wishes to comply with *mitzvot* and the problem may arise only because he or she can at times be coerced by their negative disposition.[40] However, in light of the Divine imperative for education,[41] Divine assistance ensures victory in this confrontation, even in the face of daunting odds.[42] Thus, in education:

(i) the educator should focus on the student's limitless Divine potential;

(ii)   since G-d has mandated the universal Noahide Laws
        instilling basic morality, this implies the attainability of
        the goal to influence moral behavior worldwide; and

(iii)   Education is thus perceived as an endeavor of univer-
        sal significance. Here, Maimonides' principle[43] of the
        learner viewing the world as a precariously balanced
        universe where their next thought, speech, or action is
        of cosmic significance becomes particularly relevant to
        this understanding of education.

Educational Aims, Methodology and Responsibility

An understanding of the authority for education also has implications for the aims of education. It follows that prerequisite goals
of education include the learner's awareness and mindfulness of
the Higher Authority as a tangible presence in his or her life that
guides their moral choices. Also, R. Schneerson's educational philosophy emphasized the life of virtuous deeds and selfless altruism
as educational goals.

Following from his understanding of the authority for education,
the responsibility for education will be heightened by the expectation that the educator is engaged in a Divinely entrusted venture.
Consequently, the educator needs to show meticulous concern for
the task that goes far beyond a financial or contractual arrangement.

The methodology of education should be proactive, pre-emptive,
confident, and extraverted, and the policy of education will be influenced by this understanding. Similarly, the content of education
needs to reflect this Divine component as inclusion of information
that encourages student sensitivity to the supernatural dimension,
and sustained reflection on Divinity will be integral to the curriculum.

R. Schneerson's understanding of the authority for education
reveals that his understanding is consistent with the Judaic or covenantal perception of authority as distinct from a contractual view.
This means that the preoccupation with rights that characterize

discussions of those who adopt the contractual position, such as the philosophers of Ancient Greece, Renaissance Italy, and the writings of John Stuart Mill, is not found in R. Schneerson's educational discourse. R. Schneerson views education as a Divine imperative prerequisite for virtuous living which is so vital and basic that it does not require a specific Biblical command. Also, as a fundamental, all-encompassing responsibility, it transcends the category of a particular *mitzvah* that applies to specific regulations, surpassing all these.

Indeed, this Divine imperative for education has implications for the nature and aims of education. For example, it follows that the individual is capable of, and Divinely empowered to meet, this expectation of a virtuous life. R. Schneerson's understanding of educational authority also has consequences for the responsibility for education, its methodology, and content. His perception of the authority for education is axiomatic to his understanding of the content, practice, and policy of education, as well as to his concept of the responsibility and methodology for education.

In summary, the educational process is seen as geared to a successful outcome where the reformability of the individual is achievable,[44] particularly as children are considered receptive to adopting upright ideals at the hands of those who educate them.[45] There is potential within everyone equally, the quality of self-sacrifice is shared,[46] and the soul is filled with all abilities needed for it to succeed in its mission,[47] with Divine assistance enabling the overcoming of negative impulses.[48] To underscore the attainability of educational aspirations, R. Schneerson highlighted a number of other sources. R. Schneerson's insistence that self-mastery and self-cultivation are attainable educational goals and that the individual is Divinely empowered to succeed in these tasks find their earliest precedents in Jewish mystical literature, as expounded in early Habad-Hasidic texts.[49] Throughout R. Schneerson's discourse, he states that the educational enterprise is attainable and achievable because "G-d only demands according to the potential possessed by a person" and the person is endowed with that potential.[50]

Notes

1. Curren, 2007:151.
2. Of thirty-one anthologies of R. Schneerson's educational writings, only three cite sources of R. Schneerson's writings on the authority for education, while twenty-three anthologies cite sources on the nature of education, twenty-four on the aims of education, twenty-one on the responsibility for education, twenty-four on the method of education, twenty-one on the content of education, and eighteen cite sources in R. Schneerson's writings on the practice of education.
3. Sacks, 2007:69-74.
4. *Op. cit.*, 71.
5. *Op. cit.*, 69-72. Sacks also noted (*op. cit.*:73) that "one of the ironies of the post-modern West" was "that the triumph of freedom over totalitarian regimes has gone hand in hand with an erosion of the moral bases of freedom. Morality has been relativized into self-fulfillment. Responsibilities have taken second place to rights. The very idea of objective standards of right and wrong has become suspect. If history teaches any lesson at all it is that this, if unchecked, is a prelude to disaster. The man who said so best was an unlikely figure, Bertrand Russell. Russell, hardly a religious man, thought that the two great ages of mankind were to be found in ancient Greece and Renaissance Italy. But he was honest enough to admit that the very features that made them great contained the seeds of their own demise: What had happened in the great age of Greece happened again in Renaissance Italy: traditional moral restraints disappeared . . ."
6. *Op. cit.*: 70.
7. Biblical notions of the covenant abound. See Genesis, 17:9-14.
8. Sacks, 2007:71.
9. Rabbi Sacks (*op. cit.*, 70) explained that marriage is the ideal expression of a covenantal relationship as it meshes two individuals who concur with uniting their futures as one, with each holding the other in high esteem so that they maintain and defend each other. Marriage also encapsulates covenantal society in that each marriage partner holds the trustworthiness of the other in the highest regard, thereby engendering a relationship characterized by co-operative affiliation. Also, marriage and covenantal society both draw their power from affection, dependability, eagerness to assume care, and viewing the other's concerns as if they were one's own, rather than through coercion.

10. Rabbi Sacks noted that the covenantal society is an expression of freedom *par excellence* because it depends on moral obligation rather than coercion for its effectiveness. In this way, it differs significantly from societies based on class or caste where hierarchic considerations are all-important. It is thus superior to nationalist or fascist societies which limit the individual's significance to his or her function as a contributor to the nation as a whole. It is also preferable to democracy which, while valuing the individual above all else, is ultimately a contractual system based on the individual's self-interest. In the contractual system, the individual benefits by relinquishing a portion of his or her autonomy to the jurisdiction of the ruling body that regulates through legal enactments to protect the domain and supply various utilities which enhance the life of the individual to a level far superior to that had he not relinquished some personal autonomy.

11. Sacks, 2007:71.

12. Sacks has noted that this has a great advantage in that the Jewish people, who, if faithful to this mutual commitment, enjoy a liberty that surpasses that experienced by other nations in contemporary or bygone eras. This is because if the covenant is impressed upon the psyche of its civilians, coercion by law-enforcement agencies becomes unnecessary. Real liberty comprises self-restraint without requiring external control and willingly undertaking ethical self-limitation. If this self-restraint is not present, freedom deteriorates into immoderation and the public arena becomes a venue for conflicting predispositions and passions.

13. For a full scholarly exposition of R. Schneerson's analysis of this issue, see *LS*, XXXV:61-9. A similar rendition of R. Schneerson's position, written in a style appropriate to a different target audience and with differing emphases, was edited by R. Schneerson and approved for publication. See I.Z. Weisberg's rendition of this address in Althaus, P.T. (*ed.*), (1999) :381-93. See also *TM-HIT-5747*, III:431-2 and *SH-5748*, II:614-6.

14. Biblical verses only allude to an imperative for training a child from a young age to act appropriately without legislating a formal commandment. For example, the patriarch Abraham is identified in Genesis, 18:19 as an individual "who instructed his children and his household after him to follow in the way of G-d, doing charity and justice...". While he is a recipient of Divine blessing as a result of this conduct, this is a communication of Abraham's life-style rather than a specific command for all to emulate his example. Similarly, the Rabbinic interpretation (Talmud, *Yevamot* 114a cited by Rashi) of Leviticus 21:1 derives an obligation where adult *Kohanim* (priests) are cautioned regarding their children that they must ensure that the children who are priests adhere to the laws of priesthood. Still, this is a command that applies exclusively to laws of priesthood and is not an all-encompassing obligation to train children to act appropriately in all circumstances. The Biblical command (Deuteronomy, 11:19) to "teach [words of Torah] to your children to discuss them when you sit in your house, when you walk by the way, when you

lie down and rise up" refers to the obligation to teach Torah but does not include training children to practice its commandments. Because the verse "Educate the child according to his way so also when he grows older he will not depart from it" is from Proverbs 22:6, it does not have the authority of one of the six-hundred and thirteen legal commands derived from the Pentateuch, and is considered to be sagely advice from King Solomon rather than a Divine imperative.

15. *SH-5748*, II:614.

16. *TM-HIT-5747*, III:431-2.

17. R. Schneerson pointed out (*SH-5748*, II:615) that "...there is a fundamental and essential distinction to be drawn between education and other preparatory Biblical requirements [in that] the Torah study of children...is not merely a preparation for their Torah study and fulfilment of Biblical commands upon their reaching maturity.... Torah study and fulfilment of Biblical commands by children are superior to those of adults, as confirmed by many statements of our Sages (Talmud, *Shabbat* 119b) concerning the exceptionally elevated status of "the breath of young infants who study the Torah" which is untainted and characterised by innocence..." This observation renders all the more significant the question of why this all falls under a Rabbinically-ordained obligation rather than a Torah imperative.

18. *SH-5748*, II:614.

19. He cited (*LS*, XXXV:62) examples of prerequisite requirements which are "incorporated" in the *mitzvah*, including acquisition of *tefillin* [phylacteries] (See Exodus, 13:16) prior to a *bar mitzvah* boy's thirteenth birthday, the construction of a *sukkah* [booth] in readiness for fulfillment of the Biblical command to dwell for seven days in a *sukkah* (See Leviticus, 23:42), the prior acquisition of palm branches, willows, myrtle and *etrog* [citrus] for the fulfilment of this command during the *Sukkot* festival (See Leviticus, 23:40) and possessing a *shofar* [ram's horn] and practising sounding it so as to perform its *mitzvah* (See Leviticus, 23:24).

20. *Shulchan Aruch HaRav,* beginning of *Hilchot Talmud Torah* and *Orach Chayim*, Chapter 343:2.

21. *LS*, XXXV:64.

22. *Op. cit.*, XXXV:67-8.

23. He likened this (*op.cit.*, XXXV: 66-9) to the Torah's allowing a time lapse of almost six months between the Torah command (Exodus, 25:8) to construct a sanctuary on *Tishrei* 11th (See Rashi's commentary to Exodus, 30:16) and completion of this project (Exodus 40:17) on *Nissan* 1st. Because this period allowed for engagement in indispensable activity such as collection of funds and materials as well as the actual construction of the sanctuary and the highly skilled fashioning of its vessels, this time-consuming process was still considered to be in fulfilment of the *mitzvah* of "You shall make for Me a sanctuary". Similarly, as long as one is engaged in the process of destroying leavened food substances before or during Passover

according to the natural order of events, no Torah requirement has been transgressed. Also, the Biblical description (Genesis, 24:1) of Abraham as "coming in days", referring to his achievement of a life of consummate perfection, includes those years when he was still engaged in investigating and formulating his monotheistic world-view.

24. *SH-5748:615.*
25. *LS*, XVII:71-7.
26. See letter of *Tevet* 26th, 5742 [Jan. 21st, 1982] in *Letters from the Rebbe*, VI: 190-4, Letter 133.
27. Hebrew letter of *Ellul* 2nd, 5723 [Aug. 22nd, 1963] in *IK*, XXII:494-7, Letter 8,664 [Addenda to *LS*, XXII:393-5].
28. Address of *Shabbat Parashat Devarim*, 5746 [Aug. 9th, 1986] in Addenda to *LS*, XXIX, 247-8; Address of the Eve of 3rd night of *Sukkot*, 5747 [Oct. 19, 1986] in *TM-HIT-5747*, I:206-13.
29. Besides the need for student humility in the cognitive domain of education, R. Schneerson explained (*IK*, II:314-6, Letter 343 [Addenda to *LS*, XX:584-5]) the required dynamic of willing submission of the mentee before the mentor in the domain of moral education (in the case of learning spiritual growth from one's Hasidic spiritual master) in *Yechidut* or private intimate meeting which will ideally result in: (i) Clarification of the spiritual standing of the mentee; (ii) Identification of his or her ideal path of service; (iii) Forging an ongoing spiritual devoted connection from mentee to the mentor. These three aims can only be attained through a genuine heart-to-heart communication, not via a merely superficial, external communication.
30. *Bamidbar Rabba*, 12:3.
31. *Avodah Zara* 3a. This idea is similarly expressed in the dictum (Talmud, *Ketubot* 67a) "According to the camel is the load."
32. See *Reshimot*, IV:175 & 177.
33. *Op. cit.*, IV:175-81 [*Reshima* No. 130].
34. *Bamidbar Rabba*, 12:3.
35. *IK*, I:283-4, Letter 152 [Addenda to *LS*, II:680-1]; *IK*, I:284-6, Letter 153.
36. *Op. cit.*, I:119-20, Letter 72 [Addenda to *LS*, II:679-80]; *IK*, I:283-4, Letter 152 [Addenda to *LS*, II:680-1]; *IK*, I:284-6, Letter 153.
37. *Ibid.*
38. *Op. cit.*, I:283-4, Letter 152 [Addenda to *LS*, II:680-1]; *IK*, I:284-6, Letter 153.
39. Citing Maimonides, *Laws of Divorce*, end of Chapter 2. This was explicitly enunciated to Rabbi Dr. Jung in *IK*, I:284-6, Letter 153.
40. *IK*, I:284-6, Letter 153.
41. *Op. cit.*, I:119-20, Letter 72 [Addenda to *LS*, II:679-80]; *IK*, I:138-9, Letter 83 [Addenda to *LS*, XXIII:422]; *IK*, I:194-6, Letter 108.

42. *IK*, I:119-20, Letter 72 [Addenda to *LS*, II:679-80]; *IK*, I:186-7, Letter 102 [Addenda to *LS*, XIV:381-2]; *IK*, I:283-4, Letter 152; *op. cit.*, I:284-6, Letter 153; *op. cit.*, XXI:45-6, Letter 7795; *op. cit.*, II:168-9, Letter 246.

43. Maimonides, *Mishneh Torah, Laws of Teshuvah*, 3:4.

44. *IK*, I:283-4, Letter 152; *op. cit.*, I:284-6, Letter 153.

45. *Op. cit.*, I:119-20, Letter 72 [Addenda to *LS*, II:679-80]; *IK*, I:283-4, Letter 152; *op. cit.*, I:284-6, Letter 153.

46. *Op. cit.*, I:110-2, Letter 65 [Addenda to *LS*, XXI:492].

47. *IK*, I:186-7, Letter 102 [Addenda to *LS*, XIV:381-2].

48. Talmud, *Sukkah* 52b; *IK*, I:194-6, Letter 108. R. Schneerson authored (*op. cit.*, I:141-53, Letter 85) an extended exposition of the redeemability of every Jew whereby every Jew has a place in the World to Come. Further examples of the attainability of educational aspirations cited by R. Schneerson are: (a) The depletion of the soul's love and fear of G-d during its terrestrial existence is compensated by the sublime unity achieved through Torah and *mitzvot* (*op. cit.*, I:194-6, Letter 108); (b) A sudden descent into exile is matched by the sudden ascent (through *teshuvah*) that is without gradation (*op. cit.*, I:194-6, Letter 108); (c) The Midrashic statement that "A staff thrown to the air lands on its root" was interpreted by R. Schneerson (*op. cit.*, I:197-8, Letter 110) to imply that though the staff is now dry, due to extensive dislocation from its source, the power of its source and root can again be awakened in it; and (d) An innate eager anticipation to receive and internalize the Torah is characteristic of the Jewish people as symbolized by counting the *Omer* (*IK*, XVIII:365-7, Letter 6,855).

49. See *Chassidut M'vueret—Tanya* (Boymelgreen Edition), Vol. 2, Pages 43-4, citing early Habad sources that developed this idea which is based on Kabbalistic precedents.

50. *IK*, III:246-8, Letter 566 [Addenda to *LS*, IV:1,248-9] citing *Bamidbar Rabba*, 12:3.

Chapter 5

THE RESPONSIBILITY
FOR EDUCATION

> Educators must dedicate their first waking thought and
> final deliberation at the conclusion of each day to the wel-
> fare of their students.
>
> —Rabbi Menachem M. Schneerson[1]

Discussion of educational responsibilities—pertaining to both society and educators—is a pivotal element of educational philosophy.[2]
This encompasses discussion of the extent of the educator's responsibility to educate, to be a catalyst for a better society,[3] and for the
development of student potential. The delineation of responsibility
for the enhancement of student potential also includes equity in
special education, overcoming the myths of learning disabilities,[4] a
capability perspective on impairment, special needs,[5] and advancing both mainstream or average students.

Within educational philosophy, understanding the role and
responsibility of the educator follows from a conception of the nature and aims of education. For example, educational academic
H.C. Black viewed[6] the definition of the role of educator and the
responsibility for education in light of the basic understanding of
education which an educational thinker adopts. Having defined
education as "the cultivation of life at higher levels," Black wrote:

> Another implication of this point of view is that the
> training of the teacher is extremely important. It means

that the teacher himself must develop a mature, integrated personality, must receive an education which
means cultivation of life at its higher levels, and must
have a well-rounded knowledge of the social heritage.[7]

Given the centrality of educational responsibility to an educational philosophy, R. Schneerson's educational discourse is
examined with respect to the responsibility for education.

An Awesome Responsibility

R. Schneerson's understanding of the nature of education whereby
he viewed "everything as educational" impacts directly on the role
of the educator and the responsibility of everyone for education. To
R. Schneerson,[8] the educator should emulate the Talmudic ideal[9]
epitomized by the Talmudic exemplar of the consummate peda-
gogue, Rabbi Shmuel ben Shilat, an educator who was concerned
for his students even when off-duty. This Talmudic passage relates
that Rav once encountered Rabbi Shmuel bar Shilat, a teacher of
small children, standing in his garden. Rav confronted him as to
how he was able to contemplate his garden at length and abandon
his students. Rabbi Shmuel ben Shilat replied that thirteen years
had passed since he had last seen his garden and that contrary to
appearances, even now, in the garden, his mind was focused on his
students as he had not deflected his attention from them. Citing
this episode, R. Schneerson explained:

> It is understood that Rabbi Shmuel ben Shilat's students
> benefited from his thinking about them.[10] The challenge
> addressed to him as to why he had left his students was (not
> just that he was not doing his job but) precisely through this,
> there was something that the students were missing. There-
> fore it must be that his intention in answering, "My mind
> is upon them" is that as a result of his thinking about them,

the students receive edification... From this we can derive a lesson for teachers, heads of *yeshivot* and *metivtot*, *mash-gichim* and *mashpi'im* regarding the extent to which they must be devoted to their students...[11] Being that this is his vocation, even if he leaves it once in thirteen years, and even if his departure is connected to spiritual matters[12]... still, if his mind was not on his students in a way that the students also derived benefit from this, he would then be subject to the criticism of abandoning his profession.[13]

R. Schneerson repeatedly stated that in education, no moment is too early,[14] no detail inconsequential,[15] no interaction inciden-tal,[16] and no exertion ever unproductive.[17] Similarly, no teacher is too advanced to have outgrown the responsibility of seeking a moral mentor of his or her own.[18] No student is too unlettered that he or she cannot be a teacher of others at some level.[19] Little wonder that to R. Schneerson, the role of the educator entails an awesome responsibility,[20] while simultaneously being a unique privilege.[21]

Because he viewed learner potential as awaiting urgent activa-tion and beckoning the educator to reveal it, as explained in the Nuclear Metaphor for education, R. Schneerson urged an extro-verted and proactive approach to educational responsibility, since the consequence of failure to initiate educational interaction can leave the learner's potential tragically undeveloped.[22] Clearly, R. Schneerson's insistence on the educator's application to his or her role is a crucial subject worthy of exploration.

R. Schneerson recommended that educators invest all mental and emotional resources, including latent, unrealized potential, in the ed-ucation of children.[23] He applied this responsibility first and foremost to parents of children, with the additional concern for the children of others. There is a daily obligation to reflect on the educational requirements of the members of the household, comparable to don-ning *Tefillin* (phylacteries), which requires total application of mind and heart;[24] similarly, educators should approach this task with self-lessness,[25] devotion,[26] self-discipline,[27] and self-sacrifice,[28] devoting themselves with all their soul to the education of youth.[29] The educator is also duty-bound to contemplate the soul of his or her student[30] and seek ways to best attract and inspire the student wherever possible to Torah and *mitzvot*; in addition, there is a responsibility that Divine Providence has placed on every individual to exert a positive influence on the community and every person with whom we interact.[31]

An educator's failure to work to their full capability is considered to be in blatant contradiction of G-d's Will.[32] This responsibility is intensified by the realization that the children and students of today are the Sages of tomorrow, as the *Midrash*[33] states, "If there are no young goats [kids], there will be no adult goats"; upon this is contingent the drawing down of the presence of the *Shechina* (Divine Presence).[34] In contrast to educators who belittle the importance of education for women and girls, R. Schneerson suggested that this responsibility applies particularly to females, as female graduates will become builders of their own homes.[35] This premium importance of girls' education is further underscored by the *Midrash*'s assertion[36] that the Giving of the Torah at Mount Sinai was dependent on its prior acceptance by women.[37] Indeed, R. Schneerson emphasized the collective responsibility for supporting girls' educational institutions and seeing to their quantitative expansion by increasing the number of students and qualitative enhancement by upgrading the quality of teaching.[38]

Ideally, the educator should be motivated by whole-hearted dedication to fulfillment of his or her sacred task.[39] Also, an expansiveness is required where the educator displays "generosity of the soul,"[40] encompassing a devotion to the point of *mesirat nefesh* (self-sacrificing idealism).[41]

R. Schneerson employed a horticultural metaphor[42] to encapsulate educational endeavor and to urge[43] educators to be mindful that there are profound, long-term benefits derived from even minor educational advancements in the young child. Based on this premise, he argued that the educator's additional effort for Jewish education was imperative, as it impacted on areas that exert a crucial influence on the entire future life of the child. Every small educational achievement resulting from the educator's extra application and effort becomes amplified as every educational action is of utmost consequence.[44] It is apparent R. Schneerson's view of educational responsibility is greatly influenced by his understanding of the nature of education.

The Parameters of the Educator's Responsibility

R. Schneerson believed that educational leadership must take responsibility for the inappropriateness of people's conduct:[45] the educator should not be satisfied while even one Jewish child is not receiving *chinuch al taharat hakodesh* (authentic Jewish education),[46] nor simply accept the number of children currently under his or her influence.[47] Indeed, the responsibility of the educator extends even beyond the learner's independence from the teacher and continues for the duration of the learner's lifetime.[48] The educator has an obligation to supervise not only what goes into the mouth of a child, by ensuring that his food is kosher, but also what is internalized by the child's mind.[49] R. Schneerson pointed out that the educator's potent influence extends beyond limitations of his or her particular subject area, as a student's affection and honor for a teacher are not constrained by such considerations.[50] He argued that if a person can, they must disseminate authentic Judaism irrespective of their particular profession, a responsibility certainly applicable in the teacher-student relationship. In light of the exceptional influence bestowed upon the educator, he or she must be mindful of avoiding even subtle negative educational influences that might inadvertently be exerted on a student.[51]

In addition, the educator's responsibility also extends to education that takes place off the school premises and outside school hours. During the school year, when students in an educational institution apply themselves diligently to their studies, the obligation rests on their educators to maintain their focus to ensure that their students' conduct and lifestyle are appropriate even after school hours.[52] It follows even more that during summer vacation, educators should take an active interest in the whereabouts and activities of individual students, assisting them to behave in a correct, upright way.[53] Moreover, the educator's role has an additional dimension of responsibility: specifically, to rescue a child who years later will become the foundation of the home when becoming a parent.[54] R. Schneerson also argued that the establishment of educational institutions was contingent on finding a dedicated individual who would willingly take responsibility for the entire project, without exorbitant payment.[55] While parents carry a general responsibility for their children, both as parents and educators, this applies particularly in the summer months when this responsibility rests exclusively on parents' shoulders.[56]

Educational responsibility even extends to children described as coarse, defiant, and cynical. R. Schneerson thus wrote:

> Our Sages[57] comment that the Torah mentions the obligation incumbent upon the elders (in knowledge) to educate the youth (in knowledge) in three contexts: (i) the prohibition against partaking of blood... [to teach one that one should never argue that] 'Since those whom I am trying to educate are sunk in the desires of their hearts, of what avail will my efforts be to give them a good education?' (ii) the prohibition against partaking of small crawling animals. A person who partakes of these does so solely to anger his Creator[58] for even he is disgusted by them. And so a person might think: What hope is there in speaking to him? (iii) the priests' obligation to observe ritual purity: The concepts of ritual purity and impurity are not able to be explained within the scope of the intellect.[59] Moreover, the subject is relevant only to priests who were chosen to stand before G-d. Therefore an educator may think: "How is it possible for me to explain these matters?" And particularly, there is the possibility that the listener will reply: "I will be like all the other nations."[60] I don't want to be part of "a nation of priests, a holy people."[61] Therefore

in these instances, the Torah commanded us regarding education, so that a person should not despair. On the contrary, we are commanded to try to do whatever is possible on behalf of every member of the Jewish people, endeavoring to set him on the path of truth and to arouse the Jewish spark within him.[62]

Educators' Awareness of Their Responsibility

The educator must be aware he or she is Divinely empowered[63] and in receipt of Divine assistance for the educational task.[64] This awareness should inspire in educators a sense of responsibility, mindful of the Heavenly delegation of care for His vineyard, namely children.[65] The educator must also be aware of the pre-eminence of his or her role, as evident in the Torah's reference[66] to Abraham's activity as an inclusive educator serving as the climax of his life's work, even beyond his overcoming of other trials and challenges.[67] All of this applies to all parents who "carry the great responsibility for their children as parents and educators simultaneously."[68]

Moreover, the Habad educator is expected to be mindful that he or she is an agent[69] of RJIS who, when he could have been engaging in the most profound, mystical Torah matters, showed self-sacrifice and devoted his energy to sustaining even basic Jewish education.[70] This self-sacrifice is a prerequisite for successful Jewish education for it is only a genuinely G-d-fearing educator speaking with *mesirat nefesh* (self-sacrifice) and sincerity who can access and penetrate learners.[71] No self-sacrifice can be too great, especially where there are no other volunteers to undertake an educational task.[72] The educator must also be constantly aware of the goals and outcome of education and their fundamental aim, namely, the revival of the student whose potential lies dormant. In the case of students who are already "alive" and alert to Jewish educational ideals, there is an obligation to add a further dimension of "essential light"[73] to their lives.

R. Schneerson understood education to be of universal significance with enormous consequences, particularly in light of
Maimonides' requirement[74] that every individual view his or her
every future action, speech, or thought to be of crucial cosmic
significance in a precariously balanced universe. Likewise, an educator has a responsibility to view the world as evenly balanced and
his or her educational activity as the key to producing both a moral
human being and a better world.[75]

R. Schneerson repeatedly stressed that tending G-d's vineyard
involves not only a tremendous responsibility, but also an awesome
privilege[76] where involvement in an educational initiative benefits
the educator as well as the student.[77] The seriousness of the educational responsibility is thus counterbalanced by an associated
emphasis on the blessing and privilege that accompany education.

The Educator's Illustrious Privilege

One area repeatedly and prominently accented in R. Schneerson's
discourse is the privilege of engagement in education.[78] This element shows that he considered education to include enormous
advantages. R. Schneerson spoke of the great merit of "illuminating hearts and homes through education"[79] and asked, "What can
resemble or equal the pleasure generated Above through education?"[80] In contrast to practitioners who were preoccupied with
the educator's unfortunate circumstances and who perceived
their rewards to be incommensurate with the stress involved, R.
Schneerson emphasized the privilege of involvement in education.
In response to correspondence from teachers who bemoaned the
challenges of their situation,[81] R. Schneerson would point out that
theirs was the "fortunate lot"[82] with a "blessed vocation."[83] In the
Jewish context, initiating a child into Jewish tradition and moral
instruction in all things Jewish were key means of providing a child
with education for their lifetime and even for generations to come.

One unique privilege of educators is that their small deeds bring immeasurable positive outcomes,[84] especially being able to instill in the student moral values and piety for their lifetime.[85] For example, R. Schneerson wrote:

> Happy is your lot in that you have been given the opportunity to exert a positive influence on and participate in forming the character of Jewish youths, which will quite possibly exert an influence for the entire duration of their lives, meaning for decades to come and including their setting up of their homes when they marry. My application of the term "happy is your lot" to your educational assignment has a dual implication: If the "happy lot" refers to the possibility of you assisting someone materially or spiritually even in a one-off instance and only for a · short duration, how much more so does this apply to providing simultaneous assistance to both the material and spiritual aspects of life, for a lengthy duration and perhaps for even their entire lifetime![86]

The ideals communicated and the good deeds inspired by the educator are unending, as expressed in the concept that "the words of the righteous live on forever."[87] R. Schneerson applied this principle to many practical areas of education, citing it particularly when encouraging extraverted educational initiatives. For example, he argued that the merit of enrolling students in a *yeshivah* defies description, and that if saving a single child physically is considered most meritorious, this principle certainly applies even more to rescuing a child spiritually.[88]

He further argued that the privilege of education implies that educators "must stand in the front row" as those "that ignite the light of 'the candle of G-d [which] is the soul of man' in children, position them in a 'ray of light' so that those children will become exemplary members of the Jewish people."[89] The educator's fortunate lot also means he or she should be appreciative because while earning a livelihood, they are spared the ordeal of "treading in mud," therefore avoiding enduring the rigors of the world of commerce to earn their income.[90]

R. Schneerson viewed education as a vessel that contains blessing,[91] with a reward associated with its involvement[92] that cannot be truly estimated[93] because it has enormous positive effects for the educator.[94] R. Schneerson's ideal is educators working to the very best of their abilities without extrinsic motivation or self-interest, such as incentives of honor and pride.[95] He nevertheless viewed an educator undertaking an educational activity, consciously motivated by the determined attempt and purpose of actualizing Divine blessing, as positive.[96] Through engaging in education a person acquires in a single moment a portion in the World to Come for themselves and others.[97] Thus R. Schneerson wrote:

> Happy is your lot in that Divine Providence has placed you in the most fortunate position of one engaged in *chinuch*, which draws near the hearts of Jewish children to our Father in Heaven. The great reward for this defies description, apart from the primary and ultimate reward, whereby "the reward of the *mitzvah* is the *mitzvah* itself."[98] Furthermore, this activity is one of those things about which it is written, "One eats of the fruits in this world while the principal remains for the World to Come."[99] This endeavor incorporates the *mitzvah of* Torah study, which "is the equivalent of all the other *Mitzvot*"[100] as well as *gemilut chasadim*, (kindness) which is even greater than *tzedakah* (charity)[101] and is the primary form of divine service in our time,[102] just prior to the advent of *Mashiach*.[103]

Having outlined central aspects of R. Schneerson's view of the responsibility for education and the need for the educator's awareness of it, his emphasis on the benefits and privileges of engaging in education is also incorporated. In order to understand the duality of his argument for continued engagement in education even when facing challenges, it is necessary to examine the specific privileges that he associated with educational engagement.

(i) *The Educator's Reward*

An awareness of the privilege of education is even more inspirational when people consider that the rewards and blessings for education are "measure for measure," being commensurate with effort.[104] In the context of Jewish education, R. Schneerson constantly reminded others of his predecessor's teaching, that "G-d does not remain indebted," but repays all those engaged in establishing kosher Jewish education with both spiritual needs and the material means to fulfill these aspirations.[105] R. Schneerson viewed educational activity as the portal for success in all endeavors[106] and repeatedly gave examples of the benefits and blessings which include:

(i) *Nachat* (Pride) in One's Own Children

R. Schneerson argued that the educator will derive satisfaction from his or her own children as the reward, "measure for measure," for involvement in drawing people's children close to G-d.[107] Involvement in education elicits G-d's blessing in particular, the educator deriving true fulfillment and pride from their own children[108] and reward by raising them in "the candle [which] is the *mitzvah* and the light [which is] the Torah..."[109] He cited his predecessor's statement that "to exhaust oneself for the welfare of 'G-d's children' is repaid by G-d with *Yiddishe* satisfaction from one's own children..."[110]

(ii) Mutual Enlightenment

Another reward for the educator's endeavor is the mutual enlightenment of educator and student,[111] so that through teaching others, the educator gains a quantitatively enhanced, qualitatively improved, and swifter comprehension in their own studies.[112] Because education is a form of spiritual charity, it follows that just as charity refines the philanthropist's mind so that an individual succeeds in their study "a thousand times more than one would have otherwise achieved,"[113] similarly, engagement in education achieves the same outcome.[114]

(iii) Exalted Spiritual Status

Educators merit an exalted spiritual status in both this world and beyond, as in this world they are located in "a ray of light" due to their educational endeavors.[115]

(iv) Health of Educators and Their Offspring

Educational engagement is the facilitator of physical healing for the educator[116] and the educator's offspring.[117]

(v) Material Sustenance

As education is considered spiritual charity, it secures salvation, livelihood, and sustenance, no less than the blessings achieved by giving material charity.[118]

(vi) A Life of Happiness

Education assists the educator in his or her search for a marriage partner[119] and benefits the educator, his fiancée, and their resulting life of happiness.[120] As well, educating young people was also seen as a means of correction for personal youthful failings.[121]

(vii) The Additional Privilege of Habad Educators

Addressing Habad educators, R. Schneerson spoke of "the fortunate lot of those on 'RJIS's wagon.'"[122] Indeed, engagement in activities urged by his predecessor, RJIS, is of critical contemporary importance and everlasting significance, given that "the words of the righteous live on forever."[123] The Habad educator is also privileged to be granted a portion in the radiance and splendor of Torah, namely, the Hasidic philosophy that he or she disseminates.[124]

For the educator to succeed in this calling, he or she is responsible for acquiring several attitudes and attributes.

The Characteristics of the Ideal Educator

(i) Confidence

One reason that educators often declined educational opportunities or sought to abandon a teaching position was their lack of confidence.[125] R. Schneerson challenged educators' self-doubt, where they thought they should be doing something more worthwhile than education.[126] He also urged them to overcome seductive arguments of the destructive impulse that challenged them with arguments like, "Just who are *you* to influence others?"[127] Even in exceptional cases of aspiring educators who discovered that, irrespective of training, application, and external intervention, they were simply not successful in the classroom, R. Schneerson urged them to make a different contribution to education such as recruiting students or fund-raising for educational causes. He argued that if a person had been assigned an educational task it meant that they are capable of fulfilling it successfully in one way or another.[128] In most cases, the actual responsibility indicates Divinely bestowed abilities to enable the individual to meet this responsibility in the best manner.[129]

Discouragement or a spirit of defeatism should not be permitted to creep into the educator's mind-set, with doubts such as "What can I do?" or "I am alone in the field" causing potential loss of enthusiasm if unchallenged. He responded to these claims by referring to Abraham, our patriarch, who taught us the extent of what one individual can achieve, citing the Biblical verse,[130] "One was Abraham, yet he inherited all the earth." R. Schneerson recommended that the educator view the learner positively, because his or her mistaken negative perception of students may often contribute to teacher despondency. R. Schneerson further argued that an educator's minimizing his or her self-worth is a strategy of the destructive inclination[131] because only educators with self-assurance,[132] inner strength, and steadfast resolve are respected and their directions observed. The words of such individuals, even when spoken gently, are heeded[133] because ultimately, heartfelt words have an effect.[134] Furthermore, an educator's lack of desire, confidence, or enthusiasm leads him or her to believe that he or she is unable to achieve, which causes him or her to abandon the task at hand and become emotionally distraught.[135]

R. Schneerson believed that the educator must display independence and confidence,[136] and the educator's self-concept must allow no room for despondency[137] or despair regarding a learner's situation.[138] Though repeated attempts by the educator may be required before they are effective, he urged educators not to tire of speaking many times until eventually their words are effective.[139] There was no place for melancholy or unnecessary doubts which are the implements of the *yetzer hara*,[140] nor ever for despair.[141]

He thus encouraged hesitant educators to know their strengths, suggesting that many apparent difficulties disappear when they begin their endeavor and they see that with G-d's help, they can achieve.[142] Disappointment and frustration, such as children who are not observant, are never sufficient[143] for abandoning a task, as the educator must employ good ways, words, and entreaties.[144] Feelings of frustration never justify inactivity about a challenging situation.[145] In the American context, he argued that the educator must have an inner resolve, confidence, and optimism, similar to the Biblical spies Joshua and Caleb,[146] so that the conquest of the American Jewish landscape for authentic Jewish education is indeed possible.[147] Joy and unreserved trust in G-d[148] were also viewed as a prerequisite for educational success, with joy and humility working hand in hand.[149] The educator's success in influencing others would become the educator's own joy and purpose.[150]

An unenthusiastic educator must realize that the very word *mitzvah* (commandment) is derived from the root *tzavta* (literally, connection) because the fulfillment of a *mitzvah* like education enables the educator to connect to the Designator of the command: there is no greater eliciting of vitality than this realization and its practical application.[151] Moreover, an educator's lack of perception of this mystical connection, given the power of the possible negative impulses in the life of the human being, in no way reduces the reality of the G-dly connection.[152] Similarly,[153] R. Schneerson proposed that in order to provide an antidote to despondency, an educator should reflect on Divine benevolence and the Biblical injunction[154] to "serve G-d with joy."[155]

(ii) Proactivity

In light of the educators' responsibilities and privileges, every educational effort is worthwhile from the educator's perspective as well as from the learner's. The educator must initiate and repeatedly try to make even one minor improvement in educational policies impacting on students' conduct, especially for fundamental educational reforms because these can exert influence through the learner's entire lifetime.[156] Such policy issues include gender separation beyond the hours of prayers and religious studies.[157] Similarly, proactive efforts should be made to enroll students so that they receive authentic religious education.[158] From his earliest writings, R. Schneerson advocated a proactive approach to educational initiatives.[159] For example, he urged communal workers who were involved in education to endeavor, even during their vacation in the countryside, to enlist those whom they encounter for the first time to assist *yeshivot* and explain the benefits of supporting Torah education.[160]

(iii) Sensitivity

Applying the horticultural metaphor, the educator, as a sensitive gardener,[161] must extend concern to every individual[162] because paying attention to the collective welfare of the class as a whole is insufficient. R. Schneerson found Biblical support[163] for the ideal of concern for the individual in the lessons of Judah's taking personal responsibility for Benjamin.[164] R. Schneerson's leadership, even after his formal assumption of Habad leadership, was characterized by concern for the individual's welfare.

(iv) Meticulous Concern for Detail

An educator's responsibility extends to the cognitive domain and includes a preparedness to extract lessons that pertain to learner edification from a text. R. Schneerson believed that educators should display a willingness to emphasize the derivation of life-lessons from a text as well as extracting its higher-order application and relevance.[165] The educator should also use age-appropriate terminology and show meticulous concern for detail, prioritizing what is user-friendly to the learner over other considerations.[166] This requires deletion of any information that detracts from the principal area of focus and may cause student confusion or overload.[167] This concern for detail and his insistence that educators ensure that public perception of an educational initiative is appropriate was also demonstrated by R. Schneerson himself, when he disapproved of a plan to distribute tickets for attendees of *Mesibat Shabbat* (Sabbath afternoon gatherings for children), due to anticipated misperception that meant these could be carried on *Shabbat* to the *Mesibat Shabbat* meetings.[168]

(v) Time Management and Organization

As well as an educator's proficiency in pedagogy, a responsibility also exists in educational policy. The educator must be aware that wasted time is an irretrievable loss[169] and therefore they have a duty to be well-organized in order to optimize their time with students.[170] This practice is particularly relevant when engaged in educating youth, as they themselves have additional responsibility, in light of their gifts from G-d which have limited time to actualize.[171]

A methodical, organized approach applies not only to the educator's personal work habits, but similarly to a teacher's precision in his teaching, as well as his or her personal organization, especially applicable when teaching subjects like science and secular wisdom. This is unlike less formal educational activities, which are subjects based on clearly defined rules of logical deduction. In particular, students of science have been educated to value a serious and methodical approach to life. R. Schneerson extended this requirement into teaching religious studies, arguing that when these students of science study Jewish studies, they must be taught to apply these same attitudes from their scientific endeavor to their special Jewish duties and responsibilities.[172]

(vi) Exemplar of Ideals

R. Schneerson was insistent that the educator exemplify the ideals he or she seeks to convey[173] with sincerity, especially in light of the Judaic teaching[174] frequently cited by R. Schneerson[175] that "words emanating from the heart penetrate the heart." As all educators are considered by others as exemplars, they need to correct themselves so as to be completely "in order"[176] or appropriate to influence others.[177]

Consequently, R. Schneerson encouraged educators that their words, when heartfelt, will be effective and have an impact.[178] For this reason he argued that no student is too impenetrable to accept change. Ultimately, a G-d-fearing educator acts in accordance with the ideals they embody[179] being someone who speaks with genuine *mesirat nefesh* (self-sacrifice) and can touch the mind and heart of the listener.[180] Indeed, the educator's own Torah observance enables his or her self-assurance and confidence.[181] In keeping with his predecessor's teaching,[182] R. Schneerson considered an educator unable to motivate others as pitiable,[183] as it is imperative that they inspire others, either directly influencing that individual or indirectly serving as a role-model, perhaps without knowing the specific impact.[184] The role of exemplar applies to the home as well, because parents teach by example, and it is through a mother's modesty and father's integrity that their children internalize these values.[185]

R. Schneerson noted that an awareness of this educational assignment was especially pertinent to students of his predecessor, RJIS.[186] These students embody the ideal of "candles that illuminate" and of "living people who give vitality to others," thereby fulfilling their purpose in life.[187]

(vii) Positive Perspective

To R. Schneerson, a vital prerequisite for educators to be able to fulfill their responsibilities is their adopting a positive view of their students. In Biblical times, on the breast-plate of the High Priest who served in the portable Sanctuary or the Jerusalem Temple were twelve precious stones corresponding to the twelve tribes of Israel. These precious stones were embedded in settings that surrounded them that thereby highlighted the beauty of the stones that they framed. R. Schneerson's predecessor, RJIS,[188] had likened engagement in the educational task of education to the Biblical settings that enhance their pre-existent beauty. R. Schneerson was similarly insistent that educators adopt a positive view of all students, viewing them as possessing immense latent potential and able to be influenced.[189]

The educator must never despair of the learner's situation,[190] nor be daunted by obstacles, but rather must constantly advance the student to higher levels.[191] Even an inability to achieve specific educational objectives is not cause for dejection, but should be considered motivation to seek other creative ways to ensure its most favorable implementation.[192] This applies particularly to the case of the depraved, defiant, and cynical learners.[193] All those endowed with a pedagogical talent should provide assistance to dislocated souls because the educator is Divinely empowered to undertake this responsibility;[194] consequently, the educator's self-concept must be indefatigable and undaunted,[195] being someone for whom challenges bring forth latent power.[196]

Besides addressing the educator's responsibility for Down-syndrome learners, R. Schneerson also insisted that there is a parallel responsibility for individuals facing physical disability,[197] detainees of corrective institutions,[198] the elderly,[199] the disenfranchised,[200] the disadvantaged,[201] and the antagonistic.[202] In a pastoral Chanukkah letter R. Schneerson wrote inclusively to Jewish detainees:

When a person finds himself in a situation of "after sunset," when the light of day has given way to gloom and darkness—as was the case in those ancient days under the oppressive Greek rule—one must not despair, G-d forbid, but on the contrary, it is necessary to fortify oneself with complete trust in G-d, the Essence of Goodness, and take heart in the firm belief that the darkness is only temporary, and it will soon be superseded by a bright light, which will be seen and felt all the more strongly through the supremacy of light over darkness, and by the intensity of the contrast. And this is the meaning of lighting the *Chanukkah* Lights, and in a manner that calls for lighting an additional candle each successive day of *Chanukkah*—to plainly see for oneself, and to demonstrate to others passing by in the street, that light dispels darkness; and that even a little light dispels a great deal of darkness, how much more so a light that steadily grows in intensity. And if physical light has such quality and power, how much more so eternal spiritual...[203]

In short, no setback was too daunting in R. Schneerson's educational thinking. He considered that the elderly are never too old,[204] nor the juvenile ever too immature,[205] as society's supposed failures are never beyond hope. Therefore, society has a responsibility to address the education of the most challenging educational circumstances, even long-established failures. Consequently, society has a responsibility to initiate educational opportunities to transform their lives. R. Schneerson also viewed the education of the elderly as vital[206] and the responsibility for educational advancement of such individuals equally applicable to education of the youth. Moreover, because even one individual can transform an entire community, as did our patriarch Abraham, every individual[207] has a responsibility to exert a positive influence on society in general, without the community's influence over the individual.[208]

The Education of the Educator

(i) Pedagogical Professional Development

As it is rare for an educator to possess all these qualities instinctively, and accepting that educational talent requires nurture and enhancement, it is unsurprising that the process of pedagogical education was seen as imperative in R. Schneerson's vision. Thus, besides continual personal self-cultivation, an educator can meet his or her educational responsibility by regularly engaging in pedagogical training and professional development.

Before assuming the leadership of the Habad movement in 1942, as head of its educational arm R. Schneerson highlighted the need for evening classes for pedagogical training of teachers as a priority for *Merkos L'Inyanei Chinuch* (Habad's educational organization over which he presided).[209] His predecessor, RJIS, wrote:[210]

> ... even the most gifted and experienced educators need to periodically discuss educational methodologies which are most appropriate for their particular student body. This principle certainly applies to younger, less experienced educators who are duty bound to do all possible to widen their knowledge of education and guidance. It is upon this knowledge that much of their success in this area of utmost responsibility is dependent.

As seventh *Admor*, one of R. Schneerson's first educational initiatives was the establishment and expansion of educational activities in North Africa. He stated that the objective for these communities was to train their own educators[211] so that they gained professional training and thereby educational qualifications,[212] with special attention through appropriate courses in pedagogy.[213]

(ii) Self-Development

To spiritually enliven others, the educator must be "spiritually alive."[214] A stagnant spirituality is therefore insufficient for this undertaking and educators must replenish their aspirations, akin to RJIS demanding additional daily efforts more than the previous day.[215] In the Habad context, the ideal where a person's service must continually increase[216] as taught by Habad's fourth *Admor*, the Rebbe Maharash, is applied by R. Schneerson to the educational context with the paradoxical question, "Because good is good, better isn't better?"[217]

Consequently, R. Schneerson argued that just as education is similar to lighting the *menorah*, educators must elevate themselves to a higher level before seeking to enlighten others. Educators must also periodically increase their educational efforts for others,[218] constantly broadening their educational deeds and activities rather than concentrating on receiving the fruits of their personal labors.[219] Moreover, it is essential that the educators conduct an honest reckoning regarding what happens in the area of tangible action, assessing the situation without embellishments or enhancement based on their love of the Jewish People.[220]

Responsibility Not to Abandon or Delegate

R. Schneerson compared the educator who opted out of the teaching profession to a soldier who abandons the front.[221] Because he viewed educator involvement as imperative,[222] he considered cases of educator indifference to be immoral, challenging passive educators who stood on the sidelines and thereby disconnected from the full force of education.[223] He was particularly concerned if an educator abandon those distant from Torah and *mitzvot*, thereby disregarding the significance of extracting "the precious, upstanding person from the corrupt,"[224] an undertaking with inestimable exalted significance.[225] He believed that an educator's efforts cannot be curtailed without causing a diminution in the area of a child's spiritual well-being and thereby inevitably resulting in ill-effects for the child's spiritual well-being.[226] Similarly, R. Schneerson was insistent that implementing the aims of education must not be the exclusive domain of religious institutions or law-enforcing agencies. Having written[227] that "It is necessary to engrave upon the child's mind the idea that any wrongdoing is an offense against the Divine authority and order," he disapproved of delegating this educational responsibility solely to religious leaders. He wrote:

> At first glance this seems to be the essential function of a house of prayer and of spiritual leaders. However, anyone who does not wish to delude himself about the facts of house of prayer attendance, both in regard to the number of worshippers and the frequency of their visits, etc., etc., must admit that shifting the responsibility to the house of prayer will not correct the situation. Nor can we afford to wait until the house of prayer will attain its fitting place in our society, and in the lives of our youth in particular, for the young generation will not wait with its growing-up process.[228]

He similarly argued that implementing the aims of education cannot be relegated to law-enforcement agencies, writing, "We cannot leave it to the law-enforcing agencies to be the keepers of the ethics and morals of our young generation."[229]

R. Schneerson believed that imbuing the new generation with ethics and morals was the responsibility of the educator and parent, while acknowledging that every individual shares this responsibility.

No Individual Is Absolved of Responsibility

R. Schneerson's conception of education carries implications for his educational thinking on who is considered an educator. To R. Schneerson, education is a collective responsibility shared by everyone.[230] Just as the pauper is Halachically required to apportion some charity from his meager income for material charity,[231] so too, the spiritually poor individual has an obligation to give spiritual charity,[232] each according to his or her individual ability.[233] Similarly, R. Schneerson considered[234] the educational directives described in his writings to be universally imperative and absolutely not restricted to professional educators.[235]

Though more applicable to professional educators, R. Schneerson[236] believed the process of education to be an all-encompassing responsibility unlimited by a person's professional obligations.[237] He argued that everyone is capable of making an educational contribution and therefore nothing should be considered an obstacle.[238] However, he did acknowledge[239] a category of individual whose paramount task was education with other religious responsibilities preparatory[240] to that task. Indeed, R. Schneerson wrote categorically:

> No one is exempt from this sacred task for at least a certain amount of time every day, week and month. The more gifted the individual in this educational work, the more time they should devote to it... Everyone must serve as an educator to G-d, Torah and *mitzvot*, and participate in the educational "call of the hour."[241]

To R. Schneerson,[242] no one is so important that it precludes responsible involvement in the education of the youngster or the beginner.[243] Furthermore, education must never be below anyone's dignity or not befitting their standing,[244] as the most elevated individual must still interact with, and exert influence on those on the periphery, particularly currently,[245] including the teaching of simple matters such as *Aleph-Beit*.[246] He further argued[247] that "no matter a person's station in life or how important their activities seem to be, they must first and foremost dedicate at least some part of their time and efforts to the most important of all causes, saving our young generation..." and cited further Rabbinic sources that emphasize this responsibility.[248]

Given the comprehensive nature of this responsibility, it follows that everyone endowed with a pedagogical talent should engage in contributing to education and especially to providing assistance to lost souls[249] and not display misplaced modesty.[250] Even though a student might aspire to contribute to Jewish education through pursuing a commercial career and thereafter providing financial assistance, the contemporary dearth of successful educators coupled with a paucity of venues providing authentic, inspirational teachers meant that the education profession was to take priority.[251] Concerning the educator's responsibility, R. Schneerson wrote:

> The extent of one's duty is in direct proportion to one's station in life. It is all the greater in the case of an individual who occupies a position of some prominence, which gives him, or her, an opportunity to exercise influence over others, especially over youths. Such persons must fully appreciate the privilege and responsibility which Divine Providence vested in them to spread the light of the Torah and to fight darkness wherever and in whatever form it may rear its head. This is your duty and privilege as one of the student officers in relation to your co-religionist colleagues and student body in general. I should also like to convey this message to your colleagues in the JCF. You are all no doubt aware of this, but perhaps there is room for added emphasis and the conviction that "it cannot be otherwise."[252]

The unusual energy of youth bestows a distinctive responsibility on them to be at the forefront of those who are active and inspire others to dispense spiritual charity generously to the underprivileged in their understanding of spiritual matters.[253] This led R. Schneerson to argue often that an educator's dissatisfaction was unjustified[254] and that the educator should not abandon his or her task, but rather consider it as imperative.

Society's Responsibility

R. Schneerson believed that every society has a collective responsibility to ensure the best education of all of its citizens. Society's educational responsibility includes justice in special education; overcoming the myths of learning disabilities,[255] impairment, and special needs;[256] nurturing gifted children;[257] and even advancing average students. Addressing the education of mainstream students, R. Schneerson urged educators to apply the principles of educational responsibility and effort to them too. He explained:

> Of every 100 students, there is a 20% minority that are of such standing that they will develop even independent of the influence of the educator. There is another 20% upon whom the educator has a very minimal influence. It is the remaining 60% who are in the middle. One must devote oneself to them to ideally move them toward the standard of the elite 20%. If one neglects them, they can fall by the way to follow the negative example of the problematic 20%.[258]

R. Schneerson argued for an inclusive approach for students considered by many to be unworthy of educational investment or effort. In short, no obstacle was too daunting in R. Schneerson's educational thinking. Because he considered society's failures to be never beyond hope, it follows that society has a responsibility to address the education of the most challenging educational circumstances.

The Contemporary Responsibility

It is important to document R. Schneerson's argument for the intensification of this educational responsibility when assessed in the context of contemporary times. To R. Schneerson, the decline in moral standards and rise of inappropriate behavior by youth meant greater responsibility for education was necessary as the antidote for these problems. In his correspondence[259] and addresses,[260] he referred to this situation as a state of emergency that required urgent attention, where education has a key role to play. He saw the alarmingly low attendance at Jewish educational institutions and a rising rate of intermarriage as two pressing problems; he linked this contemporary crisis to an intensification of educators' responsibility to rectify the situation.[261]

In an address of 1981 after the unsuccessful assassination attempt on the life of US president Ronald Reagan, R. Schneerson argued that education is not the mere acquisition of skills and knowledge. This situation meant a greater responsibility for educators to extend the breadth of the curriculum to include values education, as R. Schneerson believed that the inculcation of ethics and morals serves to equip children to be respectable citizens. He believed that if education is amoral or value-free, it represents a dangerous indifference to one's obligations to society. Analyzing the root causes of the assassination attempt, he stated:

> The blame can be laid squarely on the education that he [the perpetrator], and many other children, have received and continue to receive. An education, which imparts only knowledge, and gives no direction as to how that knowledge is to be applied usefully and constructively, is not worthy of the name "education." Technical skills are essential instruments for later life; but when unaccompanied by education in ethics and morality to form character, to learn right from wrong, they are dangerous tools. Although they may be used for good, they can also destroy. The failure to instill in children an awareness of G-d, an omnipresent real G-d who sees and judges, has inevitably produced the selfish, egocentric lifestyles so prevalent

today—the "Me" generation. The desistance of parents and schools from "intrusion" into a child's life replaced by blanket permission to run free of any moral restraints or limits has seen its tragic results. It has created an entire generation of unbridled passions, the inevitable offspring of an amoral, value-free education. Rather than inculcating children with the knowledge that the foundation and aim of their learning is to equip them to be decent and productive citizens, schools propagate the pathetically inadequate warning to refrain from crime solely to avoid punishment. The inevitable result is the belief that one need not necessarily refrain from wrongdoing, but only be "smart" enough to avoid being caught and punished...[262]

In the context of Jewish education, R. Schneerson also believed that the obligation to rescue souls through education is even more applicable after the enormous losses of the Jewish people due to the Holocaust.[263] As well, today there exists a greater educational responsibility as the established educational landscape is more accepting of a kosher Jewish education in its fullest measure.[264] Furthermore, before the arrival of *Mashiach*, there is an additional obligation to fulfill the *mitzvot* of loving our neighbor as ourselves and bringing merit to the community, both of which find real, concrete expression in education.[265]

Thus, the unique opportunities and responsibilities of the times in which educators currently find themselves mean that the general principles for the responsibility for education as explained by R. Schneerson are even more valid and pertinent, with an added dimension of urgency.

Notes

1.   Address of *Av* 20th, 5737 [Aug. 4th, 1977] in *SK-5737*, II:388-9.

2. For example, Curren (2007:223) questions whether educational responsibility is synonymous with "adults' *roles* as parents, as citizens of political communities that have collective responsibilities to children, as do government officials who act on behalf of those communities, as school administrators, and as teachers."

3. See Meira Levinson and Sanford Levinson, "Getting Religion": *Religion, Diversity, and Community in Public and Private Schools*, 2003.

4. See G. E. Zuriff, *The Myths of Learning Disabilities*, 1996.

5. See Lorella Terzi, *A Capability Perspective on Impairment, Disability, and Special Needs*, 2005.

6. H.C. Black, 263-8.

7. *Op. cit.*:265.

8. *SH-5749* [1988-89], I:29.

9. *Talmud Bavli, Bava Batra*, 8b.

10. See *LD-RJIS*, I:1, explaining that "thought is potent."

11. At this juncture R. Schneerson dismissed (as simply not an excuse) the argument that "the educator works many times more than required according to the salary which he earns and that he has already exceeded the hours of employment for which he was hired, being that he is not paid his wage on time, etc..."

12. R. Schneerson pointed out that this certainly applies to Rabbi Shmuel ben Shilat, who was a sage of the Talmud who clearly, when standing in his garden, was fulfilling the Biblical injunction (Proverbs, 3:6) to "Know G-d in all your ways" where "all *your* ways" in the case of Rabbi Shmuel was complete and an integral part of *his* contribution to refining the world.

13. *LS*, V:376-7.

14. *TM-HIT-5742* [1982], IV:2190.

15. *IK*, VI, 282.

16. *SH-5749* [1988-89], I:29.

17. *IK*, II, 81-2.

18. In 1986 R. Schneerson inaugurated a campaign that every individual appoint a moral mentor in the fulfillment of the Mishnaic dictum "Provide yourself with a teacher" (*Avot*, 1:16). See *LS*, XXIX:247-8, Address of *Shabbat Parashat Devarim*, 5746 [August 9th, 1986].

19. *IK*, XV:371-2, Letter 5,697 of *Ellul* 1st, 5717 [August 28th, 1957] to R. Yaakov Eliezer Herzog of Melbourne, Australia. Here R. Schneerson encouraged the empowering of capable senior students with the role of teaching of younger classes for a limited period each day.

20. As previously encountered, RSB, in his address of *Simchat Torah* 5660 [July 27th, 1890, cited in *HaYom Yom*:13, entry of *Tevet* 22nd; *IK-RJIS*, IV:186] had likened the educational obligation toward one's children to that of the Biblical obligation (Exodus, 13:16; Deuteronomy, 5:8) to don *tefillin*. He stated, "Just as wearing *tefillin* every day is a *mitzvah* commanded by the

Torah to every individual regardless of standing in Torah, whether deeply learned or simple, so too it is an absolute duty for every person to spend a half hour every day thinking about the Torah education of children and to do everything in one's power—and beyond one's power—to inspire children to follow the path along which they are being guided." Noting that *tefillin* are worn on the head (symbolic of full devotion of intellectual faculties to Divinity) and on the arm facing the heart (symbolizing devotion of one's emotional attributes to Divinity), R. Schneerson (*LS*, I:9) argued that Rabbi Shalom DovBer's comparison underscored the duty and responsibility of the educator and parent to totally devote mind and heart to the task of religious and moral education. See also *IK*, V:67-8.

21. *LS*, VI:309; *IK*, I:82-3, Letter 52, Letter of *Shevat* 11th, 5703 [Jan. 17th, 1943].

22. Address of *Tammuz* 13th, 5722 [July 19th, 1962]; Letter of *Nissan* 11th, 5715 [April 3rd, 1955] in *IK*, XV:33-7.

23. Addenda to *Torat Menachem-Reshimat HaYoman*:462.

24. *Ibid.*

25. *IK,* I:165-6, Letter 92.

26. *Op. cit.*, IV:56-7, Letter 812.

27. *Op. cit.*, I:75-8, Letter 48.

28. *Op. cit.*, IV:56-7, Letter 812; *op. cit.*, IV:305-6, Letter 1,029.

29. *Op. cit.*, XXI:142, Letter 7,899.

30. *Op. cit.*, II:95-6, Letter 210.

31. *Op. cit.*, IV:242-3, Letter 972.

32. *Op. cit.*, I:57-8, Letter 35.

33. *Vayikra Rabba*, 11:7; Prologue to *Esther Rabba*, sec. 11.

34. *IK*, I:69-70, Letter 44 citing Jerusalem Talmud, *Sanhedrin*, 10:2.

35. *Reshimot*, II:260-8 [*Reshima* No. 30].

36. *Mechilta* cited by Rashi [and *Shemot Rabba*, 28:2] commenting on *Shemot* 19:3: "...Thus shall you say to the House of Jacob and tell the Children of Israel."

37. *IK,* II:80-1, Letter 203.

38. *Op. cit.*, XXI:102-3, Letter 7,851.

39. *Op. cit.*, XXI:142, Letter 7,899.

40. *Op. cit.*, IV:56-7, Letter 812.

41. *Op. cit.*, I:249-50, Letter 136.

42. *Op. cit.*, II:82; *op. cit.*, V:56; *op. cit.*, VI:3; VIII:190-1 and multiple Hebrew letters; English letter of *Ellul* 28th, 5730 [Sept. 29th, 1970] published in *Return to Roots*:222 and *Letters from the Rebbe*, II:84-5, Letter 33.

43. *Ibid.*

44. *IK*, XXI:141-2, Letter 7,898; *op. cit.*, V:169-70, Letter 1,373. Applying the horticultural metaphor to the study of a *yeshivah* student, R. Schneerson utilized the notion of "ploughing" to refer to the student's meticulous observance of the *yeshivah* schedule, even when it means less devotion to sleeping and eating and when it means that he will prioritize activity antithetical to his desire to

be lazy or lacking in devotion and application. Also, for a *yeshivah* student, "sowing" means studying with appropriate devotion and application.

45. *Reshimot*, III:75-7 [*Reshima* No. 52] citing Deuteronomy 1:13, as interpreted by *Sifri* and Rashi.
46. *Op. cit.*, II:260-8 [*Reshima* No. 30]; *IK*, XXI:126-7, Letter 7,881.
47. *IK*, IV:54-5, Letter 811.
48. *Op. cit.*, I:83-4, Letter 53.
49. *Op. cit.*, IV:458-9, Letter 1,181.
50. *Op. cit.*, XVIII:296, Letter 6,790.
51. Note the Habad custom that does not approve of children "snatching" the *Afikoman* [portion of *matza* needed on the Passover *Seder* night] and using it to ransom a reward (*Haggadah Shel Pesach Im Likkutei Ta'amim, Minhagim U'Biurim*:11).
52. *IK*, IV:371-3, Letter 1,090.
53. *Ibid.*, citing Talmud, *Bava Batra*, 8a and *Chiddushei Aggadot, loc. cit.*
54. *Reshimot*, II:260-8 [*Reshima* No. 30].
55. *IK*, III:231-2, Letter 555.
56. *Op. cit.*, IV:328-9, Letter 1,051.
57. Talmud, *Yevamot*, 114a.
58. Talmud, *Horayot*, 11a.
59. Rambam, *Mishneh Torah*, the conclusion of *Hilchot Mikva'ot*.
60. Ezekiel, 25:9.
61. Exodus, 19:6.
62. *IK*, I:119-20, Letter 72. This theme also pervades (with textual variations and variant derivations) two other letters, namely, *op. cit.*, I:283-4, Letter 152 and *op. cit.*, I:284-6, Letter 153.
63. *Ibid.*
64. *IK*, III:310-1, Letter 618. "One who seeks to purify [others] receives assistance" (Talmud, *Yoma* 38b, as explained by RSZ in *Likkutei Torah*, discourse *Havaya Lee B'Ozray*:89d-90a, Paragraph 5).
65. *IK*, I:82-3, Letter 52.
66. This notion is confirmed by Genesis, 18:19, which identifies the cause of G-d's choosing Abraham to be "...because he commanded his household after him" and because Abraham was an individual "who instructed his children and his household after him to follow in his way."
67. *IK*, I:139-40, Letter 84.
68. *Op. cit.*, IV:328-9, Letter 1,051; see also *op. cit.*, III:435-6, Letter 730, where R. Schneerson expressed his belief that parents must entreat G-d that their children, irrespective of the challenges their children face in their future lives, remain Jews and good Jews, both in areas "between man and G-d," as well as in their relationship with their parents and in the area of interpersonal relationships.
69. *Op. cit.*, III:316-7, Letter 623 citing Talmud, *Kiddushin*, 42b.

70. *Op. cit.*, IV:170-1, Letter 914.
71. *Op. cit.*, I:249-50, Letter 136.
72. *Letters from the Rebbe*, III:15-6, Letter 12.
73. *IK*, III:265-6, Letter 579.
74. Maimonides, *Mishneh Torah, Laws of Teshuvah*, 3:4.
75. *IK*, I:110-2, Letter 65.
76. *Op. cit.*, I:82-3, Letter 52; *op. cit.*, XXI:107, Letter 7,857; *op. cit.*, V:66-8, Letter 1,281, §6.
77. *TM*, IV [*TM-5712*:I]:237-8.
78. A collection of pivotal expressions of R. Schneerson's enunciation of this theme are anthologized in Kehot Publication Society's *HaMechanech* (2009) compiled by Rabbi Eliyahu Friedman (1989) and translated by Solomon (2009) as "The Educator's Privilege."
79. *IK*, IV:93-4, Letter 841.
80. *Op. cit.*, IV:113-4, Letter 858.
81. See *op. cit.*, XV:28-31, Letter 5,355 and *IK*, XVII:339-41, Letter 6,490.
82. *Op. cit.*, VIII:227; *op. cit.*, XIV:511-2; *op. cit.*, XIV:525-6; *op. cit.*, XX:236; *LS*, XVI:553; *op. cit.*, XXII:356, *op. cit.*, 399; *op. cit.*, XXIV:347.
83. *Op. cit.*, III:254-5, Letter 572; *op. cit.*, XXI:126-7, Letter 7,881; *op. cit.*, XXIII:357, Letter 8,962.
84. *Op. cit.*, XXI:30-1, Letter 7,779.
85. Address of Shabbat *Parashat Vayeishev, Shabbat Chanukkah, Kislev* 26th, 5733 [Dec. 2nd, 1972].
86. *IK*, XX:336-8.
87. *Op. cit.*, XXI:126-7, Letter 7,881.
88. *Op. cit.*, IV:371-3, Letter 1,090.
89. *TM-5710* (1992 edition):7-8.
90. *SK-5689-5710* [1929-1950]:154-5, Paragraph 15.
91. *IK*, XXI:126-7, Letter 7,881.
92. *Op. cit.*, IV:423-4, Letter 1,143; *TM*, IV [*TM-5712*:I]:237-8.
93. *IK*, IV:423, Letter 1,142.
94. *Op. cit.*, IV:113-4, Letter 858, citing Talmud, *Temura* 16a.
95. *Op. cit.*, I:57-8, Letter 35.
96. *TM-HIT*, III [5711, II]:333-5.
97. *IK*, III:320-1, Letter 626.
98. *Pirkei Avot*, 4:2.
99. *Pe'ah*, I:1.
100. *Ibid.*
101. Talmud, *Sukka*, 49b.
102. *Tanya, Iggeret HaKodesh*, Chapter 9.
103. *IK*, XVII:313.
104. *Op. cit.*, IV:458, Letter 1,180; *op. cit.*, IV:469-70, Letter 1,188; *op. cit.*, IV:503-4, Letter 1,218.

105. *Op. cit.*, XXI:126-7, Letter 7,881.
106. *Op. cit.*, IV:83-4, Letter 832.
107. *Op. cit.*, IV:469-70, Letter 1,188; *op. cit.*, IV:503-4, Letter 1,218.
108. *Op. cit.*, XXI:126-7, Letter 7,881, citing *RJIS*.
109. *Op. cit.*, IV:423-4, Letter 1,143.
110. *Op. cit.*, IV:458, Letter 1,180.
111. *TM*, IV [5712, I]:77.
112. *IK*, IV:113-4, Letter 858.
113. *Op. cit.*, IV:113-4, Letter 858 citing Talmud, *Temura* 16a on Proverbs, 29:13 and end of *Hakdamat HaMelaket* to *Tanya* (See *TM-HIT*, III [5711, II]:224-6).
114. *IK*, V:66-8, Letter 1,281, §6.
115. *Op. cit.*, IV:113-4, Letter 858; *op. cit.*, XIII:198-200, Letter 858.
116. *IK*, III:251, Letter 569*; *op. cit.*, V:304, Letter 1,503; see also *op. cit.*, XVIII:189-90, Letter 6,693.
117. *Op. cit.*, III:251, Letter 569*.
118. *Op. cit.*, III:462-4, Letter 749.
119. *Op. cit.*, IV:72-3, Letter 825.
120. *Op. cit.*, III:396, Letter 695.
121. *Op. cit.*, IV:109-10, Letter 854.
122. *Op. cit.*, III:396, Letter 695.
123. *Op. cit.*, XXI:126-7, Letter 7,881.
124. *Op. cit.*, III:284-6, Letter 595.
125. English letter of *Adar–Rishon* 20th, 5711 [March 28th, 1951], Addressee: Ms. Dena Mendelowitz, Vice-President, Jewish Culture Foundation, N.Y.
126. *IK*, IV:56-7, Letter 812; *LS*, III:792-4.
127. *Op. cit.*, III:265-6, Letter 579. He urged (*op. cit.*, III:469-71, Letter 753) such individuals to emulate "a soldier who does not understand the workings of a rifle or military tactics but devotes himself to the general [in this case RJIS] and does so with joy and is thereby victorious." As well, regarding one's shortcomings, R. Schneerson taught that one may not speak negatively about even oneself.
128. *Op. cit.*, IV:390, Letter 1,107.
129. *Op. cit.*, IV:10-1, Letter 775.
130. Ezekiel, 33:24.
131. *IK*, I:73, Letter 46.
132. *Op. cit.*, IV:489-90, Letter 1,205; *TM-HIT*, III [5711, II]:333-5.
133. *IK*, III:481-2, Letter 761.
134. *Op. cit.*, I:138-9, Letter 83 citing Rabbi Moshe Ibn Ezra in *Shirat Yisrael*.
135. *Op. cit.*, III:284-6, Letter 595.
136. *Op. cit.*, I:38-40, Letter 22.
137. *Op. cit.*, I:73, Letter 46.

138. *Op. cit.*, I:118-9, Letter 71; *op. cit.*, I:283-4, Letter 152. In a particular case, R. Schneerson argued (*op. cit.*, V:80-1, Letter 1,293) that it was imperative that his correspondents communicate with their daughter-in-law about observance of Family Purity, *Kashrut*, and Shabbat observance upon which the happiness of her husband and her children is contingent. He argued that their involvement was imperative.

139. *Op. cit.*, V:80-1, Letter 1,293.

140. *Op. cit.*, III:353-4, Letter 655.

141. *Letters from the Rebbe*, III:16, Letter 13.

142. *IK*, I:66-7, Letter 42. Arguing against despair despondency, R. Schneerson (*op. cit.*, II:384-5, Letter 398) cited RJIS's aphorism citing his father, RSB (*HaYom Yom*, entry of *Adar-Sheini* 8th), that "One positive deed is better than a thousand sighs."

143. *Op. cit.*, II:384-5, Letter 398; *op. cit.*, V:70-1, Letter 1,285; *IK*, V:80-1, Letter 1,293.

144. *Op. cit.*, V:80-1, Letter 1,293.

145. *Op. cit.*, II:384-5, Letter 398.

146. Numbers, 14:6-9.

147. *IK*, I:295-6, Letter 157.

148. *Op. cit.*, III:316-7, Letter 623; *op. cit.*, III:353-4, Letter 655.

149. *Op. cit.*, III:316-7, Letter 623 citing *SM-RJIS-5710*:238-41, §9-§10.

150. *Op. cit.*, III:320-1, Letter 626.

151. *Op. cit.*, II:308-9, Letter 337.

152. *Ibid.* An individual soul thereby also becomes connected to its "all-encompassing soul."

153. *Op. cit.*, III:366, Letter 668; *op. cit.*, III:401, Letter 700.

154. Psalms, 100:2.

155. To Habad devotees R. Schneerson (*IK*, III:366, Letter 668) urged that they reflect on how Habad *Admorim* had shown self-sacrifice that their missions be carried out with kindness and mercy.

156. *Op. cit.*, II:81-2, Letter 204.

157. *Op. cit.*, XIV:433-4, Letter 5,212; *op. cit.*, XV:28-31, Letter 5,355.

158. *Op. cit.*, I:114-5, Letter 68.

159. *Op. cit.*, I:63-4, Letter 40.

160. *Op. cit.*, IV:371-3, Letter 1090.

161. *Op. cit.*, I:82-3, Letter 52.

162. *Op. cit.*, I:81-2, Letter 51.

163. *Bereishit*, 43:9 and 44:18-34.

164. *LS*, I:94-5.

165. *IK*, XXI:12-3, Letter 7,764.

166. *Op. cit.*, I:36-7, Letter 20.

167. *Ibid.*

168. *Op. cit.*, I:120-1, Letter 73.

169. *Op. cit.*, I:53-4, Letter 32.

170. *Op. cit.*, IV:56-7, Letter 812.
171. *Ibid.*
172. *TM*, III [5711, II]:333-5.
173. *Reshimot*, III:75-7 [*Reshima* No. 52].
174. Rabbi Moshe Ibn Ezras in *Shirat Yisrael*.
175. *IK*, I:138-9, Letter 83; *op. cit.*, IV:56-7, Letter 812; *IK*, IV:170-1, Letter 914.
176. *TM-HIT*, III [5711, II]:224-6.
177. *TM*, III [5711, II]:333-5.
178. *IK*, I:138-9, Letter 83.
179. *Op. cit.*, III:246-8, Letter 566.
180. *Op. cit.*, I:249-50, Letter 136.
181. *TM-HIT*, III [5711, II]:333-5.
182. *HaYom Yom* for *Adar-Rishon* 30th.
183. *IK*, III:320-1, Letter 626.
184. R. Schneerson cited the teaching of *Chiddushei HaRim* based on *Psalms* 106:32.
185. *LS*, III:792-4.
186. RJIS was viewed by R. Schneerson (*IK*, III:328-9) to be the exemplification of application to the rescue of Jewish children, particularly through education. R. Schneerson (*op. cit.*, III:333-4, Letter 637) told his adherents that all must seek to emulate his example, adding that "if we but desire, we are capable of emulating RJIS's personification of self-sacrifice, his being a *Gaon*, possessing exemplary character traits, a *Tzaddik*, a recipient of Divine inspiration and one accustomed to miracles."
187. *Op. cit.*, III:375-6, Letter 677, citing *Avot*, 4:2.
188. *Klallei HaChinuch V'HaHadracha* [The Principles of Education and Guidance], Chapter 14.
189. *IK*, I:119-20, Letter 72; *op. cit.*, I:283-4, Letter 152; *op. cit.*, I:284-6, Letter 153.
190. *Op. cit.*, I:119-20, Letter 72; *op. cit.*, I:284-6, Letter 153.
191. *Op. cit.*, III:316-7, Letter 623.
192. *Ibid.*
193. *Op. cit.*, I:119-20, Letter 72.
194. *Op. cit.*, I:197-8, Letter 110; see also *op. cit.*, I:199-200, Letter 112, where R. Schneerson explains that one assists a "dislocated" soul by disturbing lethargy and tranquility to ensure a return to the source.
195. *Op. cit.*, I:284-6, Letter 153.
196. *Sefer Zikaron-Michtavim, Teshuvot U'Ma'anot MiKvod Kedushat Admor R. Menachem M. Schneerson MiLubavitch* [*Memorial Book in Honor of Rev Aron Dov Sufrin*], I:10-1. R. Schneerson (*TM-HIT*, IV [*HIT-TM -5712*:I]:227-31) also found confirmation of this concept in the mystical meaning of the Chanukkah lights—which take place precisely after dark, when all oils have been contaminated, and which were instituted after the destruction of the Temple. The *menorah*'s position on the left means

that one is empowered and obliged to light up someone who is really one's 'other.' [See *Bamidbar Rabba*, end of XXII; *Tanya*, Section 1:Chapter 32: "...but someone who is not his friend...One needs to draw them close...To bring them near to Torah and the service of G-d."]

197. *SK-5736* [1975-76], II:633-8; Address of *Av* 23rd, 5736 [August 19th, 1976]; *SH-5748* [1988], II:590 addressed to the Israeli Team participating in the 1976 Paraplegic Olympics. R. Schneerson elaborated on the principle that a physical deficiency is indicative of a greater spiritual potential, enabling the individual to more than compensate for the deficiency.

198. *SK-5736* [1975-76], I:548-49; *LS*, XXV:514-5.

199. Addresses of *Shabbat* of *Av* 20th and Saturday night, *Av* 21st, 5740 [August 3rd, 1980], in *SK-5740* [1979-80], III:880-903.

200. Pastoral letter of *Nissan* 11th, 5717 [May 12th, 1957] published in *IK*, XV:33-6.

201. R. Schneerson's view was predicated on the Midrashic statement (*Bamidbar Rabba,* 12:3) that G-d only requires of individuals according to their abilities. From this principle, R. Schneerson argued that negative circumstances are indicative of Divine bestowing of greater latent abilities.

202. Address of the Last Day of *Pesach, Nissan* 22nd, 5712 [April 17th, 1952] in *LS,* I:128; *op. cit.,* I:27-53; Letter of *Nissan* 11th, 5712 [April 6th, 1952] in *IK,* V:308-9, Letter 1,507.

203. Hebrew/English letter of *Kislev* 15th, 5738 [Nov. 25th, 1977] in *Letters from the Rebbe*, II:187-9, Letter 87.

204. *LS*, XXIX:263-71.

205. *TM-HIT-5742* [1981-2], III:1,456.

206. Address of *Shabbat Parashat Ekev*, 5740 [Aug. 2nd, 1980] in *Sichot Kodesh-5740*, III:89733-901.

207. *TM*, II [5711:I]:315-9, §20-§23.

208. *IK*, III:475-6, Letter 756.

209. *Op. cit.,* I:56-7, Letter 34.

210. *IK-RJIS*, IX, Letter of *Adar* 29th, 5707 [March 21st, 1947], Letter 2,999, in a letter addressed to the Board of *Merkos L'Inyonei Chinuch*, suggested the speedy implementation of courses to enable *Yeshivah* heads and primary and secondary Jewish Studies teachers, to expand and develop their knowledge concerning educational methodology. In a letter of the same day (*ibid.*, letter 3,000) RJIS wrote to the educators of the New York *Lubavitcher Yeshivah* and its subsidiary branches throughout America. He urged all education faculty of *Tomchei Temimim* to attend those courses for the above-mentioned purpose and to obtain formal accreditation for these skills. As a result of this directive, weekly pedagogic courses were conducted for senior students of RJIS's *Yeshivah* and *Kollel*, the post-graduate academy for Talmudic studies for married students (multiple interviews between 2010 and 2014 with Rabbi Moshe Pesach Goldman).

211. *IK*, III:237-8, Letter 559.

212. *Op. cit.*, III:308-9. Letter 616.
213. *Op. cit.*, IV:242-3, Letter 972.
214. *Op. cit.*, III:265-6, Letter 579.
215. *Op. cit.*, XXI:28-9, Letter 7,777; *op. cit.*, I:103-4, Letter 61.
216. *Op. cit.*, I:57-8, Letter 35.
217. *Op. cit.*, XXI:28-9, Letter 7,777.
218. *Op. cit.*, II:314-6, Letter 343.
219. *Op. cit.*, III:320-1, Letter 626.
220. *Ibid.*
221. *Op. cit.*, XI:125, Letter 3,509.
222. *Op. cit.*, IV:298, Letter 1,024.
223. *Op. cit.*, V:66-8, Letter 1,281, §6.
224. Jeremiah, 15:19; Targum & Rashi, *loc. cit.*
225. *IK*, XXI:81, Letter 7,828.
226. *Op. cit.*, III :1-2, Letter 406.
227. English letter of *Nissan* 26th, 5724 [April 8th, 1964] in *Letters from the Rebbe*, IV:64-74, Letter 38.
228. *Ibid.*
229. *Ibid.*
230. *IK*, XXI:107, Letter 7857. He wrote here, "Every man and woman shares some responsibility for education."
231. *Shulchan Aruch, Yoreh De'ah*, Section 248.
232. *IK*, III:462-4, Letter 749.
233. *TM*, III [5711, II]:85-92, §19-§27 & §29. See also *IK*, IV:242-3, Letter 972 where education is viewed as leading the student out of darkness to light, arguing that everyone must assist in showing the way from darkness to light.
234. While viewing the educational task to be the obligation of all, including those in other professions, R. Schneerson simultaneously supported the cause of pedagogic training for those who would take on the educational role in a professional capacity. See *IK*, XV:353, Letter 5,698 of *Ellul* 1st, 5717 [August 28th, 1957].
235. R. Schneerson (*LS*, III:792-4, §13) believed that everyone shares a responsibility for education and not only the professional educator, in the same way that all must contribute to extinguishing a fire, not only professional fire-fighters. This analogy is in harmony with R. Schneerson's citation (*op. cit.*, I:98-102) of RJIS's utilization of a conflagrational metaphor, which likened the futility of compromising educational ideals to attempting to extinguish a fire with kerosene.
236. *IK*, XV:28, Letter 5,355.
237. *Op. cit.*, III:466-7, Letter 751. Also, and even especially, *yeshivah* students are duty-bound to devote a portion of their time to awakening and educating others.

238. *Op. cit.*, I:61-2, Letter 38; *op. cit.*, I:62-3, Letter 39; *op. cit.*, I:63-4, Letter 40; *op. cit.*, I:65, Letter 41; *op. cit.*, III:333-4, Letter 637.

239. In the same letter (*IK*, XV:2) R. Schneerson wrote, "The circumstances of the individual endowed with special talent in communal affairs differ from those whose communal undertakings are done out of a sense of duty and self-discipline." Concerning those individuals who are totally committed to religious education, R. Schneerson wrote (unpublished letter to R. Yehuda Cohen) that "One who has been active in *chinuch* has special G-d-given gifts and capacities for it, and whose qualifications go hand-in-hand with his total commitment to Torah and *mitzvot*—is obviously duty-bound to continue to carry on this great responsibility, which is also a great *zechut* (merit)." To R. Schneerson the educator thus possesses a Divinely bestowed pre-disposition to the pre-requisite ability and potential to discharge his or her educational responsibility. The educator is, in fact, the delegated representative of the Creator, who as emissary and envoy must not shirk from the educational responsibility. This is in keeping with the theme of pre-ordained victory.

240. The Talmudic concept (*Shabbat* 118b) of an individual *mitzvah* "with which one is more meticulous" is cited by R. Schneerson (*IK*, XV:28-31) as evidence for this distinction. This Talmudic source is elaborated by RSZ (*Tanya, Igeret HaKodesh*, end of Ch. 7) and by RJIS (*SH-RJIS-Summer-5700* [1940]:22) to imply the existence of a particular religious observance through which all other human initiatives proceed and through which a Divine response is primarily activated.

241. *IK*, XV:29.

242. *IK*, V:252-3. Pastoral letter of *Adar* 7th, 5712 [March 4th, 1952], addressed to "All Participants Involved in Authentic Religious Education and Especially Those Involved in the Education of Small Children."

243. He believed (*IK*, III:256-7, Letter 574) that there is a responsibility to provide leadership as well as with financial, material, and spiritual assistance to the masses of uneducated people.

244. *Op. cit.*, IV:56-7, Letter 812.

245. *Op. cit.*, VIII:254-5, Letter 1,443.

246. *LS*, III:792-4, 12.

247. Pastoral letter of *Adar* 7th, 5712 [March 4th, 1952], addressed to "All Participants Involved in Authentic Religious Education and Especially Those Involved in the Education of Small Children" (*IK*, VIII:254-5, Letter 1,443).

248. The *Midrash* (*Esther Rabba* 8:7, 9:4; *Yalkut Shimoni, Esther*, paras. 1057-8) relates that when Haman's intended decree of annihilation of the Jews became known, Mordechai, the leader of Jewry at that time, went out into the streets and gathered some twenty-two thousand children, whom he taught Torah and with whom he prayed for G-d's mercy. R. Schneerson observed that Mordechai was a head of the *Sanhedrin* (religious court), indeed the greatest Jew of his time, who nevertheless disregarded his

elevated status and proceeded to imbue young children with a spirit of selfless devotion to Torah.

249. *IK*, I:197-8, Letter 110.
250. *Op. cit.*, III:481-2, Letter 761.
251. *Op. cit.*, III:466-7, Letter 751 [Addenda to *LS*, IX:305-6] argued that providing education in this day and age is in the category of "a *mitzvah* that cannot be delegated to others."
252. English letter of *Adar–Rishon* 20th, 5711 [March 28th, 1951] addressed to Ms. Dena Mendelowitz, vice-president of the Jewish Culture Foundation of N.Y.
253. *IK*, III:466-7, Letter 751. Youth who engage in this work also share the privilege of being connected to G-d and the Torah.
254. *Op. cit.*, III:284-6, Letter 595; *op. cit.*, XIII:198-200.
255. See G. E. Zuriff, 1996.
256. See Lorella Terzi, 2005.
257. See Laura Purdy, 2000.
258. *Yechidut* of Rabbi Moshe Herson of the Rabbinical College of Morristown, New Jersey.
259. For an example of the linkage of contemporary crisis to enhanced responsibility, see English letter of 1964 entitled "The House Is on Fire and Our Children Are Inside" in *Chayenu* of the week of *Parashat Lech L'cha*, 5714 [Oct. 26th–Nov. 1st]. R. Schneerson wrote: "When an emergency arises, however, all theoretical differences must be put aside in order to deal with the emergency.... At such a time there can be no difference of opinion as to the imperative need to fight the blaze and save the trapped ones. This is the duty of everyone who is nearby, even if he is not a trained firefighter, and even if those trapped inside the burning house are strangers. The obligation is immeasurably greater, of course, if those inside are one's own relatives, and especially if one has had experience and has been successful in fire-extinguishing activity.... More compelling still is this duty to one who has tried his ability in the field of education and has met with success."
260. See edited address of 2nd night of Pesach, *Nissan* 16th, 5714 [April 19th, 1954] in *LS*, I:98-102.
261. Address of Shabbat *Parashat Lech L'cha*, *Cheshvan* 8th, 5741 [Oct. 18th, 1980] in *SK-5741*, I:367-76, *Sicha* #2, §33-§52 & *op. cit*, 392-4, *Sicha* #4, §84-§87.
262. Address of *Nissan* 11th, 5741 [April 15th, 1981].
263. *IK*, IV:176-7, Letter 920.
264. *Op. cit.*, IV:455-7, Letter 1,178. While in this correspondence R. Schneerson applied this principle specifically to the people of Morocco, the contemporary acceptance of kosher education worldwide infers its applicability to a variety of situations.
265. *Op. cit.*, I:56-7, Letter 34.

Chapter 6

THE METHODOLOGY
OF EDUCATION

Education and guidance constitute a comprehensive discipline with many principles concerning the proper preparation of both educator and pupil.
　　　　　—Rabbi Yosef Yitzchak Schneersohn[1]

R. Schneerson's account of educational methodology would appear to be predicated upon his understanding of the nature and aims of education and the nature of educational authority and responsibility. His understanding that "everything is educational" has implications for the methodology where use of all educational opportunities becomes a key educational strategy. This perception in turn influences R. Schneerson's understanding of educational responsibility which also implies a process that requires the educator to seize teachable moments and be present in the moment. The notion of education being an endeavor of universal significance with implications for the individual, the wider community, and redemption, making education a life-saving rescue, leads inexorably to a methodology where urgency and proactivity are crucial. Thus, enthusiasm must characterize educational endeavor as revealed in R. Schneerson's horticultural metaphor where an active approach implies that education is characterized by constant, incremental advancements. These examples of methodological implications of R. Schneerson's understanding of education are indicators of a coherence to the elements of his educational discourse.

R. Schneerson's aims of education have been presented in Chapter 3. These aims call for a methodology where education is permeated with self-sacrifice, devotion, and sanctity and where ideals are not compromised. Moreover, the aims lead directly to empowering students to be exemplars and role models, becoming educators and even disciplinarians themselves.

In addition, R. Schneerson's understanding of the parameters of responsibility for education is one where the educator shows concern and sensitivity for the needs of the individual, based on an inclusivism and a positive perspective of the learner, including those learners requiring special education. Other methodologies include ensuring that a unity and harmony characterize efforts by educators, employing educational methodologies that encourage student focus and guarantee that the language of instruction is secondary to an emphasis on content.

The discussion of methodology will be subdivided into the following categories:

(a) Methodologies Emerging from R. Schneerson's View of the Nature of Education
   · utilization of all educational opportunities;
   · urgency and enthusiasm must characterize educational endeavor; and
   · a proactive approach to education with constant incremental advancements.

(b) Methodologies Emerging from R. Schneerson's View of the Aims of Education
   · education must be permeated with self-sacrifice, devotion, and sanctity;
   · ideals must be communicated without compromise;
   · teaching must take place in a way that empowers the learner to be an exemplar;
   · empowering the learner to be an educator; and
   · empowering the learner to be a disciplinarian.

(c) Methodologies Emerging from R. Schneerson's View of the Responsibility for Education
- showing concern and sensitivity for the needs of the individual;
- inclusivism must characterize educational endeavor; and
- the positive view of the learner must prevail.

(d) Methodologies beyond Texts Encountered
- unity and harmony must characterize educators' efforts;
- education must encourage student focus; and
- language of instruction must be secondary to content.

Utilization of All Educational Opportunities

It was R. Schneerson's belief that all information can provide inspirational teachings for moral edification.[2] Based on this premise he derived many lessons from the game of chess[3] and other worldly phenomena.[4] Similarly, he was insistent that seasons and festivals occurring during the Jewish year provide auspicious moments for education.[5] Such festivals, like *Purim*,[6] *Pesach*,[7] and *Shavuot*,[8] provide unique educational opportunities. For example, R. Schneerson wrote regarding *Shavuot*:

> G-d Almighty said to the Jewish people, "Bring for Me reliable guarantors that you will guard the Torah and I will then give it to you." When those who were to receive the Torah declared, "Our children will be our guarantors" [meaning that they would educate their children in the path of Torah], G-d responded, "These are certainly good guarantors and because of them, I will give the Torah to you."[9] *As it was then, so it is now.* It behooves each and every one of us, in preparing him or herself for the forthcoming festival of Shavuot, the Season of the Giving of the Torah, to now do all in his or her capacity for

the education of Jewish boys and girls in the path of the
Torah. We should make a firm resolve and take upon
ourselves to endeavor in this matter with even greater enthusiasm after the festival of the Giving of the Torah. *All
Jews are responsible for one another.* The above-mentioned
effort, when focused exclusively on the *chinuch* of our
own sons and daughters, is utterly insufficient. Each of
us is *definitely* able to influence, at least to some extent,
the *chinuch* [religious education] of Jewish boys and girls
in our immediate environment and also exert influence
on the *chinuch* received by those geographically removed
from us, even those children in another country...[10]

In the life of the individual, birthdays[11] also provide inspirational opportunities[12] when the educator can be both pre-emptive
and proactive.[13]

Urgency and Enthusiasm Must Characterize Education

The critical urgency[14] that characterized R. Schneerson's recommended methodology for education[15] can be viewed as an outgrowth
of the metaphor whereby he compares education to life-saving rescue. Because education is seen as the spiritual equivalent of saving
lives, it requires immediate and energetic special attention, and
must become the focus of all the educator's powers and applied with
much eagerness.[16] As well, because R. Schneerson viewed education
as key to activating learner potential, education takes on an urgency
where it assumes priority over virtually all other considerations. R.
Schneerson would repeatedly recommend beginning working toward an educational objective immediately, without delay.[17]

From the horticultural metaphor, R. Schneerson inferred that
just as the farmer must be at the right place at the right time, so
too educational success is contingent upon the educator's being

at the right place at the right time,[18] activated immediately and energetically.[19]

Factors that R. Schneerson believed should be set aside to facilitate urgent fulfillment of the imperative educational task included even pressing financial issues. Thus, in a letter of *Shevat* 22nd, 5735 [February 3rd, 1975], R. Schneerson wrote:

> Time is particularly of the essence in the area of education... for when one embarks upon ambitious educational programs, involving financial problems, it is clear that the financial difficulty can be overcome in due course, while, if it were to curtail an educational activity, or even to delay it, the loss may be irretrievable. A Jewish child who is deprived of proper Torah *Chinuch* not only suffers an immediate loss, but he or she may fall under undesirable influences from which it might later be difficult to extricate him or her.[20]

Consequently, he also encouraged[21] the investment of substantial resources into education, arguing that G-d is the source of financial wealth.[22] He urged people to devote generously to education, aware that Judaism viewed expenses relating to children's religious education as predetermined at the outset of the creation.[23] Moreover, R. Schneerson[24] extended the application of this principle to the Torah study of all children,[25] arguing that the extra expense incurred was "on G-d's account."[26] Even working on personal self-improvement did not justify an educator keeping others waiting for their educational assistance.[27]

In keeping with the urgency and proactivity which he saw as vital educational methodologies, citing Halachic evidence,[28] R. Schneerson argued[29] that religious education must not be deferred, but rather is to be commenced from the earliest moments, insisting that it is never too early to embark upon education.[30] Quantitatively he believed that the more meaningful education that is given, the better the outcome.[31] Unsurprisingly, he encouraged a variety

of educational initiatives for children from newborns to pre-*Bar*-
and *Bat-Mitzvah* youth.

Along with the eagerness which R. Schneerson demanded be
applied to education,[32] he agitated for pre-emptive intervention
and action,[33] believing that to act proactively ensures that one is in
time to guarantee an education that guides children along the good
and upright path from childhood onward.[34] Any matter concerning youth was to assume priority status.[35] A practical way that this
proactivity was exemplified was through establishing educational
institutions which guarantee Jewish continuity,[36] particularly institutions of girls' education. Their urgency meant that an educator
must be aware that these vital tasks must never be deflected or de-
layed,[37] with full application to the task at hand.[38] R. Schneerson
considered an educator's responsibility to preclude abandonment
of his calling, challenging an educator who had ceased his full
involvement in education:

> ... how is it possible for you to stand on the side and not
> be involved with all your energy and strength? Consider
> the following scenario: were you to stand on the bank of
> a river studying a Talmudic theme at a point where your
> heart desires to study and you were to see an individual
> drowning in the river, surely you would interrupt your
> study and involve yourself in rescuing a human life?[39]

Thus, R. Schneerson's approach to education included a constant
call for the widest possible circulation and maximum dissemination of educational material to the community.[40] He encouraged
use of the media to publicize educational activities and active
outreach,[41] recommending lenient acceptance policy to a Psalm-
Recital Society that he was promoting.[42] This extraverted outreach
which aimed to draw irreligious people near to G-d through gentle
words[43] rather than by rejecting them[44] required one individual
to proactively desire for there to be another.[45] While he spoke of
"stretching out 'a long arm' to provide assistance," he was equally

insistent that this outreach be careful not to compromise the educator's personal standards, but acting only to elevate others to the educator's level of religiosity.[46]

However challenging a situation, R. Schneerson's insistence on an urgent approach meant that he displayed little tolerance for complacency and considered complaining about the situation to be an unsatisfactory response,[47] and silence was completely unacceptable in the face of an educational crisis.[48] For R. Schneerson, the only acceptable response was to proactively address the shortcomings immediately.[49] Only the dual method of reaching out to others coupled with a refusal to compromise ideals provides the winning strategy for successfully "extricating the precious from the corrupt."[50] Indeed, the proactive methodology that he advocated requires an expansive, inclusive approach to education rather than a parochial view of others.

An Innovative Approach to Education

R. Schneerson's predecessor, RJIS, viewed educational activity as being like any living entity which must proceed and grow, constantly developing and broadening.[51] To R. Schneerson, education must proceed from the premise that "tomorrow must be different"[52] where even small, steady incremental changes are vital. When viewed in this light, R. Schneerson's constant call for educators to expand the student population of their institutions and increase the numbers of helpers[53] is understandable. Besides this quantitative expansion, he believed that also, qualitatively, educational efforts must progressively increase periodically.[54] He envisaged a constant advancement in education where a mediocre education was improved to a good education, and from a good education to an even better one.[55] Educators must therefore always replenish their aspirations.[56] The vital methodologies that aimed to ensure an educator's improvement of his or her aspirations were an outgrowth of R. Schneerson's understanding of the responsibility for education.

Arguing that sanctity must be on the ascendancy, he cited the obligation to kindle the *menorah* at the outer doorway of the home without shame as symbolic of the ideal where people illuminate the outer environment represented by the public thoroughfare in an increasing measure each day.[57] He believed that small beginnings can and must lead to exalted ends.[58] Citing mystical teachings that confirmed this ideal, R. Schneerson observed that the progressive increase in revelation of heavenly light[59] requires a corresponding increase in "awakening from below," or at least an increase in the creation of practical vessels to contain this light.[60]

Education Must Be Permeated with Self-Sacrifice, Devotion, and Sanctity

Selfless altruism without an ulterior motive[61] was an ideal of Habad Hasidism since the movement's inception.[62] Unsurprisingly, self-sacrifice for education, fearless resistance to inhibition of Jewish education, and heroism for the sake of education were hallmarks of Habad[63] under the leadership of RJIS,[64] particularly in its fight against Communist oppression in the USSR. In keeping with this ideal, R. Schneerson urged that efforts for education be to the point of self-sacrifice.[65] Genuine self-sacrifice, where the educator is permeated by a whole-hearted dedication to this sacred task,[66] is an essential educational methodology that is always successful on some level.[67]

The need for the educator to devote himself or herself with self-sacrifice[68] and abnegation of the ego[69] is underscored by R. Schneerson's observation that historically, whenever there was self-sacrifice, the matter for which the sacrifice was displayed resulted in a permanent victory.[70] As well, R. Schneerson[71] emphasized that it was the self-sacrifice of women that saved our people. Moreover, the educator must show self-sacrifice for the individual, not only for the group.[72] In this context one can understand the intense and ardent educational campaigns recommended by R. Schneerson.[73] This self-sacrifice should be accompanied by teacher sincerity, where words that emanate from the heart were able to penetrate the heart of the learner,[74] as frequently cited by R. Schneerson.[75]

R. Schneerson endorsed and argued for the ideal of *chinuch al taharat hakodesh*, meaning "education in pure sanctity."[76] This meant that both educator and student should approach the study of Torah with reverence, and rather than seeking mere mastery of factual Torah knowledge, the student must be mindful that the Torah being studied is from G-d, and education is focused on gaining an appreciation of its inner truth.[77] The learner must be conscious of the transcendent essence of the Torah[78] while actively engaging his or her rational faculties to probe its meaning as much as humanly possible. This approach to Torah study is dependent on the concept of the ongoing gift of Torah as it was at Sinai,[79] where the Giving of the Torah is an ongoing event, and that Torah study today is a reliving of the Giving of the Torah.[80] Even the legalistic dimensions of Torah such as *halacha* (Jewish law) are a source of spiritual content.[81]

Moreover, such Torah study both inspires and is characterized by self-sacrifice,[82] with even disregard for personal considerations.[83] This disciplined attitude to Torah study is integral to the process that leads ultimately to acquisition of a genuine passion for Torah study.[84] R. Schneerson also argued that even the communication of general knowledge should be *al taharat hakodesh* (in pristine sanctity).[85] Therefore, penetrating the heart of the student can only occur when the educator is G-d-fearing and speaks with *mesirat nefesh* (self-sacrifice). The educator must address "the point of faith" within the learner, however hidden. Even though externally the educator communicates only intellectual reasoning, in the same way that the seed is concealed within the fruit and its peel, which have taste, appearance, and fragrance,[86] the factors that really infuse the educator's words with vitality and enthusiasm are the educator's personal devotion and idealism. R. Schneerson believed that from this convergence of factors will emerge a student like a tall tree bearing fruit and branches.[87]

Selfless idealism was not only the domain of the educator, but should also be the hallmark of the student. R. Schneerson believed the greater the level of selflessness and self-cultivation that infuses the educational setting, the more receptive the learner can be.[88] Even the student's rational and intellectual capacities must aspire to attain a level of dedication and self-sacrifice that transcends rationality.[89] The greater an individual's rational or strong-willed nature and the more self-assured, the more challenging is the self-transformation that the learner aspires to achieve and the more deficient is the learner's spiritual preparedness.[90]

Ideals Must Be Communicated Uncompromisingly

Another ramification of this methodology is that education must be without compromise of ideals.[91] Arguing that people should now recognize the absolute necessity to abandon any compromise, R. Schneerson wrote:

> If in years past there was room to discuss the legitimacy of sacrificing one aspect of faith in order to retain another, more basic principle, certainly now, after the trial of several decades, the matter should be perfectly clear. (I write explicitly "discuss" being that the conclusion even then was unequivocal: Once one begins to sacrifice a portion of the foundation, one ends up forsaking it entirely.) One can clearly see that the various forms of compromise have led to awful results. Clearly, one must stand strong, resisting any compromise on the foundations of Torah education. Then and only then can we hope to rescue the young generation, and effectively the middle-aged and elderly as well. The trial of the previous generation has also shown us that the children themselves denounce those who adopt the approach of compromise, saying, "had those who compromised genuinely believed in the opinions they professed, they wouldn't have compromised at

all, especially with matters concerning G-d's Torah." For, certainly, no person or authority has the right to compromise with the affairs of the Almighty.[92]

He also explained that young people raised on compromises are "deprived of enthusiasm and zeal for Judaism for the rest of their lives. The scar inflicted on their soul during their youth may, Heaven forbid, render them spiritually disadvantaged."[93] R. Schneerson urged an extensive campaign in every appropriate manner for all Jewish children and adolescents to be given an authoritatively Jewish education following in the traditions of our people and without compromise.[94]

In keeping with this principle and Habad's disdain for compromise and for whatever might lead to deflection from the scrupulous maintaining of an educational ideal, the Habad custom was, and still is, for parents and children to desist from the widespread practice of snatching the *Afikoman*[95] at the Passover *Seder* service, with tacit parental approval, thereby using it as leverage for extortion of gifts before allowing the Passover *Seder* service to proceed to its conclusion.[96]

The Learner as Exemplar

Empowering the student is a crucial methodology in R. Schneerson's educational writings, reaching its fullest realization with the notion of *shlichut* (an emissary) which was central to R. Schneerson's educational agenda. The role of a *shaliach* is based on the Talmudic principle[97] of the individual in whom the principal has invested his powers.[98] R. Schneerson wrote:

> It is a truism that every student grows up to be an educator, whether as a parent or a teacher, or even simply as a member of the society in which one lives. Directly or indirectly every person influences the immediate surroundings, to a greater or lesser degree, since no person

lives in isolation. No effort should therefore be spared in providing for the young generation the kind of education that will produce the best possible educators. This is particularly true in regard to Torah education. What children and youths will absorb in their formative years will set the stage for their adult and family life and will be reflected in their children and grandchildren in an unbroken chain....An investment in Torah education is certain to produce the cumulative dividends of inestimable value for all who will be touched by it in this and future generations.[99]

A pivotal methodology recommended by R. Schneerson was the empowering of students in two critical roles: as exemplars of ideals[100] as well as active educators of others.[101] A general observation for all students of *Tomchei Temimim yeshivot* was that they become "shining lights" of the *yeshivah*'s ideals.[102] R. Schneerson wrote that his predecessor's educational ideal was that "He demanded the kind of Torah education that would make the students *neirot leha'ir*—shining lights, spreading the light of Torah and *Mitzvot* around them even after concluding their studies at the *Yeshivah*; and the boys did not disappoint him."[103] He further explained in a letter to a resident of Northridge, California, that there is always a positive outcome, even if initially unrecognized by the exemplar:

> If this seems far-fetched and mystical, the following episode will illustrate what even a comparatively small effort can accomplish. You may have heard that many of our senior students volunteer their summer vacation to travel to distant places in order to reach out to fellow Jews in need of encouragement to strengthen their identity with, and commitment to, our people and the Torah way. In the course of this program it so happened that one of the students visited a small Jewishly isolated town where he found only a few Jewish families, and,

as he later reported, he was disappointed to have accomplished nothing there. But several months later, our *Merkos L'Inyonei Chinuch* which sponsors this program received a letter from one of the families in that town. The writer, a woman, related that one summer day she happened to stand by her front window when she saw a bearded young man, wearing a dark hat, his *Tzitzis* showing, approaching her door. She confessed that when she admitted the young man and learned of the purpose of his visit, she was not responsive, for she and her family were not prepared at that moment to change their lifestyle. Yet for a long time after that encounter, the appearance of the young man haunted her. He reminded her of her grandfather and had refreshed her memories of the beautiful Jewish life she had seen at her grandparents' home, though the material circumstances were incomparably more modest than she had come to know in her married life. Finally—the letter went on—she decided to make the change. She made her home kosher, and the family began to observe Shabbat and Yom Tov, and she is raising the children in a Torah way. Since then her home was filled with such contentment and serenity that she decided to write to the *Merkos L'Inyonei Chinuch* and express her profound gratitude.

Now, if all that was the result of a brief encounter with that young man, though unbeknown to him of his lasting impact, how much more can be achieved by an American Jewish family, whose influence is not limited to a few minutes conversation, but serves as a shining example of the kind of daily life and conduct that should be the privilege and blessing of every Jewish family.[104]

The ideal is that learners are actively engaged in sharing knowledge with others less knowledgeable than themselves, especially by serving as educators.

The Learner as Educator

R. Schneerson believed firmly in the empowering of students to participate in what he termed life-saving educational endeavors.[105] For example, he encouraged newly arrived Yemenite children in Israel to become educators and guides of other Yemenite children.[106] Similarly, he empowered students to publicly review Hasidic discourses for those of limited understanding, urging students to be prepared so that within a short time, each would be able to recite a Hasidic discourse that is effective and has an impact on listeners, including those who are not intellectuals or experts in Hasidic philosophy. In 1953, R. Schneerson wrote[107] that he was very pleased to learn of the sending of students to address Synagogue worshippers. He expressed his hope that this would influence both those who listened and the students themselves.

He recommended[108] that even individuals who considered their religious knowledge insufficient should assume an educational role. R. Schneerson interpreted the Mishnaic directive that a person "establish many students" to imply more than that they teach many students. R. Schneerson considered that it included developing one student to a point where that student proceeds to inspire their own students, in such a way that the educational initiative has an ongoing effect.[109] He also established a system where students of Habad *yeshivot* would be "travelling rabbis" to distant communities during their summer vacation.[110]

Professor Reuven Feuerstein, world expert on the education of Down-syndrome children, confirmed[111] that R. Schneerson's suggestion to empower such children to assume a leadership role was particularly radical when viewed against the educational climate of 1979. In a pioneering correspondence, R. Schneerson wrote:

> Part of the above approach, which, as far as I know, has not been used before, is to involve some of the trainees in some form of leadership, such as captains of teams, group leaders, and the like, without arousing the jealousy

of the others. The latter could be avoided on the basis of seniority, special achievement, exemplary conduct, etc.[112]

Additionally, R. Schneerson also believed in empowering young children and teenagers.[113] R. Schneerson[114] similarly urged that all students should be empowered with the responsibility for maintaining discipline of other students. He urged that even students who were not particularly disciplined themselves should be included in this project, recommending a rotating system, whereby everyone could take responsibility for a month.

The methodology of mindful concern for the individual learner's situation and paying special attention to the learner's specific circumstances was evident in many of R. Schneerson's personal educational practices and those that he managed.

Inclusivism

In R. Schneerson's educational writings, inclusivism is a pervasive theme, whereby he insisted that the educational agenda must encompass everyone[115] and be non-parochial.[116] In a typical expression of this ideal penned at the beginning of his leadership, he wrote:

> When a young man who is a Torah scholar is found in a city, it must be evident that there is a Jewish person in the city... You must take the youth in hand. All of the four types of sons are included in this category: The wise, the wicked, the simple and the one who does not know how to ask. There are no exceptions, as implied by the promise (Joshua, 24:3) "I will multiply his descendants."[117]

In the same letter, he explained that only "by adopting an approach that is appropriate for every young man and woman," Divine assurance for success in the educational task is actualized. When he wrote about outreach, he included even deeply estranged

youth whom he referred to in the context of the four sons of the
Pesach *Seder* service, as "the fifth son":

> While the "Four Sons" differ from one another in their
> reaction to the *Seder* Service, they have one thing in com-
> mon: they are *all* present at the *Seder* Service. Even the
> so-called "Wicked" son is there, taking an active, though
> rebellious, interest in what is going on in Jewish life
> around him. This, at least, justifies the hope that some day
> also the "Wicked" one will become wise, and all Jewish
> children attending the *Seder* will become conscientious,
> Torah-and-*Mitzvot*-observing Jews. Unfortunately, there
> is, in our time of confusion and obscurity, another kind
> of a Jewish child: the child who is conspicuous by his ab-
> sence from the *Seder* Service; the one who has no interest
> whatsoever in Torah and *Mitzvot*, laws and customs; who
> is not even aware of the *Seder-shel-Pesach*, of the Exodus
> from Egypt and the subsequent Revelation at Sinai.
>
> This presents a grave challenge, which should command
> our attention long before Passover and the *Seder*-night.
> For no Jewish child should be forgotten and abandoned.
> We must make every effort to save also that lost child, and
> bring the absentee to the *Seder* table. Determined to do so,
> and driven by a deep sense of compassion and responsibil-
> ity, we need have no fear of failure...There is no room
> for hopelessness in Jewish life, and no Jew should ever be
> given up as a lost cause. Through the proper compassion-
> ate approach of love of one's fellow, including even those
> of the "lost" generation can be brought back to the love
> of G-d and love of the Torah, and not only be included in
> the community of the "Four Sons," but in due course be
> elevated to the rank of the "Wise" son.[118]

It is consequently not surprising that he was insistent that his
educational endeavors be accessible to everyone, requiring of the

"*Mishnah* by heart" initiatives that he co-ordinated prior to becoming the seventh *Admor* of Habad, that "Ideally, the address [of the organization promoting the programme] should not be that of the Habad *yeshivah* [in Montreal], so as to underscore that this was in no way the initiative of one particular group..."[119] R. Schneerson advocated[120] compassion and understanding for those whom he termed "as-yet non-observant," refusing to categorize them as definitively irreligious.[121] He argued that the Biblical command[122] to love our neighbor as ourselves should inspire great compassion for someone who has not yet returned to observance through *teshuvah*.[123]

R. Schneerson was adamant that everyone avoids the approach of shutting themselves within their community, at the same time cautioning that inclusivism does not imply connecting to all aspects of secular society.[124] He also advocated that matters be structured so that children would not feel compelled to adopt norms of observance that they may consider too rigorous.[125]

R. Schneerson insisted that this inclusive approach be applied to a person's own children but extended it[126] to all students. For R. Schneerson, like at the Giving of the Torah, had there been 600,000 minus one individual, the Torah could not have been given, so too, no individual can be excluded from any educational activity.[127] R. Schneerson's inclusivism implied that it was imperative that we love each member of the Jewish people simply because that individual is a member of the Jewish people as this is the gateway for Divine service,[128] by focusing attention on simple people[129] to draw them close to their spiritual heritage.

R. Schneerson argued[130] that through the inclusion of special children in Jewish educational activities,[131] the child will receive "a sense of belonging and attachment, and a firm anchorage to hold on to, whether consciously or subconsciously." He wrote that "Eventually a subconscious feeling of inner security would pass into the conscious state, especially if the teacher will endeavor to cultivate and fortify this feeling." Consequently, R. Schneerson believed that we can assist and re-embrace a dislocated soul by disturbing his or her lethargy and tranquillity to ensure that soul's return to its source.[132] Clearly, adopting this inclusive educational ideal places the educator face-to-face with students who were possibly hostile to the educator's attempt at communication. R. Schneerson suggested that this barrier be overcome through adopting a positive view of the learner, irrespective of evidence to the contrary.

Positive View of the Learner

R. Schneerson[133] wanted the educator to remain focused on the learner's positive potential, citing evidence from Talmudic[134] and Halachic[135] texts that confirmed the appropriateness of this attitude. For example, he raised the legitimacy in Jewish law of a divorce given under duress where "We compel [the husband] until he complies." He explained this in light of Judaism's perception of the husband's inner desire to cooperate, despite the need for external enforcement to enable him to reveal his deepest preference for good over non-compliance. R. Schneerson thus urged educators to focus on the redeemability of every person and not despair of anyone, for however deep their failing, everyone can emerge to great light, especially with Divine assistance that always awaits everyone.[136] The educator must therefore encourage the individual to awaken his will and the inner point of his Jewishness,[137] and the educator must also be mindful that he or she will ultimately achieve improvement of the students.[138]

R. Schneerson's belief in the educator's need to focus on the power of the individual and adopt an optimistic approach[139] is consistent with his nuclear metaphor for education, whereby the minuteness of the atom parallels the small individual's power of self-sacrifice and nullification of ego which enable him or her to transform entire cities and direct the world positively.[140] The educator must be utterly convinced of the reformability of the individual learner,[141] thereby leaving no place for despondency or weak application of effort.[142]

R. Schneerson believed that, in the context of the *Chanukkah* episode, this principle applied to the extent that even when people say there is insufficient oil, they must be convinced there is sufficient oil to continually and increasingly illuminate their surroundings and lives.[143] He also derived the message from *Chanukkah*'s miraculous existence of one uncontaminated cruse of oil that it is therefore never recommended that anyone totally abandon a successful enterprise like education.[144] This methodology of finding the positive in every individual has its practical expression in R. Schneerson's recommended educational policy, where there is sensitivity to and concern for the needs of each individual, including those whom others may overlook.[145]

This optimistic approach[146] had ramifications for the banishing of apathy and lethargy from the educational environment. Teachers and students should be imbued with the pervasive belief that every good purpose will be successfully achieved, the only question being whether sooner or later.[147] This was considered by R. Schneerson vital, as apathy leads to rationalizing inactivity, whereas everyone should be doing everything possible toward appropriate goals, each person according to his or her ability.[148] Indeed, an intensification of educational endeavors was considered imperative for anyone who wishes to receive the Torah.[149]

R. Schneerson believed in an optimistic approach for the education of Down-syndrome children as "a pre-condition for greater success."[150] He argued that the educator's "very confidence that such progress is in the realm of possibility will inspire greater enthusiasm in this work, and hopefully will also stimulate more intensive research." Here we have application of the Habad principle[151] of "positive thoughts engender positive outcomes" for education. A second reason for this positive approach was proposed by R. Schneerson in an argument similar to Robert K. Merton's 1948 "Self-Fulfilling Prophecy,"[152] but radical in its application to Down-syndrome children.[153] R. Schneerson argued:

> Just as the said [positive] approach is important from the viewpoint of and for the worker and educator, so it is important that the trainees themselves should be encouraged—both by word and the manner of their

training—to feel confident that they are not, G-d forbid, "cases," much less unfortunate or hopeless cases, that their difficulty is considered...only temporary and that with a concerted effort of instructor and trainee the desired improvement could be speeded and enhanced.[154]

He was particularly concerned "to avoid impressing the child with his or her handicap." At the same time, R. Schneerson did caution that "care should be taken not to exaggerate expectations through far-fetched promises, for false hopes inevitably result in deep disenchantment, loss of credibility, and other undesirable effects."[155]

Professor Reuven Feuerstein[156] stated that when consulting with R. Schneerson regarding a particular circumstance that challenged the professor's characteristic optimism, R. Schneerson's confidence in a positive outcome was undiminished and his encouragement unrelenting for a breakthrough.

Unity and Harmony

R. Schneerson cited his predecessor's positive interpretation of the Talmudic dictum[157] "All Jews are *areivim* [responsible] for one another," where *areivim* is understood to mean:

(i)   "sweetness," i.e., to view one's fellow as sweet;
(ii) "intermingled," i.e., to realize that our destinies are inextricably intertwined; and
(iii) "guarantor," i.e., to realize we have a mutual responsibility for each other.

R. Schneerson was insistent[158] that education be above factionalism and party-political considerations and that every educational endeavor be directed to rescuing all groups.[159] The educator's foremost concern must be for issues affecting our people collectively, because they are of paramount importance.[160]

Similarly, he viewed division and disharmony as completely undesirable.[161] He was adamant[162] that children should not be entangled in an internal disagreement between educators, nor suffer because of a temporary dispute between parents and administration,[163] noting that while the dispute may be temporary, when it comes to educating children, one cannot change negative consequences at whim. To R. Schneerson, working peacefully is always the preferred option, and only when there is no other option may protest be used.[164]

Student Focus

R. Schneerson believed that education must not be preoccupied with *tachlit* (livelihood, both spiritual and physical)[165] and that this applies even more to children at the beginning of their education, who cannot predict the source of their income when adults.[166] Student memorization of religious texts has traditionally been seen as a means for students to focus their intellect on meaningful knowledge during free time and avoid distraction. An example of Habad Hasidism's recognition of the value of this activity is found in the writings of R. Schneerson's predecessor, RJIS, who encouraged rote recitation of *Mishnah* and wrote:

> When someone walks down the street and mentally reviews passages from *Mishnayot* or *Tanya*, or sits in his store with a *Chumash* or *Tehillim*, this is more cherished [above] than [in previous ages], when the streets shone with the light of Torah. We must not go about in the street empty-handed. One must be equipped with words of Torah... that he can review from memory as he walks.[167]

Associating this with the cleansing of the atmosphere, RJIS stated:

> The world needs to have its air purified and this can be accomplished only through the letters of Torah [that

one recites]. These letters of Torah afford both universal and individual protection. The division of the Six Orders of the *Mishnah* (to be studied by heart) fulfills [the mandate to study Torah] "while you walk on your way" (Deuteronomy, 6:7). Every single *Mishnah* that a person reviews [from memory], wherever he may be, lights up the connection between the Jewish people and G-d. Significantly, the word *Mishnah* shares the same letters as *neshamah*—"soul." It is difficult to find the appropriate words to express the great benefit, and the universal and individual protection that will be gained through the constant review of *mishnayot*. And there are no words to describe the great gratification that [such review] gives the Creator of the World.[168]

RJIS further enunciated this idea of cosmic purification through recitation of religious texts, stating:

A person's life depends upon the air around him: without air one cannot live. Moreover, the kind of air in which one lives determines the quality of one's life. When a person lives in an atmosphere of Torah and *mitzvot*, his life is healthy... Whoever is familiar with Torah learning must have something on call that he has learnt by heart, be it Chumash, *Tehillim, Mishnah, Tanya*. This will enable him to review the holy words of Torah— mentally and verbally—at any time and in every place.[169]

R. Schneerson embraced this concept[170] and wrote long expositions[171] of the value of memorization and recitation and the resultant "purification of one's environment" especially through the memorization of *Mishnah*,[172] arguing that even when the student was not actually reciting these texts, they remained engraved in a learner's mind.[173] Moreover, he believed Torah learned by rote recitation provided the antidote to untoward thoughts as a more focused mind is less prone to allow inappropriate thoughts, and when such notions do occur, they can be easily dismissed.[174]

Content above Language

Given the centrality of piety and virtue to the aims of education, the language of instruction was viewed by R. Schneerson as a means that must never impede the desired ends of education and which must not become an end in itself. In 1943, he recommended that students should be initially taught religious studies in English and only after extra-curricular efforts ensured students had mastered Yiddish was religious instruction permitted in that language.[175]

In a *yechidut* (private meeting), he told English educator Rev. Aron Dov Sufrin,

> Tell the parents who want everything taught in *Yiddish* that they most probably also want their children to grow up to be *Shomrei Torah Umitzvot*—Torah-observant Jews. If the children will be taught in Yiddish, which is a strange language to them, they may develop distaste for everything they learn. This will affect them in their future development of their *Yiddishkeit*. It is appropriate to speak to them in Yiddish during playtime, or breaks, or when telling a story; this will help expand their familiarity with the language.[176]

Similarly, regarding the *Ivrit b'Ivrit* method, he wrote,

> The method of *Ivrit b'Ivrit* has its origin in the anti-religious drive inaugurated by the so-called *Haskalah* ("Enlightenment") movement, many years ago, which paved the way to mass assimilation. The original ambitions and motivations of this method have long been discredited. Even non-Orthodox educators recognize

the great loss of time involved in this method, which is prepared to sacrifice the child's time and education for the sake of teaching him a few phrases in Hebrew, or a Hebrew speech, which the child will anyway forget eventually. Yet, blinded by considerations which are certainly not in the interests of the child's Jewish education, some circles still cling to this method.[177]

This relegation of language to a position secondary to content is consistent with R. Schneerson's view that in the classroom, it is imperative that educators use age-appropriate terminology exclusively and delete information that might detract from the student's main focus.[178] This indicates the importance that R. Schneerson attached to the content of education as a pivotal element of his coherent educational philosophy.

Notes

1. RJIS, *The Principles of Education and Guidance*, Chapter 1.
2. *Yemei Bereishit*:337-41. Undated address at a *farbrengen* of 1947-1948, where Sabbath-observant chess champion Samuel H. Reshevsky was present.
3. *Ibid.*
4. Similarly, he suggested that while at school, a boat trip, a soccer game, or an art class provide opportunities for moral edification. (See *TM-HIT-5743* [1982-1983], III:1207ff; *op. cit.-5747* [1986-1987], IV:233-6; Address of *Nissan* 26th, 5740 [April 12th, 1980] in *SK-5740* [1979-1980], II:815-8 and letter to artist R. Hendel Lieberman publicized in *The Lamplighter*, Vol. 59:3, published by Chabad House, Caulfield, Melbourne, Australia.)
5. *IK*, IV:305-6, Letter 1,029. Semi-pastoral Hebrew letter of *Erev Rosh Chodesh Sivan, Iyar* 29th, 5711 [June 4, 1951] sent to multiple addressees; *LS*, VIII:267-8.
6. *IK*, V:252-3, Letter 1,029; *op. cit.*, V:252-3, Letter 1,453; *LS*, VI:370; Addenda to *op. cit.*, VI:387-8.
7. *IK*, IV:245-6; *LS*, IV:1,297.
8. English letter of *Shevat* 15th, 5708 [January 26th, 1948] in *Letters from the Rebbe*, III:8-9, Letter 7.
9. *Shir HaShirim Rabba*, 1:4 (1).
10. *IK*, IV:305-6.

11. *Reshimot*, I:230-3 [*Reshima* No. 7].
12. Within the Jewish community, R. Schneerson urged (*SK-5748*, II:398-407) that activities take place on or close to one's Hebrew birthday. These include: being called to the Torah on the *Shabbat* prior to, or on the day; taking out time to reflect on one's life (on the past year in particular) and considering ways to improve areas of weakness; intensifying concentration during one's prayers on the day, with greater meditation on G-d's presence; recitation of extra Psalms and the study of the Psalm appropriate to one's age; undertaking a new area of Torah study; taking on an additional *mitzvah* or enhancing a *mitzvah*; performing an act of kindness motivated by genuine concern for the welfare of one's fellow; organizing a joyous birthday gathering close to the Hebrew date, where Torah thoughts are shared with the participants and the special *Shechechiyanu* blessing is recited over a new fruit or a new garment as an expression of thanks to G-d for reaching this stage of life; when the birthday falls on a weekday, extra charity is given both morning and afternoon.
13. English letter of *Shevat* 15th, 5708 [January 26th, 1948] in *Letters from the Rebbe*, III:8-9, Letter 7.
14. *IK*, I:78-9, Letter 49.
15. He argued that engaging in educational endeavor must be done immediately and energetically. See also *IK*, I:38-40, Letter 22; *op. cit.*, III:252-3, Letter 571; and *op. cit.*, IV:93-4, Letter 841.
16. *Op. cit.*, III:328-9, Letter 634.
17. *Op. cit.*, III:350, Letter 652; *TM*, IV [*HIT-TM-5712*:I]:227-31.
18. *IK*, V:56-7, Letter 1,272.
19. *Op. cit.*, I:38-40, Letter 22.
20. Letter addressed to I.I. Cohn of Detroit, Michigan, published in *The Uforatzto Journal*, Summer 5735 (1975), III, No.4 (12):19, (*ed.*) M.S. Rivkin.
21. *TM*, III [5711, II]:85-92, §19-§27 & §29.
22. Haggai, 2:8.
23. *Beitza*, 16a; RSZ, *Laws of Torah Study*, 1:7.
24. *TM*, III [5711, II]:85-92.
25. He applied this principle to the case of providing aid for the education of children from Yemen, Morocco, and Iraq upon their arrival in Israel, and R. Schneerson implored educators and benefactors who were sensitive to his recommendations that they ensure these children study *Aleph-Beit*, *Chumash-Rashi*, and wear a *tallit* and lay *tefillin* (which he saw as part of *Talmud Torah*).
26. The Russian equivalent of this phrase is that it is "on the King's account" (*TM*, III [5711, II]:85-92).
27. Excerpt of an English letter of *Adar-Sheni* 19th, 5711 [March 27th, 1951] distributed as monograph.
28. See *Shulchan Aruch* of RSZ, beginning of *Laws of Talmud Torah*.
29. *IK*, IV:110-1, Letter 855.

30. *Op. cit.*, IV:11-2, Letter 776; *op. cit.*, IV:155-6, Letter 897; *op. cit.*, IV:374-5, Letter 1,093; *op. cit.*, IV:447, Letter 1,169; *op. cit.*, V:11-2, Letter 1,233; *op. cit.*, V:21-2, Letter 1,242.

31. *Op. cit.*, IV:11-2, Letter 776.

32. *Op. cit.*, XXI:107, Letter 7,857, and *op. cit., IK*, III:337, Letter 642.

33. He noted that RJIS had demanded that urgency be applied to education along with an extraverted and proactive approach to spirituality (*op. cit.*, I:53-4, Letter 32). R. Schneerson's emphasis on a proactive and pre-emptive approach to education based on the horticultural metaphor stands in sharp contradistinction to Pestalozzi's and Froebel's utilization of the horticultural metaphor to justify educators desisting from intervention.

34. *Op. cit.*, XXI:45-6, Letter 7,795.

35. *Op. cit.*, XXI:142, Letter 7,899.

36. *Op. cit.*, XXI:45-6, Letter 7,795.

37. *Op. cit.*, I:110-2, Letter 65.

38. Hebrew letter of *Kislev* 7th, 5712 [Dec. 7th, 1951] in *op. cit.*, V:66-8, Letter 1,281, §6.

39. *Op. cit.*, V:67.

40. *Op. cit.*, I:61-2, Letter 38; *IK*, I:62-3, Letter 39; and *IK*, I:69-70, Letter 44.

41. *Op. cit.*, IV:455-7, Letter 1,178; *Yechidut* of *Shevat* 5751 [late Jan. or early Feb., 1951] with Gershon Kranzler in "A Visit with the New Lubavitcher Rebbe": *Jewish Life,* Sept.-Oct., 1951.

42. *IK*, I:63-4, Letter 40.

43. While advocating "gentle words," he wanted these words to be spoken with inner strength. (See *TM-HIT*, III [5711, II]:224-6.)

44. *IK*, V:114, Letter 1,324.

45. *Op. cit.*, I:127-8, Letter 77.

46. *Op. cit.*, V:114, Letter 1,324.

47. *Op. cit.*, III:328-9, Letter 634.

48. *Op. cit.*, IV:121-2, Letter 865.

49. *Op. cit.*, IV:455-7, Letter 1,178; *TM,* IV [*HIT-TM-5712*:I]:227-31.

50. *IK*, V:114, Letter 1,324.

51. *Op. cit.*, III:320-1, Letter 626.

52. *Op. cit.*, III:308-9, Letter 616.

53. *Op. cit.*, III:310-1, Letter 618; Addenda to *LS*, XXIII:497.

54. *IK*, II:314-6, Letter 343; Addenda to *LS*, XX:584-5.

55. *IK*, XXI:81, Letter 7,828.

56. *Op. cit.*, I:102-3, Letter 60 [Addenda to *LS, XXI*:494]; *IK*, I:103-4, Letter 61.

57. *TM-5710* (1992 edition):7-8.

58. *IK*, III:236, Letter 558; Addenda to *LS*, XI:204.

59. *Tanya, Iggeret HaKodesh*, Chapter 14.

60. *IK*, II:308-9, Letter 337.

61. *Op. cit.*, I:165-6, Letter 92.

62. The founder of Habad, RSZ, had interrupted his prayers in order to chop wood and prepare soup so as to personally provide food for a woman after childbirth who was without support at home. (See R. Schneerson's Discourse *Bati L'Gani-5711*, Paragraph VI in *SM-Melukat*, I:7.)

63. *IK*, IV:170-1, Letter 914.

64. See A.B.Z. Metzger (1999).

65. *IK*, IV:202-4, Letter 940; *SM-5711*:178; Addenda to *LS*, XI:346-7; *IK*, IV:204-6, Letter 941; Addenda to *LS*, VI:369.

66. *IK*, XXI:142, Letter 7,899; *op. cit.*, V:124-5, Letter 1,333.

67. *Op. cit.*, IK, IV:342-3, Letter 1,062.

68. *Op. cit.*, V:124-5, Letter 1,333; *op. cit.*, IV:84-5, Letter 833.

69. *Op. cit.*, IV:305-6, Letter 1,029.

70. *Ibid.*

71. Addenda to *LS*, XXX:311-4; *TM*, IV [*TM-5712*:I]:232-6.

72. *LS*, I:94-5.

73. *IK*, IV:93-4, Letter 841.

74. "Words emanating from the heart penetrate the heart" was attributed to Rabbi Moshe Ibn Ezras in his *Shirat Yisrael*.

75. *IK*, I:138-9, Letter 83; *op. cit.*, IV:56-7, Letter 812; *op. cit.*, IV:170-1, Letter 914 *et al.*

76. *Op. cit.*, IV:245-6, Letter 975.

77. *Op. cit.*, I:122-4, Letter 74.

78. *TM*, IV [*TM-5712*:I]:232-6; Edited address of *Tishrei* 27th, 5725 [Oct. 3rd, 1964] in *LS*, XV:1-6.

79. *Ibid.*

80. *IK*, I:128-9, Letter 78.

81. *Op. cit.*, I:130-31, Letter 79.

82. *Op. cit.*, IV:384, Letter 1,102. In the Habad context, R. Schneerson noted that this devotion was exemplified and inspired by RJIS.

83. *Op. cit.*, I:126-7, Letter 76. This devotion includes the requirement that one maintain a spiritual connection with one's Torah teacher and spiritual masters even when they are in a distant location, with the student viewing them as tangibly present.

84. *TM*, [5711, I] II:91-3, §13-§16.

85. *IK*, XVII:140, Letter 6,287.

86. Hebrew letter of *Shevat* 21st, 5704 [Feb. 15th, 1944] and *Shevat* 27th, 5704 [Feb. 21st, 1944] in *op. cit.*, I:249-50, Letter 136.

87. The seed with no taste from which the tall tree ultimately emerges is symbolic of selfless idealism.

88. *IK*, II:314-6, Letter 343 [Addenda to *LS*, XX:584-5].

89. *Ibid.*

90. *Ibid.*

91. *IK*, III:370-1, Letter 672.

92. *Op. cit.*, VII:238-9, Letter 2,100.

93. *LS*, I:81-5.

94. *IK*, III:466-7, Letter 751.

95. *Afikoman* refers to the portion of the middle of three *matzot* (unleavened bread), which is divided and set aside at an early stage of the Passover evening to be eaten as the conclusion and culmination of the festive meal.

96. *Haggadah Shel Pesach Im Likkutei Ta'amim, Minhagim U'Biurim*:11. This ideal is based on the Talmud, *Berachot* 5b, which speaks of "tasting the taste of theft" in a similar context.

97. *Kiddushin*, 41a and explanation of this concept in *Lekach Tov* by R. Yosef Engel, General Principle 1.

98. *IK*, III:472-4, Letter 755.

99. Unpublished letter of *Iyar* 1st, 5740 [April 17th, 1980], addressed to "All Participants in a Dedication of the New Building of the Yeshiva College, Sydney, Australia."

100. *TM*, IV [*HIT-TM-5712*:I]:227-31.

101. *TM*, III [5711, II]:224-6.

102. *IK*, IV:94-6, Letter 842.

103. *Letters from the Rebbe*, III:231-2, Letter 153. English letter of *Erev Shabbat Kodesh Mevarchim Chodesh Tammuz, Sivan* 25th, 5745 [June 14th, 1985] addressed to "All Participants in the Annual Event in Aid of *Yeshivat Lubavitch*, Manchester."

104. English letter of *Erev Purim, Adar* 13th, 5737 [March 3rd, 1977] published in *Letters from the Rebbe*, II:184-6, Letter 85 and *The Letter and the Spirit*, I:384-6. See also *LS*, II:366-70 and *SK-5711*, address of *Av* 20th [August 22nd, 1951] as well as *TM-5715*, XIV (5715, II) [1954-5] address of *Tammuz* 13th, 5715 [July 3rd, 1955].

105. *IK*, V:131-2, Letter 1,342.

106. *Op. cit.*, V:26-7, Letter 1,246. In the Habad context, he urged students to aspire to be "a vessel" or means for the greater success of his predecessor's initiatives, where the greater the level of subservience of the student to the mission, the faster and more successful they would be in their fulfillment of the particular educational mission. See *TM*-III [5711, II]:224-6.

107. *IK-MM*, XXI:194-7, Letter 7,953 dated *Shevat* 25th, 5713 [February 10th, 1953].

108. *Op. cit.*, XVII:333-4, Letter 6,484 dated *Ellul* 19th, 5718 [Sept. 4th, 1958]. In this letter, R. Schneerson argued that a feeling of inadequacy always accompanies significant attainment, as confirmed by R. Saadia Gaon's principle (*Ikkarim* 2:30) that the more that we know, the more we are aware of what there is to know.

109. *IK*, IV:94-6, Letter 842.

110. *TM*, III [5711, II]:224-6.

111. Interviews with Professor Reuven Feuerstein, January 19th and 20th, 1998, in Sydney, Australia.

112. See *IK*, IV:229-30, Letter 960 [Addenda to *LS*, XII:148]. The principle was of particular relevance in the Habad context of the educator being the *shaliach* [emissary] of RJIS. In this paradigm, students who see themselves as agents of a spiritual mentor have the mentor's power. While the agent, such as one engaged in education, is independent to choose the correct details to best implement the mentor's vision, the educator seeks to emulate his mentor. The educator's action is not independent but rather it is that of the mentor whose power inspires the act.

113. For example, Rabbi Mordechai Einbender (2014) recorded R. Schneerson telling him in a *yechidut* at around the time of his *Bar Mitzvah*, "When you grow older you will become my personal emissary." These words were communicated after R. Schneerson had spoken to R. Einbinder's father, thereafter turning to the thirteen-year-old Einbender and communicating these words "in a manner of a general speaking to a soldier." He recorded that "these words touched [him] deeply, even at that young age. And they set forth [his] purpose in life and became [his] guiding light. In 1980, a decade later, he became R. Schneerson's emissary in an area north of Los Angeles known as The Valley. Similarly, media personality and author Rabbi Shmuel Boteach (2002:xiii-xiv) recalled a *yechidut* episode when he was a disheartened thirteen-year-old, with R. Schneerson telling him, "You are too young to be a cynic..." and thereafter empowering him to utilize his potential for positive ends.

114. *IK*, XV:435, Letter 5,760, dated *Ellul* 23rd, 5717 [August 19th, 1957]. He cited Talmudic evidence for this policy. R. Schneerson thus wrote "when the students themselves will be concerned with implementing discipline, this will comply with the Talmudic dictum that "from the very forest itself is taken the axe wherewith to fell it." This principle is also exemplified in *op. cit.*, XX:42.

115. *Op. cit.*, I:139-40, Letter 84; *TM*, III [5711, II]:85-92.

116. *IK*, I:75-8, Letter 48.

117. *Op. cit.*, IV:242-3, Letter 972.

118. *Op. cit.*, XV:33-7, Letter 5,357.

119. *Op. cit.*, I:38-40, Letter 22; he similarly wanted (*op. cit.*, I:105-7, Letter 63) all to be eligible for the "*Mishna* by Heart" Program and that a subscription to *HaChaver* be for all homes (*IK*, I:122-4, Letter 74).

120. *Op. cit.*, I:66-7, Letter 42.

121. *Op. cit.*, IV:142-4, Letter 885.

122. Leviticus, 19:18.

123. *IK*, I:66-7, Letter 42.

124. *Op. cit.*, III:355-7, Letter 657.

125. *Ibid.*

126. *TM*, III [5711, II]:85-92 citing Maimonides, *Laws of Torah Study*, 1:2 based on *Sifri* and Rashi to Deuteronomy, 6:7.

127. *IK*, IV:423, Letter 1,142.
128. Whereas BST revealed the interconnectedness of love of G-d, Torah and Israel and the Maggid revealed the intellectual understanding that underlies this unity, RSZ revealed how one can, should, and must tangibly express love of G-d, Torah, and Israel (*op. cit.*, III:469-71, Letter 753).
129. *Op. cit.*, III:284-6, Letter 595; *op. cit.*, III:469-71, Letter 753.
130. R. Schneerson strongly disapproved of what he considered an unfortunate, "prevalent misconception" that argued that given their more limited capacities, special children "should not be 'burdened' with Jewish education on top of their general education, so as not to overtax them." He decried this "fallacial and detrimental attitude, especially in the light of what [had] been said . . . about the need to avoid impressing the child with his handicap."
131. R. Schneerson explained that this inner security would result "if the child is involved in Jewish education and activities—and not in some general and peripheral way, but in a regular and tangible approach, such as in the actual performance of *mitzvot*, customs, and traditions . . ."
132. *IK*, I:197-8, Letter 110; *IK*, I:199-200, Letter 112. In these letters, as evidence of the individual's positive essence, R. Schneerson cites the statement of *Bereishit Rabba*, end of Chapter 53, "When a staff is thrown into the air, it will land on its root," meaning that it falls on the thick portion near the root. From this R. Schneerson derived "that even though the staff is now dry, for it is a long time since it has been cut from its source, it is still possible to awaken within it [the power of] its source and root" and "the staff needs assistance in this. This assistance is rendered by disturbing it, [removing it from its state of] rest, lifting it up from the earth, and throwing it in the air." R. Schneerson added that "Every person according to his capacity and particularly those whom G-d endowed with teaching skills should occupy themselves and endeavor to render such assistance."
133. *TM*, IV [*HIT-TM-5712*:I]:227-31, especially, page 228, footnote 3.
134. *Rosh Hashana*, 6a.
135. Maimonides, *Mishneh Torah, Hilchot Gerushin*, 2:20.
136. *IK*, I:122-4, Letter 74.
137. *Ibid.*
138. *IK*, IV:434, Letter 1,155.
139. *Reshimot*, IV:175-81 [*Reshima* No. 130].
140. *TM*, II [5711:I]:315-8, §19-§22.
141. *IK*, I:284-6, Letter 153.
142. *Op. cit.*, I:73, Letter 46; *IK*, III:239-41, Letter 560; English letter of *Cheshvan* 12th, 5712 [Nov. 11th, 1951] to Rev. A. D. Sufrin in *Sefer Zikaron: Michtavim, Teshuvot U'Ma'anot MiKvod Kedushat Admor R. Menachem M. Schneerson MiLubavitch* [*Memorial Book in Honor of Rev Aron Dov Sufrin*], I:10-1.
143. *TM-5710* (1992 edition):7-8.
144. *IK*, III:254-5, Letter 572.

145. Response of R. Schneerson to Rabbi Yosef Wineberg. The latter had apologized for inserting an urgent note to R. Schneerson in the door of his office, in anticipation that R. Schneerson's personal secretary, Rabbi Hodakov, would notice it. R. Hodakov's failure to detect it had caused R. Schneerson to subsequently stoop to retrieve it. R. Schneerson had dismissed Rabbi Wineberg's apology, stating, "Is not my whole function to elevate, and especially that which others have overlooked?" (interview of *Tammuz* 3rd, 5756 [June 19th, 1996] with senior Habad emissary, Rabbi Yosef Wineberg).

146. *IK*, IV:242-3, Letter 972.

147. *TM*, III [5711, II]:85-92, §19-§27 & §29.

148. *Ibid.* Examples of such confident, positive endeavors (which were antithetical to apathy) in the case of rescuing the children of Yemen where the appropriate path must be found, included voicing cries of protest, authoring letters, publishing articles, making telephone calls, or sending telegraphs to object to failure to educate Yemenite children in traditional paths.

149. *IK*, IV:299-300, Letter 1,025; *op. cit.*, IV:305-6, Letter 1,029 and *LS*, VIII:267-8.

150. Rabbi Schneerson further believed that "considering the enormous strides that have been made in medical science, human knowledge, methodology, and know-how, there is no doubt that in this area, too, there will be far-reaching developments."

151. See *IK-RJIS*, II:537, Letter 636; *op. cit*, VII:197, Letter 1,990. R. Schneerson elaborated on this principle, cited in the name of Tzemach Tzedek in *LS*, XXXVI:4-6.

152. Robert K. Merton, 1948 & 1968. See also Robert T. Tauber, 1997.

153. Interviews of January 19 and 20, 1998, in Sydney, Australia, with Professor Reuven Feuerstein, world expert on the education of Down-syndrome children.

154. Correspondence of August 15, 1979, addressed to Dr. R. Wilkes of Brooklyn's Coney Island Hospital.

155. He expressed confidence that "a way can surely be found to avoid raising false hopes, yet giving guarded encouragement."

156. Interviews with Professor Reuven Feuerstein over January 19th and 20th, 1998, in Sydney, Australia.

157. *Shavuot*, 39a.

158. *IK*, III:328-9, Letter 634.

159. He likewise urged (Postscript to *IK*, IV:1-2, Letter 766) a peaceful resolution regarding the status of youth migrating to Israel.

160. *Op. cit.*, IV:121-2, Letter 865.

161. *Op. cit.*, III:355-7, Letter 657.

162. *Op. cit.*, IV:2, Letter 767.

163. He urged the peaceful resolution of parental complaints against the school administration.

164. *TM*, III [5711, II]:85-92, §19-§27 & §29.

165. Talmud, *Pesachim* 54b.

166. *IK*, III:475-6, Letter 756 and Addenda to *LS*, XXII:418.

167. *SM-5711*:241 cited in *HaYom Yom*, entry for *Adar-Rishon* 9th.

168. *Ibid.*

169. *SH-5702*:116; cited in *HaYom Yom*, entry for *Tevet* 11th.

170. *IK*, I:105-7, Letter 63; *op. cit.*, I:126-7, Letter 76 [Addenda to *LS*, XXIII:421].

171. Hebrew letter of *Shevat* 14th, 5704 [February, 8th, 1944] addressed to R. Menachem Ze'ev Greenglass in *IK*, I:235-44, Letter 132; *Kovetz Lubavitch*, IV:66ff; *Teshuvot U'Biurim*:13-21.

172. *IK*, I:154-7, Letter 86 [Addenda to *LS*, II:691-2 and Addenda to *LS*, II (Heb.):365-6].

173. *IK*, V:169-70, Letter 1,373 [Addenda to *LS*, XXIV:509-10].

174. *Ibid.*

175. Hebrew letter of *Kislev* 5th, 5704 [Dec. 2nd, 1943] in *IK*, XXI:38-9, Letter 7,787.

176. *Yechidut* of *Adar-Sheini* 20th, 5725 [March 24th, 1965] with Rev. A. D. Sufrin (recorded in *Sefer Zikaron: Teshuvot U'Ma'anot ["Memories" in Honor of the 3rd Yarzheit of Rev Aron Dov Sufrin]*:5-7. Rev. Sufrin had communicated the following to R. Schneerson: "Most of the children in our school [Lubavitch House—Ed.] speak English at home. However in each class there are at least half the parents who would like their children to be taught in Yiddish and one child has left [the school—Ed.] because of this. There are one or two others who may leave because we do not teach in Yiddish. On the other hand there are one or two who may take their children away to other schools if we *do* start teaching the children in Yiddish, and it will also deter parents of the English and German type from sending their children to us. Yet there is the possibility that if we would go over to teaching in Yiddish, a small percentage of *frumer* [religious] children may join our school. Under the present system we have adopted we are introducing Yiddish into each class (as the Rebbe Shlita may have noticed from the curriculum I handed in) but there is still dissatisfaction amongst some parents. We therefore wish to know what our policy should be for running the school to teach in Yiddish or English...?"

177. English letter of 4th Day of *Chanukkah*, *Kislev* 28th, 5715 [Dec. 23rd, 1954] in *Letters from the Rebbe*, II:41-5.

178. *IK*, I:36-7, Letter 20 [Addenda to *LS*, IV:1260-1].

Chapter 7

THE CONTENT OF EDUCATION

Education begins with teaching a child the letters of the Hebrew alphabet.... What are the physical components of the aleph [the first Hebrew letter]? It comprises a point above, a point below, and a line in between. A child must know the first principle of the Torah: that G-d is above, the individual is below, and they are connected by a line of faith.

—Rabbi Schneur Zalman of Liadi[1]

When examining R. Schneerson's understanding of the content of education, two positions which could be viewed as contradictory become apparent. The first is his emphasis on the inclusion of sublime or esoteric subject matter, coupled with his insistence on the primary importance of teaching topics of immediate practical relevance. He also sought the harmonization of these positions and wanted no division between the esoteric and legalistic dimensions of study, as exemplified in his own expositions.

Moreover, whether it was the study of esoteric topics or mundane matters, R. Schneerson insisted that all knowledge must be used for moral edification. Consequently, he believed that a component of moral education should be included in the curriculum, an idea he conveyed to US president Ronald Reagan in 1982. He argued that an education restricted to the simplistic communication of information while neglecting to provide students with guidance about how to apply such data for beneficial and worthwhile

purposes has failed to comply with the most fundamental understanding of the term "education."[2] R. Schneerson recommended
that this dimension of moral education be integrated into the curriculum rather than merely providing additional material to an
existing curriculum, as shown by his insistence that phenomena
encountered in the learning process be employed by the educator
as opportunities for moral advancement.

The Mystical Dimension

R. Schneerson was insistent that education be *al taharat hakodesh*
(meaning "in pristine sanctity"), so that ideals of sanctity and belief are uncompromised.[3] He argued that education must begin
with imbuing a faith that transcends human intellect and surpasses
an exclusively rational approach to morality. It must encompass
supernatural faith, which lays the foundation for subsequent introduction of reason and intellectual engagement in the process of
spiritual self-realization.

R. Schneerson believed the curriculum should include miracle
stories, however astonishing they may seem to be.[4] By introducing
the spiritual or supernatural as a central component, R. Schneerson
contended that the student is thereby empowered to overcome any
obstacles to attain fullest realization of spiritual ideals. These deter-
rents often result from living in a material world whose appealing
materialism deflects from and may even obscure the individual's
innate desire for pursuing spiritual delights.[5]

Therefore, R. Schneerson insisted that education embrace
more than understanding of the purely rational and natural
world.[6] Citing RSB's rejection of a teacher who wished to delete all supernatural matters from the curriculum, R. Schneerson
supported the view that faith must take priority over the purely
rational and utilitarian.[7]

From the mystical concept[8] that we are taught the entire Torah
in utero, he found support for his agenda of making the deepest

dimensions of Hasidic wisdom accessible to all sections of the Jewish people, irrespective of their current religious position. He elaborated:

> This Talmudic teaching provides the answer to those who seek a pretext for their opposition to the study of *Hassidut* and its explication of the innermost secrets of the Torah: The Talmud tells us that the child has been taught "the entire Torah" prior to birth. "The entire Torah" includes the Torah's innermost truths and mystical dimensions as expressed in *Hassidut.* This teaches that every individual has an innate receptivity to the most spiritual teachings of the Torah. In fact, when we teach these deep spiritual concepts contained in *Hassidut,* our students are actually revising, reviewing. and relearning those ideals to which they possess a prior intrinsic affinity.[9]

Moreover, the introduction of supra-rational subject matter should start before mastery of all legalistic and rational subject matter has been achieved. Citing RSB's encounter with the pragmatic teacher, R. Schneerson firmly believed in education that begins with a faith that transcends intellect. The supra-rational approach[10] and supernatural stories should therefore be included in the curriculum, even if considered astonishing.

He further argued[11] that the inspirational power of teaching about the supernatural could elevate the individual from the lowest depths to sublime spiritual heights, thereby enabling individuals to perceive light notwithstanding the darkness engulfing them. As the inspirational power of teaching about the supernatural enabled human beings to perceive the preeminence of Divinity as the true essence of material physicality, he argued[12] for inclusion of miracles in the curriculum. In the Habad tradition, he presented reasons for the study of Hasidic philosophy before prayer,[13] stressing that the second-century Talmudic sage and mystic, Rabbi Shimon Bar Yochai, had recommended that even young children be exposed to concepts of Jewish mysticism.[14]

Prioritizing the Practical

R. Schneerson believed that however elevated the areas of educational engagement, dimensions of practical consequence in the learner's life must always take priority. R. Schneerson was often confronted by questions about what should be the priority areas of the curriculum and he frequently argued that matters of most practical application must be the principal focus.[15]

He cited[16] the Biblical ideal[17] of "Today is to perform them [the *mitzvot*]" as well as pointing to[18] the Talmudic ideal[19] of Rabbi Chiya, whose actions assured the continuation of Torah traditions. Thus, educators should strive for the students' actions to be aligned with ideals communicated by the educators, and they themselves must prioritize action in their own agenda.[20] The educator should not be satisfied with only compassion and generosity, but should strive to bring merit to many people and advantage the group by engaging in activity to benefit the wider community.[21]

R. Schneerson also maintained[22] that it is action, in contrast to philosophical discussion and theoretical deliberations, that impacts most on the learner. He simultaneously reminded educators that practical action is the domain of the educator, while success of those educational endeavors is ultimately in G-d's Hands. He believed that it is therefore necessary for educators to provide encouragement at every opportunity and appropriately so as to ensure tangible action by the student, in the spirit of "Today is to perform them" (Deuteronomy, 7:11). Thus, when considering the content of education, the practical outcome and tangible application of an ideal are of primary importance, and it must be appropriate to the learner's intellect and emotion.[23]

Synthesis of Mystical and Practical

The ideal which synthesizes mystical and practical dimensions is evident in R. Schneerson's analysis of even elementary educational practice, such as learning the Hebrew alphabet. As did his predecessors,[24] he argued that teaching the Hebrew alphabet should follow the time-honored process of ensuring the student knows the names of the vowels as independent entities, referred to as the *Kametz-Aleph-O* method. R. Schneerson insisted on following this traditional, practical procedure, and its vital importance to authentic Jewish education was traced by him[25] to a Kabbalistic source. He linked[26] the *Aleph* studied by the child at age three to the first letter of the Ten Commandments, which encapsulates the entire Torah. In this way, the teacher of Torah communicates to all pupils an appreciation that the Torah is the Will and Wisdom of G-d. R. Schneerson wrote:[27]

> My father-in-law explained that when we teach a child "*kametz-aleph-o*" [the first letter of the Hebrew alphabet and the accompanying vowel], this is connected to the *Aleph* [the first letter] of *Anochi* ["I"] of "I am the L-rd your G-d" (Exodus, 20:2). In this *Aleph*—which refers to "The Master of the Universe," is thus encapsulated the first of the Ten Commandments, "I am the L-rd your G-d," that in turn incorporates all of the Ten Commandments which alludes to the entire Written Law. And so too, the entire Oral Law [is alluded to in the initial *Aleph*] because "there is nothing not alluded to in the Torah." In other words, even before the child knows reading and writing, we implant in his heart and we imbue him with the *Aleph*—[a reference to] the Master of the Universe... The Talmud states[28] that the Hebrew word *Anochi* is an acrostic for the phrase "*Ana Nafshi K'tavit Yehavit* ["I (G-d) wrote and communicated My Very Self"]. *Yehavit* ["I (G-d) communicated..."] is indicative of "drawing down," *Ketavit* ["I (G-d) wrote..."] refers to the activity, and even *Nafshi*—["My Self"] is representative of a certain level of G-dliness. However, *Ana*—"I" refers to the very essence of Divinity—G-d's true reality and it is from this "true reality that all existence comes about."[29]

R. Schneerson explained that the very first rudimentary act of formal education thus contains profound mystical implications, indicative of a synthesis of the practical and the mystical. Similarly, R. Schneerson devoted an entire tract[30] to addressing the daily opening Morning Prayer (*Modeh Ani*) so that its levels of explanation from literal to Kabbalistic were seen as indicative of Habad mystical interpretation. His ideal in Jewish education was to seek the integration of exoteric and esoteric dimensions of Torah.[31] Furthermore, R. Schneerson's linkage of legalistic and mystical elements is found in his recommendation[32] that supervision of *yeshivah* students in the legalistic, Talmudic dimensions of Torah studies requires the supervisor's (*mashgiach*'s) prerequisite self-development in Torah's esoteric and mystical dimensions. Also, his encouragement for people struggling with Talmudic studies was one that supported perseverance based on the student's awareness of the mystical concept that, notwithstanding the difficulties, the Talmud is an expression of the Will and Wisdom of G-d.[33] It was necessary for the student of Torah to seek synthesis of its spiritual and physical dimensions.[34]

Curriculum for Moral Development

There is a further implication of R. Schneerson's integration of the esoteric and exoteric dimensions of Torah and his insistence on the inclusion of the mystical implications of exoteric texts, especially the ramifications for spiritual self-awareness. When considering the content of Torah study, he urged[35] that learning should prioritize the derivation of lessons for learner self-upliftment, which he referred to as "in a way of *Chayei HaNefesh*" (that pertains to the life of the soul), thereby integrating exoteric and esoteric dimensions of Torah. R. Schneerson simultaneously clarified that while this approach may appear new, it is actually a time-honored methodology. He thus prioritized[36] content that provides lessons pertaining to "Duties of the Heart" and the lifelong battle for self-mastery and self-cultivation over learning that provides only the student's accumulation of knowledge and *pilpul.* (*Pilpul* refers to the method of rabbinic interpretation and extrapolation that uses subtle distinctions and which subjects a text to rigorous logical scrutiny.) Matters of educational content should provide children with something of value "to warm their hearts and light up the child's home."[37] Included in the curriculum was "training children in courtesy, manners, civil or socially acceptable behavior such as appropriate conduct during a meal, helping a friend, etc."[38] He believed[39] that education without belief in G-d addresses the bodily dimension of the learner but actually undermines his or her soul. R. Schneerson's practical approach to educational content saw him campaign for the introduction of a "Moment of Reflection" in all schools at the start of the school day.

Expansive View of Curriculum

R. Schneerson recommended an expansive view of education, and his view of the curriculum reflected this position. Consequently, he urged educators to exert a positive influence even outside their specific curriculum domain. For example, a teacher of agriculture should not confine his teaching to his particular subject but must also exert a positive influence in religious education.[40] Similarly, he repeatedly emphasized[41] the vital importance of extra-curricular education, paying particular attention to the vacation period which he considered[42] a suitable time to intensify spiritual well-being.

While acknowledging that vacation is a time of rest and reinvigoration in preparation for the new school year, he stressed[43] that this does not imply a cessation of Torah study. He wrote:

> The summer recess is meant to give you an opportunity to strengthen your health of body and soul, which should, of course, go hand in hand together. For Jewish boys and girls to be truly healthy means, first of all, to have a healthy *Neshama* (soul). And a Jewish soul derives its health from the Torah and *Mitzvot*, which are "our

life and the length of our days," as we say in our prayers. Needless to say, life and health must be *continuous,* and one cannot take a vacation from them.

The Torah and *Mitzvot* are to the Jewish soul what breathing and nourishment are to the body. A healthy person seldom thinks about the vital necessity of breathing and food. However, on certain occasions one becomes acutely aware of these things. For example, when one swims under water and holds his breath, then one comes up and feels the urge to fill his lungs with fresh air. Or, after a fast-day, when the body has been temporarily weakened from lack of food and drink—one immediately feels the invigorating effect of food and drink. Now, during the school year, when a great deal of time that would be spent in studying the Torah and doing *Mitzvot* is taken up with other unavoidable occupations, such as the study of English and arithmetic, the soul becomes somewhat undernourished. At such times, your soul holds its breath, so to speak, which makes it more eager to return to Torah and *Mitzvot* whenever time is available. Come the summer recess, and your soul can now breathe more freely and more fully, for you are then released from those other unavoidable studies and occupations.

Thus, the summer vacation gives you an opportunity to apply yourselves to Torah study and Torah activities with the utmost eagerness and enthusiasm—not only to make good use of your free time, but also to make up for lost time during the past school period, and, what is not less important, to give your soul a chance to fortify herself and take a deep breath for the school period ahead. As a matter of fact, the summer vacation seems to be so well planned for this purpose, for it is a time when you can devote yourselves to Torah study and Torah activities in particularly agreeable circumstances: in a relaxed frame of mind and in pleasant natural surroundings of sunshine and fresh air...[44]

The purpose of vacation was rejuvenation to re-energize and continue and for beginners in particular to start Torah study and kosher *chinuch* with piety, application, and vitality.[45] During the long vacation days when students are free from school, *Talmud Torah*, or *Yeshivah*, they have the possibility and privilege to dedicate their free time to Torah study with greater strength. He considered[46] this intensification of spiritual activity during vacation to be essential in case bodily strength weakens the vigor of the soul.

R. Schneerson also urged a curriculum of study during Shabbat and festivals when formal *yeshivah* studies were suspended. He believed[47] that time after and physically away from school was when an educator can exert a significant influence on his or her students so that activity containing educational content should not be neglected.

R. Schneerson also believed that a child's free time, even during the school year, should be used constructively. As student memorization of religious texts was a Habad tradition,[48] R. Schneerson embraced,[49] expounded,[50] and encouraged[51] this activity as a way for students to focus their intellect on meaningful cognition during free time. Such memorization and rote recitation enable the learner to avoid distraction,[52] even when not actually reciting these texts, as they remain engraved in the learner's mind.[53]

The Jewish Studies Curriculum

While R. Schneerson was primarily engaged in promoting a curriculum of global Jewish education and a renaissance of Jewish study through his emissaries, he himself created uncharted wider curricula of Jewish studies. For example, in 1964, R. Schneerson pioneered an original approach to the study of Rashi's commentary to the Torah that continued for almost three decades. A detailed presentation of his methodology utilized in analyses of Rashi was compiled by Rabbi T. Blau and published in 1980 as *Klallei Rashi* ("Principles of Rashi"). The work provides an extensive compilation of some 217 exegetical principles that emerge from R. Schneerson's analyses of *Rashi's* commentary, as well as his application of these principles in his explanation of Rashi's commentary. An expanded version[54] of this work was published in 1990, listing an additional 182 exegetical principles and exemplifications of their application.

R. Schneerson also devoted many of his public addresses to the analysis of sections of *Mishneh Torah* being studied globally, introducing a highly original approach. In 1991, R. Mordechai M. Lauffer published *Klallei Rambam* ("Principles of Maimonides"), which cited 268 underlying axioms of Maimonides' *Mishneh Torah* brought to light through R. Schneerson's analyses of *Mishneh Torah* during over forty years of his leadership.[55]

In regard to the teaching of Jewish history, he considered[56] that exploration of past Jewish history must lead the learner to an optimistic view of the future. He cautioned[57] educators that in all subjects, educational content and its communication must be appropriate to the mind-set of the learner.[58] He charged educators[59] with enabling their students to become capable of learning *Chumash* (Pentateuch) and recommended[60] prioritization of practical applications, especially when time was limited. In light of this policy, he urged that the curriculum include familiarization of students with key prayers,[61] as well as the practical dimensions of Judaism and Jewish observance.

General Studies

There are many writings or addresses by R. Schneerson to the Hasidic fraternity where he advocated a preoccupation with religious studies to the exclusion of general studies, where this is approved by the governing educational authorities. It would appear from these writings that R. Schneerson, following his conviction that education is transformative and value-laden, considered information that exerts an incorrect effect on the learner as having a negative impact.[62]

Moreover, internalization of a negative influence makes it more difficult to assimilate an appropriate influence. This ideal was primarily communicated in addresses to or correspondence with the

Habad Hasidic fraternity and its followers, not to the wider community via cable television, where his educational message focused
on inculcation of morality through education or belief in G-d as
an antidote to juvenile delinquency.[63] From this, some people infer
that the ideal of undiluted religious studies was primarily for the
Hasidic fraternity, rather than to his wider audience where general
studies were an accepted element.[64]

In situations where the offer of a viable secular studies program
was a non-negotiable prerequisite for parents enrolling their children in a Habad school, R. Schneerson was insistent that general
studies be of a high standard.[65] At times, he asked Habad emissaries to maintain their children in these general studies where the
viability of a Habad institution was contingent on the success of
these classes, even though this required selflessness by the emissaries. Moreover, when a student was unable to engage in a full-time
Torah-study program, he considered that withdrawal from secular
studies was not recommended.[66]

Axiomatic to R. Schneerson's discussion of the place of general studies is the Judaic understanding[67] that Torah contains all
wisdom, including general studies.[68] R. Schneerson outlined[69] a
taxonomy that categorized general disciplines according to their
usefulness for Divine service. In an ascending order, these include:

(i)   to enhance a person's livelihood;
(ii)   to improve comprehension of Torah law, such as through
       astronomy;
(iii) to heal another person, such as through medicine; and
(iv)   derivation of lessons from general disciplines to resolve
       questions that conceal sanctity.

He clarified that his comment about utilization of general studies for sacred purposes applied to those who had already engaged in
their study; he did not suggest that students undertake study in general disciplines initially for such purposes, but rather spoke according
to established fact. Thus, while he discouraged university study for

his followers, he recommended that academics who made contact with him after university study advance in their studies and utilize their academic expertise for the advancement of Judaism.

R. Schneerson decried the utilitarian attitude that minimized Torah study because it viewed education as a means to ensure a more prosperous livelihood rather than as an ideal *per se*, unconstrained by financial considerations.[70] Recognizing American parents' widespread perception of education as a means to a child's future financial success, he compared interrupting a child's idealistic Torah study for financial reasons to Pharaoh's submerging Jewish male children in the Nile River, writing:

> Practically speaking: When it comes to educating children, one need not and may not immerse them in the "Nile," i.e., the national idolatry. One may not drown the children in "career-seeking." The only road to true life is a complete education in our Torah, which is the "Torah of Life." There is no point in looking at other parents whose children appear well-provided for — one with a home and another with a car; one a doctor and another a lawyer, or at the very least a shoe-polisher—and to think that by sending a child to a *yeshivah* he will grow up to be an idler and unpractical person, unable even to polish shoes for not knowing how to hold a brush. In truth, it is the Almighty who sustains and provides for all. When we fulfill His will, "and these [words of Torah] you shall teach diligently to your children, and you shall converse in them when you dwell in your house and when you go on your way, and when you lie down and when you rise" (Deuteronomy 6:7) then He will fulfill our requests of Him for both ourselves and our children.[71]

R. Schneerson was well aware that Habad schools in Australia, Great Britain, and elsewhere were legally obligated to teach general studies each day and therefore offered a dual curriculum.[72] He insisted that in such circumstances, Jewish studies be placed in first position on the daily timetable when the learner was freshest and most receptive. He stated:

> We should try to ensure that the time allocation for *Limmudei Kodesh* (Jewish Studies) will be timetabled specifically for the beginning of the day, as close as possible to the waking hours of the student, because when a child is calm and fresh, he or she is then able to study in a qualitatively superior way. [This is] in contradistinction to the end of the day, when exhaustion sets in, etc. The obligation to study Torah also applies when a person is exhausted; however, it is obvious and self-evident that one cannot compare the quality of study when one is tired to study when one is well rested. Therefore, one should try in all schools to establish that the time for *Limmudei Kodesh* (Jewish Studies) is at the beginning of the day.[73]

He found support for this requirement in the metaphorical interpretation of the Biblical injunction[74] which states, "You should set aside the first of your dough...for G-d." He explained:

> The Hebrew word *arisa* meaning "dough" also means "a bed." "The first of your dough" [*Reishit arisoteichem*] can thus also be read as "the first of your bed," meaning that the very first hours after one rises from sleep, when the body is alert and fresh, are to be devoted to Torah Study, whether taking place at *Cheder, Talmud Torah,* or *Beit Rivkah, Beit Ya'akov* and so forth. And only in the hours after that should general studies take place in those places where due to the law of the land one teaches the students general studies.[75]

Besides assigning sacred studies for the beginning of the day, R. Schneerson wanted a predominance of spiritual engagement

over the mundane and material. He wrote, "So too must you
try however possible to ensure that the hours devoted to Torah
Studies will at least be no less than those apportioned for general
studies, and ideally they should exceed them..."[76] He similarly
recommended:

> What is imperative—and there can be no compromise
> in this matter—is that the time devoted to *Limmudei
> Kodesh* [Sacred Studies] must exceed the time allocated to
> vocational studies (ideally two thirds of the time should
> be allocated to *Tefilla* [Prayer] and *Limmudei Kodesh* [Sa-
> cred Studies] and one third to vocational studies).[77]

Another interesting aspect of R. Schneerson's view of general
studies was his definition of this domain:

> I mean "general" only when compared to the stud-
> ies which are actually sacred studies [*limmudei kodesh*],
> because even the general studies must be utilized for
> sanctity [*kedusha*] in the way of preparing for a *mitzvah*
> [*hechsher mitzvah*] in order that as a result the student
> better understands his or her sacred studies.[78]

He thus encouraged educators of schools where general studies
were entrenched to do everything possible to ensure that general
studies should be *al taharat hakodesh* (in pristine sanctity).[79] This
implied that every aspect of general learning and permissible secular matter should be guarded from any impurity with no less
diligence than applies to matters of sanctity.[80]

R. Schneerson also urged the application of general studies as a
means for greater advancement in religious studies, and where possible advocated implementation of total immersion in Torah study.
Seeking to revive in America and the free world this time-honored
approach to Jewish education that had prevailed in religious communities throughout the centuries, he argued:

> Due to the law of the land, in the USA, and those countries
> similar to it...it has been ruled regarding a child...that
> a day cannot go by in the course of the school year with-
> out the teaching of general studies. Concerning this we
> must learn from...my father-in-law of saintly memory,
> who endangered his life in practice and even inspired
> other Jews to risk their lives to establish *chadarim* for Jew-
> ish children and that the Torah study in these *chadarim*
> should be *al taharat hakodesh*—in utter sanctity and
> purity, without changing, G-d forbid, the method of *chi-*
> *nuch* that was practiced by the Jewish people throughout
> all the generations. How much more so should we make
> every additional effort in our day and age in this country
> of America, and in similar countries where the situation
> is not one of physical danger, G-d forbid, that the Jewish
> education of Jewish children should be founded utterly
> upon sanctity and purity, without mixing in general stud-
> ies except for where the law does not allow this, and even
> there, in the most minimal measure that is mandatory...[81]

As a result of the diversity of approaches to the accommodation
of general studies taken by R. Schneerson, while all contemporary Habad educational institutions begin the school day with a
significant proportion of religious studies, Habad schools offer a
spectrum of possibilities that aspire to comply with R. Schneerson's
directives, each facilitating a differing emphasis on Torah studies
in relation to general studies. Still, the ideal graduate remains the
person whose preoccupation with and application to Torah studies
takes priority over his or her engagement in general studies.

As stated, R. Schneerson did not advocate university attendance
for his followers. For example, he advised against a Habad emissary
attending college as he felt it would deflect him from his mission
and involve disruptive matters. He also felt the emissary's choice
would serve as a poor example to the congregants, who would consequently send their children to college.[82]

A concern which led R. Schneerson to discourage his followers from college study was disorientation that it might have on "the sense of awe and holiness" of a religious student. He thus wrote:

> One of the serious dangers that is inherent in college edu-
> cation has to do with its influence on the thought process
> of the college student. The college student is trained to
> think in secular terms and categories. In all courses (ex-
> cept theology) G-d is banished from the classroom. This
> often leads to the tendency of leaving G-d out of the
> Torah study as well. When, and if, the college student re-
> turns to the *Gemara*, he is likely to approach it with the
> same mental process. He may still admire the wisdom of
> the Torah, and may still derive pleasure from its study, but
> he will not be able to recapture the sense of awe and holi-
> ness with which he had once approached G-d's Torah...[83]

Another area of concern was the lack of morality that character-ized life on college campuses. He wrote:

> The obvious dangers when a *yeshivah* boy is subjected
> several times during the week to such radical changes
> of atmosphere and ideology as exist between the *yeshi-
> vah* and the college, where the majority of students are
> gentiles, and the majority of the Jewish students are
> unfortunately not religious, etc. It is impossible for a
> student to avoid contact with fellow students and pro-
> fessors. Hence, even if your son would have liked to go
> to college, it would have been highly problematical as to
> the advisability of it, as it is impossible to foresee what
> conflicts and dangers it would entail...[84]

He thus defended students whose parents sought to withdraw them from *yeshivah* studies forcibly in order to embark on college study, writing:

I am sure you will agree with me that in the case of everyone without exception, the first basic condition for happiness in life is peace of mind and the least amount of inner conflict. This has always been a fundamental principle, and it is even more so in our present generation, with its world-shattering events, confusions, conflicting ideas and ideologies. Nothing speaks more forcefully about the existing state of mind of present-day youth than the unheard-of rebellion against society in the form of juvenile delinquency and demoralization of character, all of which is a symptom of our confused age.

Therefore, the first and best thing one can do to help one's child is to endeavor to spare him the inner conflicts and to help him cultivate good religious and moral principles, so that he would not fall prey to human influences. This is especially important at the critical age of youth, when one's character and world outlook are being formed and stabilized. With this brief introduction, I return to what you consider such a problem, namely, your attempt to persuade your son to go to college and his reluctance to do so. I am sure his motives are of his purest nature, desiring to dedicate a certain period of time to the exclusive study of the Torah. At his age, to try to force him to give up something which he rightly considers in his best interests, something that is good and holy which he desires very much, would certainly upset him and inevitably endanger his peace of mind. Even if he should not show outward signs of resentment, he might well develop such a feeling subconsciously, which is sometimes even worse. It is also doubtful whether such attempts to make him change his mind would be successful.[85]

R. Schneerson also rejected economic arguments for university attendance, replying:

You think that a college education would give him greater security economically. Actually only a small percentage of college graduates directly derive their income from their college degree. In the final analysis, however, one cannot make calculations and plans about the future without taking G-d into account. For after all, G-d is not only the Creator of the world, whose direct Providence extends to every individual and detail, and success or failure is from Him; but he is also the Giver of the Torah...[86]

When conceding to the wishes of a student outside the Hasidic fraternity to attend university, his approval was conditional on the student's prior study for a year or two in a *yeshivah* as fortification against the perceived dangers of university study. He argued that "it would be obviously illogical and impossible that when a Jewish boy dedicates a few years to the exclusive study of G-d's Torah, that it would lessen his chance for happiness in life."[87] While discouraging his followers from undertaking college studies, he did encourage those who had already entered university to advance within the realm of academia and thereby exert an influence on students who look to them as role models. Thus he wrote in 1986 to "The Esteemed Faculty Members of Cornell University and Ithaca College":

I trust you do not underestimate your personal influence that is inherent in your respective prominent positions in the community and especially among the academic youth. It is a prevalent experience, human nature being what it is, that students are "often" strongly influenced by the example of their professors' everyday life and conduct regardless of the academic field that brought them together. This being so, each of you will surely readily recognize your special responsibility and extraordinary *Zechut* [*merit*] that Hashem has given you, individually and as a group, to help the young people who are fortunate to be exposed to your influence to reinforce their identity with our Jewish people and its eternal heritage; and, with emphasis on the basic principle of *Yiddish-keit* that "the essential thing is the deed," to actually strengthen their commitment to the way of the Torah and *Mitzvot* in their personal life and conduct.[88]

While recommending pursuit of religious studies in a comprehensive way, it is important to also remember that R. Schneerson interacted constantly with the world of academia and gave advice on matters concerning the content of theses and academic conferences. Interestingly, in communication with people already engaged in academic pursuits and those whom he believed could withstand the resultant transformation of such study, R. Schneerson actually encouraged even greater academic achievement and more substantive scholarly output.

Knesset member[89] Yonah Kessa (1907-1985), a childhood neighbor of R. Schneerson in Yekaterinoslav (Dnepropetrovsk), made reference to R. Schneerson's childhood diligence in Torah study together with him being well-versed in physics and mathematics.[90] R. Schneerson offered advice to then doctoral student Dr. Susan Handelman,[91] currently professor of literature at Bar Ilan University's Department of English Literature and Linguistics, regarding her prospective dissertation, and edited her essays for *Di Yiddishe Heim* magazine.[92] He also commented on the doctoral thesis written by Professor Jonathan Sacks,[93] Chief Rabbi Emeritus of the British Commonwealth.[94] In 1958, R. Schneerson encouraged Prof. Yitzchak [Irving] Block, Emeritus Professor of Philosophy at the University of Western Ontario, Toronto, to publish parts of his doctoral dissertation on Aristotle in scholarly journals. He advised Block to enlist the support of his supervisor, Dr. Roger Albitton of Harvard University, in his efforts to have the article published by Dr. Ludwig Edelstein in Johns Hopkins University's prestigious *American Journal of Philology*.[95] R. Schneerson took a personal interest in the research undertaken by Professor Herman Branover, professor of magneto-hydrodynamics at Tel Aviv and

Beer Sheva universities, encouraging Branover to deliver a critical paper at Stanford University during his first visit to America.[96] He similarly asked Dr. Velvel Greene[97] to provide him with his reports and keep him abreast of developments in micro-biology, with R. Schneerson often offering his own valuable insights.[98] American novelist Harvey Swados was amazed by R. Schneerson's reference, during a 1964 *yechidut*, to the "early works of Upton Sinclair and proletarian literature."[99] Similarly, Pulitzer Prize-winning author Herman Wouk related that in a private audience, R. Schneerson offered profound insights into the genre of fiction writing that was Wouk's area of expertise.[100] In light of these academic connections, exclusive reading of citations from R. Schneerson's writings that apply highly selective criteria might lead one to ignore his rich and broad intellectual contribution to education.

Testing and Novel Torah Thoughts

Testing has its historical precedent in Habad tradition. The third *Admor* of Habad, the Tzemach Tzedek, regularly tested his grandchildren on their religious knowledge and particularly the meaning of the words of prayer. As R. Schneerson wrote:

> The Tzemach Tzedek, as is well known, was a giant among the giants of the Torah of his time, the authority on *Halacha* as well as on *Chassidut* and *Kabbalah*, as his many works attest. In addition, he was the *Manhig* [leader] of the generation who had, on more than one occasion, been invited by the Government in Petersburg for consultations on the Jewish position. It is easy to imagine how very busy he was. Nevertheless, he used to tear himself away from his own duties and writings, and from his many public duties, in order to examine his small grandchildren once a month in order to determine their progress. He also gave them monetary prizes in order to stimulate them to

further accomplishments. Since we have been told this
story in the life of the Tzemach Tzedek, it is clear that it
contains a message for each and every one of us. It is that
no sacrifice should be too great in our efforts in the cause
of *Chinuch*, especially the education and the upbringing
of the younger generation.[101]

R. Schneerson similarly urged[102] parents to review their children's
knowledge of the weekly Torah reading during the Sabbath, stating:

As has been customary in Jewish communities, on Shabbat
evening and Shabbat day, fathers would teach their children
and test them on what they had learned during the week
and especially on the weekly Torah reading.[103] During the
remainder of the week the fathers are busy with matters of
earning a livelihood, but on the day of Shabbat they are
able to devote time and attention in a relaxed way.[104]

Mothers were also included as active participants in this testing
process at home.[105]

R. Schneerson[106] believed that the composing of *chiddushim*
(novel insights pertinent to the curriculum) by students would inspire their greater engagement and diligence in the area of study,[107]
as well as motivating other students to engage in challenging and
seeking clarification of their hypotheses. The wide publication of
such compilations would benefit fruitful scholarly interchange. The
traditional ideal of students authoring novel Torah insights was
predicated on a wealth of Rabbinic precedents,[108] especially the requirement of the *Zohar* (1:12b) to "be fruitful in creative Torah study
each day"; it was encapsulated by the statement of the founder of
Habad, Rabbi Schneur Zalman of Liadi, who wrote in *Tanya*:[109]

Every Jew is able to reveal secrets of wisdom, and to dis-
cover a new insight, whether it be in the area of *Halacha*
[Jewish law] or in *Aggadot* [homiletics], in *Nigleh* [the

revealed, exoteric dimension of Torah] or in *Nistar* [the
mystical planes of the Torah], according to the nature of
his soul's root. Indeed, one is obliged to do so, in order
to perfect his soul by elevating all the sparks that have
been allotted to it, as is known.[110]

Personal Development

R. Schneerson considered teaching matters of intimacy independent of their Torah context as potentially dangerous; therefore, he
recommended[111] that educators include such matters when teaching *Chumash* (Biblical text) as this was not problematic. He argued
that omitting matters of intimacy from their Torah context arouses
student curiosity but when taught in the context of Torah, these
matters are imbued with sanctity.[112]

Regarding the teaching of sexuality itself, he was adamant that it
not occur in a co-educational setting. Moreover, any insincere interest
by students in such discussions that might be inspired by improper motivations would need to be pre-empted and curtailed by the expert in
charge. He recommended only small group discussions of three or four
students with a mentor as considered most appropriate. He thus wrote:

> Regarding explaining to male and female adolescents
> regarding the topic of problems related to the physical
> impulse and sexuality, it is difficult to take a definitive
> position in this matter because, notwithstanding the state-
> ment of our Sages regarding the verse you cite in your
> correspondence, that "worry in the heart [of youth] should
> be discussed with others," our Sages also say in regard to
> this matter, "man possesses a small limb: starve it and it
> is satiated; satisfy it and it is hungry." It would seem that
> such discussions on matters pertaining to sexuality also
> fall within the category of satiating it, except for when the
> discussion is conducted by the most outstanding expert so

as to avoid certain inappropriate expressions and associations. And as I have seen in some places, the appropriate outcome is that with consultation with teachers on the spot, who establish the ground rules for the conduct and nature of the discussions with a particular boy (or girl) and at most another two or three compatible students who would join [the small group-discussions]. Of course, under all circumstances, these discussions must be conducted for either boys only or girls only [and not with the publicity and fanfare that is customary in some places]. Even then, great care must be taken to ensure that no one stumbles in any prohibition (be it a Torah prohibition or even a Rabbinic prohibition[113]) of "do not bring me to contemplate [that which is inappropriate]."[114]

Clearly, R. Schneerson was highly aware of the centrality of the curriculum content to his educational philosophy and he made significant contributions to the methodology and content of education.

Notes

1. Documented by RJIS in *IK-RJIS*, II:491 (letter 616) and cited in *HaYom Yom*, entry of 8th of *Adar-Rishon*. In the same entry, RJIS recorded another version of the same teaching with RSZ suggesting that the soul is symbolized by the point above, the individual's body is represented by the point below, and these are connected by a line of the fear of Heaven in the middle. R. Schneerson explained the first version of this concept in an address of *Ellul* 8th, 5718 [Aug. 24th, 1958]. (See *TM-HIT*, XXIII [5718, III]:266-8.)
2. Letter dated *Nissan* 25th, 5742 [April 18th, 1982] addressed to US president Ronald Reagan.
3. *IK*, I:56-7, Letter 34.
4. *LS*, XIX:91-3, §5-§6.
5. *Reshimot*, II:114-22 [*Reshima* No. 19]. In this text, R. Schneerson argued that faith is the foundation of the life of the Jewish people and also pertains to children.
6. *IK*, I:249-50, Letter 136.
7. *Reshimot*, II:114-22 [*Reshima* No. 19].

8. Talmud, *Nida* 30b.

9. Address of First Day (Shabbat) *Chanukkah,* 5743 [Dec. 11th, 1982] in *TM-HIT-5743,* II:677-80, §6-§8.

10. *LS,* XIX:91-3, §5-§6.

11. *Reshimot,* IV:254-62 [*Reshima* No. 138].

12. *Ibid.*

13. *IK,* IV:213-5, Letter 949 [Addenda to *LS,* XXIV:470-1].

14. *IK,* III:295-6, Letter 603 [Addenda to *LS,* XII:227] citing the 5678 [1917-18] discourse beginning with the words *Ki Ka'asher HaShamayim,* in *SM-RSB-5678*:283.

15. *IK,* IV:228-9, Letter 959.

16. *IK,* I:57-8, Letter 35.

17. Deuteronomy, 7:11.

18. *IK,* III:337, Letter 642.

19. Talmud, *Ketubot* 103b records that it was R. Chiya who suspended his personal Torah scholarship in order to engage in the arduous task of trapping deer and thereafter producing parchment for the writing of Torah scrolls with which to perpetuate Torah study, whose survival at that time was otherwise precarious. The Talmud applauds R. Chiya's efforts and exclaims, "How great are the deeds of R. Chiya!"

20. *IK,* I:57-8, Letter 35.

21. *Op. cit.,* I:66-7, Letter 42.

22. *TM,* III [5711, II]:85-92. §19-§27 & §29.

23. *IK,* III:333-4, Letter 637.

24. RJIS in *SH-RJIS-5703*:144 & 164, cited in S.Y. Cohen's anthology entitled *Likkutei Hanhagot V'Halachot B'Chinuch Al Taharat HaKodesh* (Kiryat Malachi, 1976), Section II, Chapter 4, Paragraphs 4, 5 & 6.

25. *IK,* I:188, Letter 103 [Addenda to *LS,* XXI:402].

26. *IK,* I:163-4, Letter 91.

27. *TM-HIT-5742,* IV:2,123:4.

28. *Shabbat,* 105a.

29. R. Schneerson elaborated: "So too it can be understood in regard to the word *Anochi* that the vowels accompanying the letter indicate some concept of form (e.g. the specifications and ramifications of this letter, for example, *Aleph* with a *Kamatz* vowel is the beginning of the word *Anochi* and *Aleph* with a *Patach* vowel is the beginning of the word *Anachnu* meaning 'we' and the like). Therefore, the very simplicity of the letter *Aleph*—the Master of the Universe—is reflected in the letter *Aleph* as it transcends an actual application—the essential letter without any additional vowel. Therefore, if one begins to teach a child the letter *Aleph* with the *Kamatz* vowel, without any possibility of teaching the *Aleph* on its own, not only does this not assist with the teaching and education of a child, but rather the opposite occurs, and one thwarts the possibility of implanting in the heart of a child the essential

aspect of the *Aleph*, i.e. the Master of the Universe. Through this we can now understand the great emphasis that our Rebbes of Habad laid so that, first and foremost, we teach the form of the letters independent of the vowels, thereby implanting in the heart of a child the idea that *Aleph* represents, namely, the Master of the Universe and only afterwards do we teach the child *kametz-aleph-o* as this idea is revealed in the Torah of light (when one's father teaches one Torah i.e. the *Aleph* of the word *Anochi*)."

30. *Kuntres Inyana Shel Torat HaChasidut* [translated as *On the Essence of Chassidus*]: Chapters 9-17.

31. *Reshimat HaMenorah*:74-141.

32. *IK*, IV:112, Letter 857.

33. *Op. cit.*, IV:234, Letter 964.

34. *Op. cit.*, I:130-31, Letter 79 [Addenda to *LS*, IV:1295-6].

35. *IK*, XXI:12-3, Letter 7,764.

36. *Ibid.*

37. English letter of *Shevat*, 5710 [Feb., 1950] entitled "A Message to Children on the Passing of Rabbi Joseph Isaac Schneersohn."

38. *IK*, IV:170-1, Letter 914.

39. *Op. cit.*, III:144-7, Letter 505 [Addenda to *LS*, XI:297-9].

40. *IK*, XVIII:296.

41. *Op. cit.*, III:344-5, Letter 646 [Addenda to *LS*, VIII:369].

42. *Ibid.*, citing Rambam, *Hilchot De'ot*, IV:1.

43. *IK*, IV:328-9, Letter 1,051 [Addenda to *LS*, VIII:370].

44. *IK*, XXIX (*ed.* S.B. Levin):171-3, Letter 11,151.

45. *Op. cit.*, IV:454-5; Letter 1,177 [Addenda to *LS*, IX:306-7].

46. *IK*, III:344-5, Letter 646 [Addenda to *LS*, VIII:369] citing *Zohar* I:180b & *Talmud, Shabbat*:147b.

47. *IK*, IV:357, Letter 1,076.

48. *Sefer HaMa'amarim-5711*:241 cited in *HaYom Yom*, entry for *Adar-Rishon* 9th; *SH-RJIS-5702*:116; cited in *HaYom Yom*, entry for *Tevet* 11th.

49. *IK*, I:105-7, Letter 63; *IK*, I:126-7, Letter 76 [Addenda to *LS*, XXIII:421].

50. Hebrew letter of *Shevat* 14th, 5704 [February, 8th, 1944] addressed to R. Menachem Ze'ev Greenglass, *IK*, I:235-244, Letter 132; Kovetz, *Lubavitch*, IV:66ff; *Teshuvot U'Biurim*:13-21.

51. *IK*, I:154-7, Letter 86 [Addenda to *LS*, II:691-2].

52. *IK*, V:170, Letter 1,374.

53. *IK*, V:169-70, Letter 1,373 [Addenda to *LS*, XXIV:509-10]; *IK*, V:170, Letter 1,374.

54. In a letter of *Adar* 11th, 5740 [February 28th, 1980], R. Schneerson expressed his appreciation to R. Blau for the first edition of this work and encouraged his publication of a more extensive edition.

55. Several of R. Schneerson's commentaries on Maimonides' *Mishneh Torah* are collected in Pewsner's *Yein Malchut* (I:1987 and II:1988). His *Siyumim*

and *Hadranim* [scholarly discourses delivered upon completion of a Talmudic tractate], on Maimonides' *Mishneh Torah,* and on various Talmudic tractates are collected in *Torat Menachem—Hadranim Al HaRambam V'Shas* by Lahak Hanachot (1992).

56. *Reshimot*, IV:175-81 [*Reshima* No. 130].

57. *IK,* I:36-7, Letter 20 [Addenda to *LS,* IV:1260-1].

58. For example, when a euphemism [for death] will not be understood by children, (namely, *niftar* meaning "discharged" or "absolved" or "released" from earthly existence), he recommended setting aside the more respectful euphemism, particularly when the less euphemistic and more confronting term has been previously encountered and is thus more familiar to the student.

59. *Op. cit.,* V:148-9, Letter 1,355 [Addenda to *LS,* XXII:399-400].

60. *Ibid.*

61. These included "the *Shema, Amidah,* Morning Blessings, Blessings on food, etc."

62. This is in keeping with the view of proactive inhibition, or proactive interference, which explains the psychological phenomenon of individuals who are unable to learn a new skill-set that is counter-intuitive to a previously learned skill-set. Proactive inhibition argues that an individual's old memories interfere with the way he or she retains new information. See B. J. Underwood, 1948, 1957 & 1969.

63. For examples of R. Schneerson's dedication of his televised public addresses to educational themes of relevance to society at large, see (televised) address of *Nissan* 11th, 5742 [April 4th, 1982] where R. Schneerson spoke on the importance of character education and the educator as a personal role-model, in *Hitva'aduyot-5742,* III:1197-8, §9, & 1210, §28; (televised) address of *Shevat* 10th, 5743 [Jan. 24th, 1983] on an awareness of a Higher Authority as the foundation of education and the antidote to delinquency in *TM-HIT-5743,* II:891 §11; 899-904 §23-§30; 907-9 (§36-§39) & 917 and his (televised) address of eve of *Nissan* 11th, 5743 [March 24th, 1953] on the importance of the introduction of a "Moment of Silence" in public schools, on teaching Noahide Laws and on utilization of birthdays as an educational opportunity (see *SK-5748,* II:398-407).

64. Interview of July, 2014 with a senior New York Habad educator and author who believed that R. Schneerson addressed multiple audiences, advocating intense religious studies and the minimization of secular studies for members of the Hasidic fraternity and accepting the reality of secular studies in the case of what the interviewee called "the Jew in Manhattan." A further hypothetical explanation was suggested by an international guest lecturer in the course of his address to a Habad gathering in Sydney on *Tammuz* 3rd, 5772 [July 11th, 2002]. He reminded his audience of the further consideration where R. Schneerson's addresses to his Hasidic following aimed to create a Habad fraternity who would serve as an "army"

of global outreach in the spirit of the *Tomchei Temimim Yeshivah*, where a preoccupation with religious study at the most profound level was an ideal that precluded general studies.

65. See R. Schneerson's response negating the suggestion of curtailment of general studies at Beth Rivkah Ladies' College of Melbourne in order to enable an increase in religious studies, cited in Gurewicz, 2015:195.

66. This can be understood as a reflection of Judaism's disdain for time used unproductively, which it perceived to be a cause of devastation of an individual. The Babylonian Talmud (*Ketubot*, 59b) states that idleness leads to mental illness and immorality.

67. See *Devarim* 4:6. Commenting on this verse, the Talmud in *Shabbat* 75a cites mathematical calculations of the *tekufot* and astronomical calculations as specific examples of areas of knowledge being included in Torah knowledge. See also *Ethics of the Fathers*, 5:21 [according to RSZ's allocation of *mishnayot*]: "Ben Bag Bag said: 'Delve and delve into it [the Torah], for everything is in it...'" The Maharal of Prague explained (*Derech Chaim*, comments to *Ethics of the Fathers*, 5:22 on page 275 of the Jerusalem edition published in 1960 by L. Honig and Sons) that this *Mishnah* implies that "understanding the depths of Torah leads to comprehension of all of creation."

68. *SK-5689-5710* [1929-1950]:153-4, Paragraph 12. In this address, R. Schneerson cited geometry as a specific example of an area of knowledge included in Torah knowledge.

69. *TM*, II [5711:I]:311-23.

70. *IK*, III:475-6, Letter 756 [Addenda to *LS*, XXII:418].

71. *LS*, I:98-102.

72. Conversation with Rabbi Y.D. Groner on June 30th, 1996.

73. *TM-HIT-5745*, V:3034; See also *IK*, XIII:125-6.

74. *Bamidbar*, 15:20 as explained in Habad Hasidic texts.

75. Address of *Sivan* 19th, 5747 to the Graduating Students of Beth Rivkah and the Counselors of Chabad Summer Day Camps; see *TM-HIT-5747*, III:521.

76. *IK*, X:299.

77. *Op. cit.*, IX:115; see also *op. cit.*, XII:277.

78. *TM-HIT-5747*, III:521.

79. *IK*, XXVIII (*ed.* S.B. Levin):233-6, Letter 10,803; *op. cit.*, XXVII (*ed.* S.Y. Chazan):310-2, Letter 10,192 [Addenda to *LS*, XIII:166-8]; *IK*, XXVIII (*ed.* S.B. Levin):236-7, Letter 10,804; *IK*, XXVII (*ed.* S.Y. Chazan):313, Letter 10,193 [Addenda to *LS*, XIII:168-9]; *IK*, XXVIII (*ed.* S.B. Levin):238-40, Letter 10,806; *IK*, XXVII (*ed.* S.Y. Chazan):314-6, Letter 10,194 [Addenda to *LS*, XIII:169-71].

80. As support for this notion, R. Schneerson referred the reader to Talmud, *Chagiga* 19b; *Torah Ohr* 12b; and other references as well as the end of Discourse *Zachor Et Yom HaShabbat-5626* concerning the command (Proverbs,

3:6) "Know G-d in all your ways." (as expounded in *Tur* and *Shulchan Aruch*, *Orach Chaim*, Chapter 231) [*SM-5626*:4 (Kehot Publication Society, 5749)].

81. *LS*, XVI:145-7.
82. *IK*, III:472-4, Letter 755 [Addenda to *LS*, XVII:485-7]. R. Schneerson also suggested that his correspondent's congregants would reason that if after *yeshivah* study, the emissary felt the necessity for a college education to attain human perfection, then it certainly would be of benefit to their own children. Finally, R. Schneerson told his correspondent that as an emissary of the sixth Lubavitcher Rebbe in whom the powers of the sixth Rebbe are invested, he was "dragging the sixth Rebbe onto the university campus."
83. Undated English letter of 5722 [1962-3] addressed to the editor of a NY newspaper (published in *Sparks of Chassidus for Young and Old*:111-5).
84. *Letters from the Rebbe*, I:111-13, Letter 55.
85. *Ibid.*
86. *Ibid.*
87. *Ibid.*
88. *Op. cit.*, IV:196-7, Letter 125.
89. Yona Kessa served in the Knesset between 1949 and 1965.
90. Kessa, 1997. Kessa referred to R. Schneerson's "incredible combination of knowledge" and to his being "very modest and hidden" and that "his whole existence was Torah."
91. Chabad.org/574988.
92. Chabad.org/161694.
93. From R. Schneerson's comments, R. Sacks derived that "...we cannot understand even the law of collective Jewish responsibility without first grasping its basis in mysticism."
94. Sacks, 1995:4.
95. *Living Torah*, Disc 80, Program 319. R. Schneerson constantly encouraged Professor Block to attend international conferences on Greek philosophy and to present papers at these. See "Rationalist Acting above Reason" in *Living Torah*, Disc 56, Program 221.
96. Branover, 1982:134-8. During one private audience with R. Schneerson, Branover was asked by R. Schneerson to communicate the content of material he would lecture to his students at Beer Sheva University.
97. *Living Torah*, Disc 73, Program 289. Professor Velvel Greene (1928-2011) was professor of public health and microbiology at the University of Minnesota for twenty-seven years who became an Emeritus Professor of Public Health and Epidemiology at Ben Gurion University, a Fulbright scholar, a pioneer in his field of bacteriology invited by NASA to join a select team of scientists studying the possible effects of space travel on human life. Green was an original participant in NASA's Exobiology program searching for life on Mars. He was also the director of the Jakobovits Center for Jewish Medical Ethics, at Ben Gurion University, Beer Sheva.

98. *Living Torah*, Disc 65, Program 258.

99. Swados, 1994.

100. Related by Rabbi Yisrael Deren of Connecticut on June 19th, 2015 in Sydney, Australia.

101. *Letters from the Rebbe*, VI:64-5, Letter 45. See also *SK-5726*:87-94, §5-§7 and *SK-5726*:123-4, §12 regarding *The Tzemach Tzedek* testing his grandchildren.

102. *TM-HIT-5750*, III:172; *SH-5750* [1989-90]:II, 443-59.

103. See address of *Shabbat Parashat Shelach, Shabbat Mevarchim Chodesh Tammuz, Sivan* 23rd, 5750 [June 16th, 1990] *TM-HIT-5750*, III:364: "and how much more so after he grows and studies Torah, including the weekly Torah portion in particular, as is the Jewish custom for previous generations that on Shabbat day a father tests his children on their studies for the week, and especially *Parashat HaShavua* [The Weekly Torah Reading] that he studied in *cheder* and heard just now during synagogue Torah reading."

104. See address of *Shabbat Hagadol, Nissan* 10th, 5749 [April 15th, 1989] in *TM-HIT-5749*, II:15.

105. See address of *Shabbat Parashat Emor, Iyar* 17th, 5750 [May 12th, 1990] *TM-HIT-5750*, III:172 concerning the obligation of Jewish women in *Chumash* and Torah study, "Their learning with the child is in a way of 'testing,' as is customary that the father tests his sons on their Torah study on Shabbat and such occasions.

106. *LS*, XXIII:18-9; Address of *Shabbat Parashat Vayigash, Tevet* 5th, 5751 [Dec. 22nd, 1990]; *TM-HIT-5751*, II:90; *Sefer HaSichot-5751*, I:90, footnote 47 & supra-notes and footnote 58; Address of *Shabbat Parashat Bamidbar, Sivan* 5th, 5751 [May 18th, 1991]; Address of *Shabbat Parashat Mishpatim, Shevat* 27th, 5752 [Feb. 1st, 1992].

107. "When one's novel Torah insights are published in printed form for others, then it is a person's nature (be it due to self-respect or the way of the world) that even his animal soul shows greater caution and one will look over and review in depth whatever one is submitting for publication." (See address of *Shabbat Parashat Bamidbar*, 5751 in *SK-5751*, II:561-2.)

108. For a fuller presentation of the theological and practical underpinnings of this idea, see Rabbi Shmuel Yechezkel Cohen's *Shlavei HaChinuch LaTorah B'Or HaHalacha U'Mishnat Admorei Chabad-Lubavitch* [Stages of a Torah Education in Light of Jewish Law and the Teachings of the Rebbes of Chabad-Lubavitch], Nachalat Har Chabad, Kiryat Malachi, Israel, 5752 [1992], 52-60.

109. *Iggeret HaKodesh*, Chapter 26, 145a.

110. RSZ also wrote in his *Shulchan Aruch [HaRav]* (*Hilchot Talmud Torah*, Chapter 1, end of section 4.): "The Sages of the true [wisdom] also taught (*Sefer Gilgulim*, Chapter 4; *Sha'ar HaGilgulim, Hakdamah* 11, page 16a; *Ibid.*: Introduction to *Sha'ar HaMitzvot; Aitz Chaim*, Gate 49, Chapter 5)

that in order to perfect itself, every soul must engage in the *Pardes* [the 'orchard' of the Torah] according to its capacity to comprehend and perceive. Any person with the potential to comprehend and perceive much, but due to indolence comprehended and perceived only little, must reincarnate until he comprehends and perceives everything that his soul can comprehend and perceive in the knowledge of the Torah. This includes the simple [meaning of] the laws, the allusions, the exegetical derivations, and the mystical secrets. For whatever the soul can comprehend and perceive in the knowledge of the Torah consummates its perfection. It cannot reach consummate perfection in the Bond of Life—G-d, in the Source from which it was hewn (see *Metzudat David, loc. cit.*) without this knowledge. Therefore our Sages declared (Talmud, *Pesachim*, 50a and references cited there): "Happy is he who arrives here [to *Gan Eden* in the spiritual realms] with his knowledge in hand," so that he will not have to reincarnate and [descend] again to this [material] world."

111. *SK-5689-5710* [1929-1950]:167-8, Paragraphs 7 & 8. See Addenda to *SK-5728* [1967-1968], I:506.
112. He considered omitting such matters when found in Rashi's Torah commentary to be acceptable, as student curiosity would not be aroused by this omission, as the non-inclusion of a difficult commentary by Rashi on matters of Hebrew grammar (often due to the teacher's lack of expertise in grammar) is commonplace and does not arouse learner inquisitiveness.
113. *Shulchan Aruch, Even HaEzer*, Chapter 23, par. 3; *Tanya*, Section I, Ch. 11.
114. *IK*, XX:173-5, Letter 7,597 [Addenda to *LS*, XXII:404 & 424-5].

Chapter 8

THE PRACTICE AND
POLICY OF EDUCATION

The connection between education and experience of life
is intimate and mutually effective, for each contributes to
the other in significant and profound ways.

—Professor Stephen David Ross[1]

A cohesive educational philosophy should[2] have tangible implications for educational practice and policy,[3] such that "the potency
and significance of an educational philosophy can be evidenced
by its practical application to highly specific educational circumstances."[4] This research investigated whether R. Schneerson's
educational corpus has direct implications for the practice of education and educational policy.

The Practice of Education

To R. Schneerson, education must not remain theoretical but
must impact on the learner's deeds and actions:[5] he considered
educational endeavor devoid of a practical application to be antithetical to Judaism[6] and its educational thought. Throughout his
discourse he was insistent that abstract excursions and theoretical
deliberations absolutely required resultant practical initiatives with
increased tangible educational outcomes.[7] A characteristic conclusion of R. Schneerson's discourses was his effort to make explicit

any *hora'ah* (practical directive) derived from his discussions, irrespective of their theoretical nature. Consequently, a corresponding implication for educational practice or policy accompanies his theoretical deliberations. Indeed, a vast volume of practical educational recommendations is embedded in his discourse delivered between 1951 and 1992.

Practical Ramifications of the Educational Discourse

A range of practical ramifications emerges from the themes discussed. While there are many further practical educational directives implied by his educational philosophy beyond those documented here, the ones discussed in this chapter are those mainly mentioned in anthologies of R. Schneerson's practical educational advice.[8]

There is substantive scope to R. Schneerson's practical educational initiatives implemented over more than forty-two years of leadership of Habad and the ten years prior when he headed the educational wing of the Habad movement under the direction of his predecessor, RJIS. In light of his extensive corpus of practical educational initiatives, only a sample of practical directives that emerge from the educational philosophy is included.

Practical Ramifications of the Broadest Understanding of Education

R. Schneerson advocated the adoption of an expansive understanding of education which views education as an all-encompassing enterprise[9] that incorporated everything. As a consequence of this broad understanding of education, there are many practical ramifications that he personally exemplified when communicating Jewish values and which he advocated for educators to implement.

Thus, he encouraged educators not to overlook a chance encounter with a student outside the confines of the school day, arguing that it can have even more influence than a classroom interaction.[10] He also believed that when used correctly, a chess game,[11] a boat trip,[12] a soccer game,[13] or an art class[14] can provide the educator with magnificent opportunities. One such benefit obtained from a multitude of activities was the moral edification of the learner. For example, lessons to be derived include: From chess, an educator can remind students how we must all constantly make step-by-step progression to higher spiritual levels, in the same way that chess pieces advance up the chessboard. Like the soccer player's attempts to score goals, everyone must strive to direct the world to its ideal goal, which is a more spiritual and harmonious world. Also, the artist's ability to make an inanimate canvas come alive by applying layers of paint to create an original image is similar to the attempt to look beyond the material world and enliven it by using it for doing *mitzvot*. In a letter to Hasidic artist Hendel Lieberman, R. Schneerson wrote:

> The artist must be able to look deeply into the inner content of the object, beyond its external form and to see the inner aspect and essence of the object... The viewer examining the result can now see the object in a completely different light and realizes that his previous impressions of the object were erroneous... [Similarly] an honest effort [is required of] each of us to "bring to the surface" the G-dliness inherent in everything in our lives, and to remove as much as possible the mask of physical externality obscuring the inner G-dliness.[15]

In incorporating boat travel for educational ends, he urged educators to teach students that "as the captain must steer his boat over turbulent waters, so too must each individual be sure to rise above the material world and not be dragged down by it, for soon all will reach the calm seas of time set aside each day for prayer and contemplation and particularly the tranquillity of Shabbat."

Similarly, he personally taught that the splitting of the atom,[16] breakthroughs in space exploration,[17] or even the death of Howard Hughes after a life characterized by an ungenerous disposition,[18] which were all subjects of his public addresses, were to be considered matters of didactic significance.[19]

Practical ramifications of R. Schneerson's adoption of the broadest definition of education, so that education extends from the very young to the most senior, include his recommendation[20] to surround the new-born with matters pertaining to purity and sanctity, such as verses of Torah;[21] encouraging a toddler to look at holy objects like the *Shir HaMa'alot* chart;[22] and his negating children's exposure to toys or children's decorations with images of impure animals.[23]

R. Schneerson taught[24] that the child's education "To love G-d, to fear Him, and to remember Him always" begins immediately when the child comes into the world, even prior to and during pregnancy,[25] and it gets stronger at birth when there is a *mezuzah* affixed to the doorway and a *Shir HaMa'alot* chart hanging in front of his room. It is also part of his education when the infant's father and mother look at the child, his hand and feet movements and his development, take pride in him, and give blessings and praise to G-d. R. Schneerson[26] suggested that the fact that education begins at birth is readily observed from the behavior of parents who, well before the baby even has understanding, make gestures in front of the baby, thereby teaching the baby to imitate. He acted on the principle that education begins at the earliest age by also emphasizing[27] the Halachic requirement that cautions against a child touching food prior to ritual hand washing in the morning.[28]

R. Schneerson encouraged[29] mothers to recite *Modeh Ani* on behalf of and with their infants who could not yet speak. He also recommended[30] teaching children still too young to say all of their prayers, to start each day with reciting *Modeh Ani*, whereby immediately when awaking, he or she proclaims verbally with his or her whole body that he or she has received his soul anew from G-d; we thereby teach a child that all of Judaism pertains to him or her. R. Schneerson explained[31] that this is especially imperative when the child is taught the meaning of the words as they concern him or her, as this has an effect throughout the day, even until bedtime when the *Shema* is recited.

R. Schneerson endorsed and applied the custom to teach children not yet at an age of understanding to repeat sacred names of the Jewish people such as the Twelve Tribes, the Patriarchs and Matriarchs, and names of the books of the Torah. After children learn to speak, they are gradually taught Torah verses by heart and made familiar with the *alef-beit* so that they may eventually read the words of Torah.[32] He proposed[33] teaching even very young children, who are still before the age of *chinuch*[34] and only beginning to learn to speak, to recite *brachot* (blessings) and answer *Amen*.

Similarly, his practical educational recommendations that start at birth are tangible applications of his expansive understanding of education. His campaign[35] for girls to start lighting a Shabbat candle from three years of age[36] is indicative of his expansive understanding of education. He also urged[37] boys to begin to wear *tzitzit* (a fringed four-cornered garment) from age three in accordance with Hasidic custom[38] and a headcovering from the same age.[39] R. Schneerson argued[40] that even during pregnancy, educational precautions be adopted with the welfare of the unborn child in mind, giving practical examples of applications to these principles:

(i)   Attaching *Shir HaMa'alot* to the neo-natal ward and room of the newborn child;[41]

(ii)   a campaign to encourage Shabbat candle-lighting of [a single candle] by girls from three years of age and above;[42]

(iii)   encouraging the wearing of *Tzitzit* in fulfillment of the Biblical command[43] by boys from three years of age;[44]

(iv)   recommending children's synagogue attendance to hear the reading of the Ten Commandments on *Shavuot*;[45]

(v)   encouraging children under *bar-* or *bat-mitzvah* age to acquire a letter in a Torah scroll written exclusively for them;[46] and

(vi)   promoting children under *bar-* or *bat-mitzvah* age to join *Tzivot Hashem* ("The Army of Hashem" informal educational initiative).[47]

Practical Ramifications of Education as Lifelong

Within the Jewish community, R. Schneerson inaugurated[48] the establishment of Torah study classes in every community, for men and for women, on a level appropriate to their age group. He encouraged his followers to visit old age homes and introduce Torah study classes for residents, and personally addressed gatherings of elderly individuals in Habad Headquarters in New York.

Referring to the elderly in the wider community, in 1980, R. Schneerson lamented the plight of the elderly in contemporary society and called for vigorous widespread efforts to rectify this. R. Schneerson campaigned[49] against retirement of the elderly and their placement in nursing homes, urging the elderly to continue in the work force where their expertise and years of experience could still be valuable. He considered retirement of the elderly to be a tremendous waste of human potential and squandering of invaluable resources of a priceless repository of knowledge amassed by the elderly. He even suggested that those who needed to relinquish their job or positions should be helped to redirect their lives productively for their own sake and the benefit of younger generations.

Practical Ramifications of Education beyond Formal Instruction

Informal Activities

On a practical level, R. Schneerson oversaw many informal education activities for youth. In the early years of his leadership, he established informal initiatives such as the Lubavitch Youth

Organization[50] and the Lubavitch Women and Girls Organization.[51] In 1956 he established the *Gan Israel* Summer Camps, which served as the prototype for both boys' and girls' camps currently operative throughout the world. Other informal educational activities include participation in day camps during the summer vacation and *Mesibat Shabbat* (Sabbath afternoon gatherings).[52]

Besides implementing[53] informal educational programs for Sabbath afternoons, he oversaw the texts that provided the content for these programs. R. Schneerson[54] urged educators to be concerned for their students outside the hours of formal instruction, advising them to pay special attention to children's conduct on festivals[55] and Shabbat. He wrote,

> From this can be understood that the responsibility for the conduct of the children on Sabbaths and festivals and, in general, during the hours when they are not in the appropriate institution lies also on the shoulders of their educators, even though, obviously the nature of the supervision during these days and hours is only possible when taking place in a completely different way than during formal hours of study and it frequently requires parental assistance etc. However, the planning and taking responsibility for this initiative rests with the educators.[56]

Pre-*Bar Mitzvah* and Pre-*Bat Mitzvah* Groups

In the autumn of 1980, R. Schneerson introduced a campaign specifically geared toward Jewish children beneath the age of *Bar Mitzvah* and *Bat Mitzvah*.[57] This initiative, entitled *Tzivot Hashem*, was open to all Jewish children from families of strict observance to those on the periphery of the Jewish community. Within a few years 125,000 individual students in America had become members of this youth group; subsequently over half a million children internationally have joined this group. *Tzivot Hashem* has also seen the development of the Dial-a-Jewish-Story and a Jewish Children's

Expo in Manhattan which attracted nearly 90,000 children in 1990. Pen pals are encouraged and children are invited to teach fellow members with a lesser knowledge of their Jewish heritage.

Multi-Faceted Informal Initiatives

R. Schneerson encouraged large-scale activities of an educational nature, such as huge street parades marking Jewish festivals.[58] In 1987 R. Schneerson urged children to make their own private rooms into a house of Torah study, prayer, and charity, by studying Torah there, praying to G-d, and giving charity in a charity box. R. Schneerson re-introduced the role of the *mashpi'a* or mentor in religious education. As well, to navigate the possible difficult moral challenges that people encounter in real-life situations, he encouraged individual students to acquire a personal moral mentor.[59] Students would also be empowered where appropriate to be moral mentors of others, as well as teach and lead students less capable than they are to become better people. On multiple occasions, he urged the convening of *farbrengens* in communities worldwide.

He also recommended[60] extra-curricular off-campus activities and classes of educational content, such as the running of a *cheder* for religious children after the formal hours of a kindergarten. In 1980 he established[61] a global initiative of informal Jewish education known as *Tzivot Hashem* with a children's magazine that he personally edited[62] to ensure its educational content was appropriate.

Concern for Broader Moral Education

Already in the 1960s, R. Schneerson contended[63] that the education system was no longer meeting the challenges with which it was being confronted. Noting that schools were originally designed to educate students from families with strong ethical values, he believed that they were in urgent need of overhaul as there was now a pressing need to "cultivate the [child's] purpose and mission in life, which will be reflected in the daily conduct of the boys and girls when they grow up and take their places in society." R. Schneerson observed that schools were failing in the essential task of molding moral character and behavior, which had sadly been replaced by acquisition of knowledge as the new educational priority. He reasoned that because the cultivation of codes of ethics and morality was no longer the focus of home, houses of worship, and society, this situation was doing nothing for the children's development of a concept of purpose and mission in life which is reflected in their daily conduct.

R. Schneerson argued,

> In our society, where morality and ethics can hardly be said to be at a premium, where the most prevalent criterion of what is right and proper is the claim that "everybody does it," there is no real deterrent for a child against giving free rein to his natural drives and propensities.[64]

He was concerned about what he termed "the alarming increase in juvenile delinquency" and the "increased exclusive exposure of public school students to secular morality and ethics." He felt that this crisis called for an urgent re-examination of the basic approaches to education, where leaving values education to when a child grows up is tantamount to precluding moral education.[65]

A global educational initiative launched by R. Schneerson[66] in 1983 was the promotion of a universal moral code by teaching and disseminating the seven Noahide Laws.[67] This campaign was largely aimed at government and education leaders, seeking their support for a worldwide ethical code that could become the basic foundation for ethical behavior.[68] While encouraging everyone to exert a positive moral influence, he intended this initiative to have tangible results in public schools.[69] He considered placing an emphasis on moral and values education as a vital component of the curriculum, with the study of the Noahide Laws as a pivotal aspect of the syllabus. These laws, directed to all humanity, include:[70]

- Belief in G-d and prohibition of the worship of false gods
- Respect for G-d and prohibition of blasphemy
- Respect for human life and prohibition of murder
- Respect for the family and prohibition of incest
- Respect for others' rights and property and the prohibition of theft
- The mandate to establish a system of laws, police, and courts of justice to uphold a moral society and the prohibition of political oppression or anarchy
- Prohibition of eating flesh of a living animal and, by extension, any cruelty to all living creatures

In educational terms, these seven laws require educators to imbue learners with values. The curriculum for values education would comprise the following components:

1. Children realizing that there is a Higher Authority to whom they are accountable
2. Showing kindness in speech and deed and respect for religious traditions
3. Respect for human life
4. The importance of family values
5. Respect for the property of others
6. Upholding the law
7. Respect for all living creatures

Referring to events of World War II and the Holocaust, R. Schneerson wrote:

> If in a previous generation there were people who doubted the need of Divine authority for common morality and ethics in the belief that human reason is sufficient authority for morality and ethics, our present generation has, unfortunately, in a most devastating and tragic way, realized this mistaken notion. For it is

precisely the nation which had excelled itself in the exact sciences, the humanities, and even in philosophy and ethics, that turned out to be the most depraved nation of the world, making an ideal of murder and robbery, etc.[71]

He said that while there was a time when some thinkers thought that there was no need to connect the laws of ethics and morality with Divine authority, inasmuch as these are rational principles, the fallacy of this thinking had become abundantly clear.

He wrote in reference to Nazi Germany:

For we have seen, in our own day and age, a whole nation which had boasted of great philosophic advancement and ethical systems sink to the lowest depth of inhuman depravity and unprecedented barbarism. And the reason for this was that they thought that they could establish a morality and ethics based on human reason, not subject to the authority of a Supreme Being, having themselves become a super race, as they thought.[72]

In light of this understanding, R. Schneerson repeatedly petitioned for the global dissemination of the Seven Noahide Laws as "the bedrock of society since the dawn of civilization" and an important aspect of the moral code "upon which our great nation [the USA] was founded."[73]

He believed that the child would be taught through these laws that our world is not a jungle, but rather a place that awaits our positive contribution.

As a result of these campaigns, American president Reagan[74] signed an "international scroll of honor," paying tribute to R. Schneerson and affirming "fundamental ethical values on which all civilized societies must be based." Reagan applauded R. Schneerson's work of promoting "the acceptance of the Almighty's commandments to all mankind." He added that by doing so R.

Schneerson was "combating the anti-religious forces that have caused so much misery in our lifetimes."

When it was still a possibility in the US, R. Schneerson campaigned vigorously for the introduction of a non-denominational prayer[75] at the beginning of the public school day. In 1964 he wrote,

> Certainly a non-denominational prayer in the public schools will not, in itself, provide an adequate basis for the right and complete world-outlook, but it is an indispensable first step in the direction, considering the state of our society as it is at present, and as it is likely to remain for quite a long time, insofar as it can be judged from the prevailing conditions and factors.[76]

He believed[77] that there was "no way other than to implant in the hearts of young children, from the most tender years of infancy, a firm belief in the Creator of the Universe, who actually oversees the world today."

In 1981, he repeated his position,

> A simple, brief, non-denominational prayer by children at the beginning of each day, affirming their belief and trust in G-d, is the best and most effective first step. Sincere, honest words, spoken from the heart by people who stand as living examples of those who believe and trust in G-d, will go far in inspiring children to live up to the standards set by the Bible.[78]

In 1983 he urged,

> Parents must do all possible to ensure that our children attend a school where there is mention of a Creator of the Universe, who oversees the world and its conduct. The responsibility regarding this today lies also with the schools, because our children receive most of their

education at school, rather than at home, so that it therefore behooves the school to educate its students to be
decent human beings, who are aware of G-d's authority,
of "An Eye that Sees, an Ear that Hears, and all your
deeds are recorded in a Book."[79]

Imbuing Belief in and Awareness of a Higher Authority to Instill Goodness and Values

Later, when legislation precluded a non-denominational prayer
in public schools, R. Schneerson argued strenuously[80] for the
urgent introduction of a "Moment of Silence" or a "Moment of
Reflection" into the public school day. With regard to the goal
of "implant[ing] in the hearts of the young generation a tangible
discipline," the inclusion of a "Moment of Silence" in the school
day was considered by R. Schneerson to be vital. He even encouraged[81] students to petition the government for the introduction of
a "Moment of Reflection." He saw this as potentially transformative, empowering the learner to become less self-absorbed and to
encourage more empathy and sensitivity.

In the inculcation of moral values through the "Moment of Reflection," R. Schneerson wanted schools to partner with the home
and suggested that parents, otherwise preoccupied with earning a
living, should provide this direction and guidance to their children
about the matters of importance to both the child and family upon
which the student should reflect during this time. He believed that
in the same way parents are concerned to provide for their children's needs before they leave home for school, such as equipping
them with the right clothing, as well as appropriate food, so too
and even to a greater extent, parents should supply the child with
appropriate daily spiritual nurture.[82]

These moments of thoughtful reflection at the start of each
school day were to be dedicated to meditation by the students—
with their parents' guidance—on life's purpose and their own

unique contribution as responsible citizens. Unlike organized prayer, the "Moment of Silence" aims to create an opportunity for reflection on a deeply personal level, motivating children to feel positive about themselves and their involvement in creating a better world. He believed that this time to contemplate things of importance will give context and meaning to the hours that follow, providing the "why" of their learning and not just the "how."

Because he saw a life built on a Higher calling as central to education's agenda, he wanted children to use this moment to reflect on their own Higher purpose. It is a quiet time for children to nurture their inner core and make sure they do not lose touch with the meaning of their life. For many students and parents, the "Moment of Reflection" would be a time to reflect on their responsibility to the omnipresent Higher Authority Who is aware of our most covert conduct and before Whom we are accountable for our behavior. In other circumstances, the "Moment of Silence" still provides an opportunity for children to stand back and judge their personal conduct. For example, it could still be devoted to thinking of those less fortunate than themselves, whether elsewhere in the world or even in the student's class. This was conceived as a time for a child to reflect on values such as respect, tolerance, and standing up for justice; it provides an opportunity for students to reflect on their strengths, and commit to a life of honesty and integrity. They can contemplate the deeper purpose of life and their sacred individual purpose, answering their conscience. They can reflect on ideals that are greater than the immediate moment and material success. It is a time to aspire to the ideals of subjugation of heart to mind, minimizing envy and thinking beyond oneself to becoming a better person.

R. Schneerson believed that ensuring that this "Moment of Silence" occurs at the start of the school day when students are most receptive emphasizes the importance of matters of spirituality within the curriculum and underscores its vital importance as a priority goal.

When launching an informal educational *Tzivot Hashem* project in 1982, R. Schneerson wrote:

> American children have been brought up on the spirit of independence and freedom, and on the glorification of personal prowess and smartness. It has cultivated a sense of cockiness and self-assurance to the extent that one who is bent on mischief or anti-social activity feels that one can outsmart a cop on the beat, and even a judge on the bench; and, in any event, there is little to fear in the way of punishment. As with every health problem, physical, mental, or spiritual, the cure lies not in treating the symptoms, but in attacking the cause, although the former may sometimes be necessary for relief in acute cases. Since, as mentioned, the root of the problem is the lack of self-discipline, I thought long and hard about finding a way of inducing an American child to get used to the idea of subordination to higher authority, despite all the influence to the contrary—in the school, in the street, and even home, where parents—not wishing to be bothered by their children—have all too often abdicated their authority, and left it to others to deal with truancy, juvenile delinquency, etc. I came to the conclusion that there was no other way than trying to effect a basic change in the child's nature, through a system of discipline and obedience to rules which she/he can be induced to get accustomed to. Moreover, for this method to be effective, it would be necessary that it should be freely and readily accepted without coercion.[83]

R. Schneerson personally reviewed the magazine of *Tzivot Hashem*, often making editorial suggestions of an educational nature.

Inspiring a Life of Altruism, Transforming Fellow Humans, and Influencing Society

In keeping with the ideal of learners becoming exemplars, R. Schneerson recommended that a certain portion of students of Habad *yeshivot* might serve as teachers and guides for newly arrived immigrants for a few weeks or months and even concurrently with their *yeshivah* studies.[84] He encouraged the establishment and organization of institutions of kosher education that would train their own educators.[85]

A tangible example of this ideal was his belief that capable Yemenite yeshivah students should be taught so that they become educators and guides of other Yemenite children,[86] an imperative task to occur within a short time frame.[87] This educational position also clearly underscores R. Schneerson's recommendation[88] that the Down-syndrome learner be empowered to lead other Down-syndrome children. It is also reflected in R. Schneerson's ideal[89] that the student who has mastered only the first two letters of the Hebrew alphabet be encouraged to teach other students who are still struggling to master the first letter, an *aleph*.

R. Schneerson considered that children need to be introduced to spirituality, altruism, and transcendence, so that these ideals become educational priorities, whereas egocentric life choices would be viewed as expressions of self-centeredness. To facilitate these goals, he wanted schools to collectively engage in altruistic activities and encourage individual students to embrace genuine charitable causes such as overseeing provision of interest-free loans to students of the class.[90] He encouraged school principals to assist their students personally to donate to charity, interacting with them individually in this vital endeavor and distributing charity for students to allocate.[91] The charity box was to take pride of place both in the classroom and at home.[92] Indeed, virtuous conduct would be a school priority, emphasized and rewarded in the same way as academic achievement.

The Responsibility for Education

R. Schneerson told educators and parents[93] that our broad responsibility is that "Our last thought before closing our eyes at night and our first waking thought in the morning must be about education and the Torah's exhortation[94] of 'You shall teach them to your children.'"

Because he viewed education as synonymous with rescuing an individual from life-threatening circumstances, to educate and thereby rescue even one individual is a momentous achievement, especially a child who later will become the foundation of the home when a parent.[95]

Referring to the imperative education of Yemenite children newly arrived in Israel, R. Schneerson argued that these children were powerless to rescue themselves educationally, therefore providing them with external help is a sacred obligation and privilege, even for individuals physically removed from the situation.[96] He believed that saving these youths spiritually is an obligation incumbent on every man and woman, urging, "No obstacle can prevent you from strengthening Torah and Judaism…"[97]

In response to correspondence from teachers who complained about the challenges of their situation,[98] R. Schneerson indicated that their circumstance was the "fortunate lot"[99] with a "blessed vocation."[100] While championing educators' rights to generous remuneration, he simultaneously encouraged educators to re-engage in their educational career, by drawing their attention to the unique circumstances whereby even a minor exertion and influence over students was rewarded with "cumulative dividends" for many future generations.[101]

R. Schneerson advocated a proactive approach to taking educational initiatives.[102] For example, he urged communal workers involved in education to endeavor, even during vacations in the country-side, to enlist those whom they encounter to assist *yeshivot*, explaining the exalted benefits of supporting Torah education.[103]

Educator Proactivity

Many of R. Schneerson's emissaries are stationed on university campuses, proactively encouraging student interest and inviting them to their open homes or Habad Houses, to experience Jewish religious festivities and participate in educational programs. The Habad House is a campus-based community center which provides both educational and social outreach, primarily to students of tertiary age and adults.[104] The establishment of such Habad outreach centers occurred from 1959 throughout the US.[105] In 1967, R. Schneerson established the first formal campus Habad House on the UCLA campus.[106] R. Schneerson's vision of the Habad House was that it "serves as the key to open the hearts of all who will visit it and all who will come under its sphere of influence."[107] By 1972, this Habad presence on campus was acknowledged to have "greatly contributed to the morale of the Jewish students and filled a hitherto existing void."[108]

The Habad House fulfills a role in the area of social service and rehabilitation, providing shelter and counseling. The Habad House has also played a valuable role in anti-missionary and anti-cult initiatives; some are even involved in treatment programs for victims of drug abuse.[109] In 1986 R. Schneerson called for the expansion of existing Habad Houses and the establishment of new ones where possible. By 1988, Israel's Lubavitch Youth Organization recorded 125 Habad Houses throughout Israel.[110] In the same year, *Merkos L'Inyonei Chinuch* listed over 200 American Habad Houses covering 130 university campuses, as well as another 145 such establishments worldwide.[111] Since Glasnost, Habad has opened scores of Habad Houses and educational institutions in the Commonwealth of Independent States (CIS), or former Soviet Union. To date there are over 4,700 Habad emissaries and their families worldwide in over eighty-five countries and forty-nine states of the US, an amazing achievement for Jewish outreach into the general community.

Another proactive initiative endorsed by R. Schneerson is the "Encounter with Habad" program which began in 1962, when

R. Schneerson's Habad community of Brooklyn, New York, and educational institutions there opened their doors on weekends to enable unaffiliated students to experience Hasidism. Seminars and lectures took place throughout such weekends, with attendees participating in R. Schneerson's Sabbath afternoon *farbrengen*. In 2018, over 1,000 university students from across the US, many involved locally with Habad on Campus, participated in the Encounter with Habad. This program has expanded with similar weekend events now held for teens.

Educator Sensitivity and Inclusion

Besides addressing the educator's responsibility for Down-syndrome learners, R. Schneerson also insisted that the educator show concern for individuals facing physical disability. In his address[112] to the Israeli team participating in the 1976 Paraplegic Olympics, he elaborated on the principle that a physical deficiency indicates a greater spiritual potential that enables the individual to more than compensate for the deficiency.

He had a similar approach to detainees of corrective institutions,[113] writing to Jewish detainees that as darkness is only temporary, they should aspire for light to dispel the darkness that was currently encompassing them.[114]

Regarding education for the rehabilitation of prison detainees, Habad educational initiatives encouraged by R. Schneerson have focused particularly on inmates of American state and federal penitentiaries and prisons throughout the world. A specific example of this initiative is the work of Miami's *Aleph Institute* which co-ordinates visits, religious services, and publications for Jewish prisoners throughout the United States. Religious services, including the Passover *Seder*, are conducted for these individuals, to bring a message of hope and dignity to despairing prisoners.

He similarly urged Habad educators not to abandon the disenfranchised,[115] the disadvantaged,[116] and the antagonistic.[117] His
inclusive educational policies thus included:

(i)   outreach to the widest possible audience at the furthest
      peripheries;[118]
(ii) strengthening Torah among the broadest spectrum of
      people;[119]
(iii) widely disseminating educational publications written
      in pristine purity even if their recipients are meanwhile
      distant from receiving a Kosher Jewish education;[120]
(iv) ensuring that the "Mishnah by Heart" competition is
      for everyone, and not just scholars;[121] and
(v)   instilling individuals with the realization that they
      must each desire to inspire another equally enthusiastic
      individual.[122]

R. Schneerson also disagreed with[123] the practice of students
learning in isolation and recommended replacing it with the imperative for study with study-partners who exert a positive peer
influence, as well as study partners with whom one periodically
engages in *pilpul* (Talmudic dialectics).[124] In this spirit of unity, R.
Schneerson advised that communal educational endeavors should
aim at the wider community and not be identified as Habad initiatives, in case they are perceived as insular.[125]

From the very beginning of his leadership, R. Schneerson included women, empowering them with an educational role no less
significant than their male counterparts.[126] One of the first Jewish educational institutions he established was the Beth Rivkah
girls' schools, which today have an extensive network around
the world, from elementary through tertiary levels. R. Schneerson also founded academies for women with little background
in Judaism, in New York, Minneapolis, Israel, and Australia. In
1952, he founded *Agudat Neshei Habad*, the Lubavitch Women's
Organization in Israel, an organization whose main thrust was

educational.[127] R. Schneerson always emphasized the integral role of the *shlucha* (female emissary) who is as involved in this task as her husband. For example, in R. Schneerson's Campaign for *Taharat HaMishpacha* (Torah laws governing the marital relationship between husband and wife), his *shluchot* (female emissaries)] were at the forefront of the resurgence of *mikva'ot* (pools for ritual immersion) in many communities both large and small[128] throughout the globe and in teaching the observance of *Taharat HaMishpacha*. In addition, R. Schneerson addressed several women's conventions and gatherings annually.

As Habad originated in the Soviet Union, much of R. Schneerson's inclusive educational initiative has been focused on the material and spiritual rehabilitation of Soviet Jewry. A resurgence of religious life in Russia today is largely due to the pioneering efforts of his emissaries. In the 1970s, R. Schneerson established educational programs for new arrivals of Soviet Jewry, in Israel and the free world, under the title of F.R.E.E. (Friends of Refugees from Eastern Europe), to educate these individuals formerly deprived of religious education. The Shamir Organization[129] focuses on helping Russian scientists and intellectuals who have arrived in Israel.[130] In the late 1960s and early 1970s, Habad established settlements in Israel specifically to accommodate new Russian immigrants. In 1990, with R. Schneerson's encouragement, Habad leadership took responsibility for air-lifting 500 children affected by the 1986 Chernobyl nuclear reactor disaster, providing them with physical and spiritual relief upon their arrival in Kfar Habad, Israel. To date, over 3,000 children from the radioactive Chernobyl region have been relocated to Israel by Habad. With the collapse of the Soviet Union in 1991, Habad re-established the infrastructure for Jewish education and currently runs several hundred schools and educational institutions throughout the former USSR.

Meticulous Concern for Detail by Educators

Meticulous concern for detail and insistence that educators make every effort to ensure that public perception of an educational initiative is appropriate was also exemplified by R. Schneerson himself, when he disapproved of a plan to distribute tickets for attendees of *Mesibat Shabbat* (Shabbat gatherings for children), due to anticipated misperception that they can be carried on *Shabbat* to the meetings.[131]

Similarly, he expressed[132] concerns for the educational ramifications of a common misrepresentation of the tablets of the Ten Commandments. He noted[133] that these are often prominently represented on the covers of Jewish books and on the curtain in front of the Synagogue's Ark and elsewhere as square at the base with rounded semi-circular tops. The Talmud[134] records the dimensions of the tablets to be six hand breadths in both length and width, while three hand breadths in breadth. This indicates that the "tablets" were square at both ends rather than rounded. A further confirmation of this is the Talmudic description whereby "the tablets" fully occupied the space along the length of the Ark in which they were stored, implying that they took up that entire space. To suggest rounded tops implies unaccounted space, contradicting the principle that everything is created for a specific purpose. He considered this matter to be "of far reaching consequences" rather than a mere triviality,[135] his concern being for the learner's discovered discrepancy between the educator's presentation and the Talmudic description of the tablets. He argued that such a misrepresentation undermines the learner's serious approach to the Talmudic text, as well as the authenticity of the religious educator's presentation in general.

He similarly argued[136] that representations of the *menorah* (candelabrum) in accordance with Maimonides' view replace the popular curved depiction of the branches. He noted Maimonides' handwritten sketch of the *menorah*,[137] revealing the ornamental cups face down and the branches of the *menorah* are straight (as suggested by Rashi's commentary to Exodus, 25:32).[138]

Practical Ramifications of the Education of the Educator

R. Schneerson advocated that school vacation time be used as an ideal time for educators to engage in professional development and it should be employed as an opportunity for their advancement, particularly to increase their knowledge in matters pertaining to their work.[139] When responding to a suggestion about the establishment of a seminary for teachers and classes for pedagogical training, he considered such an institution for capable but unqualified teachers to be worth serious consideration.[140] However, he stipulated that such an institution should provide pedagogic training from superlative qualified lecturers.[141] Today, Habad's "Menachem Education Foundation" has formally assumed responsibility for teacher enrichment; conferences for Habad educators are an annual event in Israel, the US, and regional Habad locations.

Practical Ramifications of Not Delegating Education

In a letter written less than a year after he formally assumed leadership of the Habad movement, R. Schneerson expressed astonishment[142] at his correspondent's lack of involvement in education for over a year, except for casual work that would not cause distress, and even then his engagement was only sporadic. R. Schneerson responded:

> How is it possible for you to stand on the side and not be involved in education with full energy and strength? Ask yourself, were you standing on the bank of a river, deeply engrossed in the study of a Talmudic topic of interest to you, upon noticing someone drowning in the river, you would certainly interrupt your study and involve yourself in saving this individual's life.[143]

R. Schneerson likened the educator who abandoned the teaching profession to a soldier who "deserts the front."[144] He similarly
expressed his shock at another educator's desire to "forsake [his]
flock" during the Hebrew month of *Tishrei*, a time he described as
"the most precious of the precious," when every moment provides
possibilities to influence students inappropriately.[145] He also viewed
talented educators leaving teaching as a serious offense because it
undermined the advancement of authentic Jewish education.[146] Similarly, he wrote to an educator who wished to lessen his engagement
in education that his diminished influence on his current students
and ambiguity concerning any future education activities[147] defied
rational explanation. He considered that the very opposite, namely,
his aspiration to exert an increased influence on his students, should
be the topic of their communication.[148]

Practical Ramifications of Being Obligated to Educate

R. Schneerson considered[149] his educational directives as universally
imperative and clearly not restricted to the professional educator.[150]
In 1952 he wrote[151] forcefully concerning the duties of parents, communal leaders and teachers of the younger generation, "Therefore, let
every Jewish mother and father, every rabbi, leader, and communal
worker and person of influence, heed the call to gather the masses of
Jewish children and bring them to the *yeshivot*, *Talmud Torah*, and
Torah-true educational institutions."[152] He recommended that those
whose ability precluded their involvement in face-to-face educating
should contribute to fund-raising for education or by assisting with
increasing enrolments,[153] working with educators performing this
task.[154] He insisted that everyone must make some effort to influence
the education of their own children and those in their environment,
even those in distant places or another country.[155]

Practical Ramifications of Contemporary Educational Responsibility

In contrast to "other Orthodox groups who built physical and psychological divisions between themselves and the outside world," the Habad movement actively confronted that world in an attempt to educate and win followers.[156] R. Schneerson began sending emissaries[157] throughout the Jewish world, including covert educational initiatives in the USSR. He turned his own movement into "an active organization of outreach to the unaffiliated, establishing centers around the Jewish world and utilizing the entire spectrum of modern techniques of communication and influence."[158]

As a global educator, R. Schneerson "developed the themes of Jewish and Hasidic teachings into a practical program of worldwide[159] outreach to alienated Jews."[160] The intensity and scope of R. Schneerson's educational program made Habad unique in the modern Jewish world:[161] there are currently over 4,700 of R. Schneerson's emissaries worldwide.

One of the clearest insights into the level of devotion inspired by R. Schneerson can be found in an anthology[162] of the addresses and writings of the late Nechoma Greisman. She was one of several *shluchot* chosen with her husband by R. Schneerson in 1975 from among his American Hasidic following to spearhead his educational initiatives in Israel.

Practical Ramifications of Utilization of All Educational Opportunities

Before the beginning of the "communication revolution," R. Schneerson quickly embraced technology in the service of dissemination of Torah concepts, stating, "Everything in this world was created for a Divine purpose. All forms of modern technology can and should be harnessed to make the world a better place and, in the case of Jews, to spread Judaism in the widest possible manner."[163] His espousal of technology for purposes of Jewish education was concurrent with his insistence that "We cannot rest until every Jewish child has a Jewish education." Examples were his encouragement of the teaching of RSZ's *Tanya* on radio[164] and his allowing the televising of his weekday addresses to Hasidic gatherings on cable television. Not surprisingly, a Habad devotee, Rabbi Y.Y. Kazen (1954-1998), is considered the "father of the Jewish internet" due to his pioneering of the employing of the internet for dissemination of Judaism in 1997, with R. Schneerson's blessing.[165] Kazen founded the Habad website, "chabad.org," whose family of websites served more than 43,000,000 visitors in 2014, with close to half a million subscribers. Chabad.org's rabbis and counselors respond to hundreds of email questions daily, and its "Ask the Rabbi" service has been responding to inquiries regarding Judaism and Hasidism since 1988. The site currently offers over 100,000 pages of information, in addition to 14,000 audio classes and 10,000 videos.

Practical Ramifications of Educator Urgency

Besides expanding existing educational institutions,[166] R. Schneerson immediately established a worldwide network of new educational facilities[167] which he continued to augment throughout his leadership.[168] When they arrived in a community, R. Schneerson's emissaries immediately established kindergartens and elementary Jewish educational facilities which subsequently developed into Jewish day schools.[169] In Habad educational institutions, R. Schneerson's teachings are studied by students as an integral component of the religious studies curriculum, as well as by senior staff for educational guidance.[170]

From 1950, R. Schneerson promoted and expanded the concept of students in his *Yeshivot* devoting their summer vacation to educational activities in outlying communities under the auspices of *Merkos L'Inyonei Chinuch*.[171] In this way he began to empower his followers with responsibility for educational leadership at the earliest possible age. While this decision was considered to be a hazardous venture, it imbued Lubavitch educational initiatives with a characteristic drive and vivacity. By 2017, Habad emissaries worldwide numbered over 4,700, each of whose responsibilities included educational initiatives at various levels of education.

Educational initiatives focused on isolated communities with limited access to Jewish resources were also among R. Schneerson's major concerns. The students of his *Yeshivot* visit such communities during their vacation, to give classes, distribute educational publications, and visit families. The agenda set by R. Schneerson for both himself and his followers, especially its unprecedented global scale, has been described as being "in a very real sense post-Holocaust Judaism."[172] Rabbi Sacks considers R. Schneerson's educational agenda to have been "the mystical answer to that unprecedented tragedy where all others fail…where a massive act of evil can be redeemed only by a massive counter-act of good; in this case, only by saving lives, souls, identities, on an unprecedented scale." Sacks thus interprets R. Schneerson's initiatives as "searching out the hidden Jews in love as they were once hunted down in hate."[173]

Many of R. Schneerson's educational initiatives can be linked to the post-Holocaust Jewish world, with him emerging as the post-Holocaust *Rebbe* who addressed the contemporary Jewish condition. His educational ventures can be viewed as a response to the alienation and secularization characteristic of this period in Jewish history. Rebuilding Judaism after the Holocaust was clearly R. Schneerson's priority for the Habad movement. He considered that subordination of the individual's selfish interests and a total change of tactics to be imperative for this task.[174] Significantly, in R. Schneerson's planned reconstruction of post-Holocaust Jewish life in America, he saw efforts to re-establish Jewish education to be of foremost importance.[175]

Empowering Learners to Be Exemplars

In a radical application of both commencing education at the youngest
age and empowering learners to be emissaries and exemplars of ideals, R. Schneerson advocated[176] that even the newborn in a maternity
ward be viewed as an emissary. He argued that by attaching the *Shir
Hama'alot* to the door of the ward, a person encouraged the perception
of the newborn as an emissary for G-d who fulfills G-d's assignment
in the world by causing sanctity to be brought into the hospital.

Another unique practical application of R. Schneerson's ideal is
evident in his recommendation that Down-syndrome children be
empowered to adopt leadership roles.

He thus wrote to Dr. R. Wilkes of Coney Island Hospital, Brooklyn, N.Y.:

> Part of the above approach, which, as far as I know, has
> not been used before, is to involve some of the train-
> ees in some form of leadership, such as captains of
> teams, group leaders, and the like, without arousing the
> jealousy of the others. The latter could be avoided by
> making such selections on the basis of seniority, special
> achievement, exemplary conduct, etc.[177]

Concern and Sensitivity
for Individual Needs

Demonstration of R. Schneerson's practical application of the
principle of concern and sensitivity for individual needs includes
evidence that he:

(i)   showed personal concern for a disoriented individual
        and argued for his acceptance in Habad's *yeshivah* in
        Montreal;[178]

(ii)   personally instigated a program of religious education for Jewish soldiers on service in WWII;[179]

(iii)   avoided compulsion or force to achieve his educational goals;[180] and

(iv)   sought feedback from the learner to the ideas communicated to him.[181]

He also urged:

(i)   children be given special supervision so that they would become accustomed to the *yeshivah* timetable;[182]

(ii)   that the customs of certain communities be taken into consideration for the religious education of girls in Habad institutions;[183]

(iii) educators to provide answers appropriate to the level of the learner;

(iv) educators to show concern for their listeners and present matters so that they will be of greatest benefit to the publicizing of these concepts, with emphasis on the internalization of the concepts;[184]

(v)   educators to select the easiest area and conditions to begin their teaching;[185]

(vi) educators to prioritize public review of discourses whose content can be understood by listeners;[186]

(vii) educators to show patience so that when including those outside the community, they allow them to progress at their own pace, with educators acknowledging that an educator's personal frustration is temporary and is incomparable to damage suffered over many years if an educator prioritizes his own personal frustration over the needs of others;[187]

(viii) educators to show a meticulous concern for detail;[188]

(ix) educators to combine an elevated involvement in Hasidic philosophy with inclusivism and a concern for the common people through action with concrete deeds;[189] and

(x)   educators to realize that a child's discomfort in their
      Jewish studies class at school was due to lack of friends
      rather than curriculum and textbooks. Educators
      conducting the class should help the child to find an
      appropriate *chavruta* (study partner) because by learn-
      ing in pairs, each person awakens his colleague,[190] so
      studying in isolation is avoided.[191]

Educators Adopt a Positive View of the Learner

R. Schneerson's belief in the limitless potential of the learner is
clearly illustrated in a pioneering letter[192] of 1979, regarding education of the Down-syndrome learner addressed to Coney Island
Hospital's assistant program director for the education of these children. In this correspondence, R. Schneerson recommended that the
educator maintain a positive view of the Down-syndrome learner
despite the prognosis, and expressed his view that enhanced educational success is dependent on this positive approach. He directed
anyone dealing with Down-syndrome learners to start from the
basic premise that the challenge is "in each case only a temporary
handicap, and that in due course, it could certainly be improved
and even improved substantially." He stated unequivocally: "This
approach should be taken regardless of the pronouncements or
prognosis of specialists in the field."

Prioritizing the Practical

R. Schneerson repeatedly urged[193] Jewish educators to ensure that
their curriculum included the study of practical *Halacha* (Jewish
law),[194] encouraging[195] publication of "A Compilation of Collected
Laws" for young students. The inclusion of memorization and rote
recitation in the curriculum was a pivotal aspect of his recommendation for educational content. In 1975, R. Schneerson initiated

a global project that involved the study and recital of *Twelve To-rah Verses and Rabbinic Quotations* by children under the age of *Bar-* and *Bat-Mitzvah*.[196] Throughout the 1970s, R. Schneerson initiated several global educational campaigns concerning Jewish religious obligations and festival observance.

Already in 1944, in his capacity as head of Habad's educational wing, R. Schneerson had created[197] a basic Jewish studies sylla-bus for Habad schools which was published by *Merkos L'Inyanei Chinuch* (The Central Committee for the Furtherance of Jewish Education). The timetable for boys included "Prayers, Jewish law, Talks, Hebrew, Yiddish, *Chumash* [Pentateuch], *Nach* [Prophets and Writings], *Gemara* [Talmud] and Jewish History," and its equivalent for girls included "Explanation of prayers, Jewish law, Talks, Hebrew, Yiddish, *Chumash* [Pentateuch], *Nach* [Prophets and Writings], *Aggadah* [homiletic texts of the Talmud and *Mi-drash*], Jewish History, Song and Music."

R. Schneerson saw a birthday as an opportunity to advance to a higher level and urged[198] that practical activities take place on, or at least in close proximity to, one's Hebrew birthday. These in-clude: being called to the Torah on the *Shabbat* prior to, or on the day itself; taking out time to reflect on one's life (on the past year in particular) and considering ways to improve areas of weakness; intensifying concentration during one's prayers on the day, with greater meditation on G-d's presence; recitation of extra Psalms and the study of the Psalm appropriate to one's age; undertaking a new area of Torah study; taking on an additional *mitzvah* or enhanc-ing a *mitzvah*; performing an act of kindness motivated by genuine concern for the welfare of one's fellow; organizing a joyous birthday gathering close to or on the Hebrew date, where Torah thoughts are shared with participants and the special *Shechechiyanu* blessing recited over a new fruit or a new garment as an expression of thanks to G-d for reaching this stage of life; when the birthday falls on a weekday, extra charity is given both morning and afternoon.

In the process of self-mastery, a student's birthday is thus an an-nual opportunity to review his or her growth and progress over the past year and thereby encourage their resolve to advance in the year ahead. On their birthday, R. Schneerson urged people to assemble family members and companions to review a significant text or idea and undertake to perform an exceptional deed of altruism. This same idea can take place at school with students pledging in the presence of peers to align with their higher selves.

An Expansive View of the Curriculum

R. Schneerson was insistent[199] that vacation provided more opportunities for educators to influence a student than during the school year,[200] and expressed[201] the necessity for urgent implementation of unique vacation programs and curricula. He considered[202] vacation to be a time for infinite advancement, particularly when a *yeshivah* curriculum for the vacation period can ensure students expand their knowledge. Vacation was also a time for *yeshivah* students to volunteer to dedicate their free time to promote the strengthening of Torah and kosher Jewish education.[203] R. Schneerson viewed[204] vacation as a time for educators to increase *yeshivah* enrollments by approaching suitable students. He wanted every location to organize an orderly campaign at this time of year to increase the number of students with zeal and enthusiasm.

Practical Ramifications for the Jewish Studies Curriculum

In 1984, R. Schneerson initiated[205] the global daily study of Maimonides' *magnum opus* entitled *Mishneh Torah,* a pivotal work that encapsulates the broad spectrum of *Halacha* (Jewish Law). On R. Schneerson's suggestion, the work is studied daily so that it can be completed either annually or over a three-year period. A special program of study for children based on Maimonides' *Sefer Ha-Mitzvot* was simultaneously inaugurated.

Throughout the 1970s, R. Schneerson initiated several global educational campaigns concerning Jewish religious obligations and festival observance. These included the *Tefillin* Campaign (initiated before the outbreak of Israel's Six-Day War in 1967), the *Mezuzah* Campaign (launched in 1974), and the *Kashrut* Campaign (launched in 1975), whereby 50 percent of the costs of expenses of converting a home to *kosher* was funded by the Lubavitch organization. R. Schneerson declared "The Year of Torah Education" in 1976 and inaugurated the Education Campaign that remains ongoing. He encouraged the use of the *mitzvah* tank,[206] a mobile center that promotes the *mitzvah* campaigns. Other global Jewish educational campaigns included those for lighting Sabbath candles, acquisition of Jewish literature, charity, Torah study, improved interpersonal relationships, and family purity. Further initiatives beyond these ten basic campaigns included drives to encourage acquisition of letters in a Torah scroll written specifically for encouraging Jewish unity.

In the early 1980s, R. Schneerson initiated a campaign to promote awareness of the attainability of the Messianic ideal. The campaign sought to educate people concerning the nature of this concept as found in Biblical and Rabbinic sources, and urged that it assume a primary importance on the agenda of his emissaries.

Testing Students and Compiling Novel Torah Insights

R. Schneerson[207] called on educational institutions to administer tests to ensure student accountability for their learning, which was most beneficial when followed by a private conversation with the student after the test. He wrote,

> Obviously the testing of students is most appropriate, and the main thing is to speak to them individually, but as we see clearly, this brings an incomparably greater benefit when besides words said at a meeting in a formal

way, there are also unofficial conversations from the person who is closest to the student and before whom the student is able to pour out his whole heart, as is obvious.... It is surely unnecessary for me to emphasize the fundamental benefit of these tests if afterwards they are used as an appropriate means to rectify the shortcomings that are found.[208]

He wrote personally to students who had received unsatisfactory test results, expressing his astonishment and dismay while at the same time expressing his hope that from now on the tests "achieve that which they are intended to achieve."[209] When expressing his disappointment to a student who had absented himself and subsequently performed poorly in tests administered by *Yeshivat Tomchei Temimim* of New York, R. Schneerson noted that these were tests "that he had personally requested."[210] R. Schneerson[211] also encouraged students to record and formally publish their *chiddushim* [original insights] in areas of the curriculum being studied.

This section has illustrated that the elements of education that comprise R. Schneerson's discussion of the nature and aims of education, the authority and responsibility for education and the methodology and content of education all have direct ramifications for educational practice that he inspired. The direct relationship between the elements and educational practice is indicative of a characteristic that is an essential feature of a coherent educational philosophy.

Notes

1.   Ross, 1966:98.
2.   Strang, 1955:163; Barrow & Woods, 1975:181-9; Peters, 1977:viii; and Burbeles, 2000:5. As stated above, W.H. Kilpatrick (1924:57) underscored the prescriptive dimension of educational philosophy when he defined it as "the determined effort to find out what education should do in the face of

contradictory demands, coming to it from the deeply rooted but relatively distinct interests of life." Stephen Ross (1966:98) has also observed that "Education is a dimension of life or experience, and life of necessity is educative."

3. Strang (1955:163) noted that "education is an applied science and a practical art" and argued that "scholarship in education is concerned with the application of knowledge." Illustrating this aspect of educational philosophy, Strang (*ibid.*) cited Woodrow Wilson's statement that "We should take the truth out of cupboards and put it into the minds of men who stir abroad," with Strang tentatively adding, "into the hearts and minds." T.W. Moore (1982:6) likewise noted that "the problems thrown up by education are not usually problems arising from conceptual confusion, but are real substantial problems arising out of practice." He saw educational theorists as "concerned with a scrutiny of what is said about education by those who practice and by those who theorize about it," and he specifically saw its impact to be "on activities like teaching, instructing, motivating pupils, advising them and correcting their work." Peters (1983:39) also viewed philosophy of education as "the complement of practice—a body of precepts and generalizations that guide actions of various sorts." Thompson (1974) argued that philosophy of education must be such that it can be utilized by "anyone seriously concerned to think purposefully and rationally about educational issues." In the category of those who would benefit from exposure to theoretical educational writings he included teachers and parents and he argued that philosophy must be capable of being utilized "to deal with practical problems." Similarly, Rusk (1979:4) considered a pivotal criterion whereby one qualifies as a great educator to include making an impact "in classrooms and studies, in high schools, nurseries and orphanages, in relations with real children, sometimes recalcitrant, sometimes 'underprivileged'... that the truth and validity of the ideas proposed were confirmed." Rusk was thus insistent that great educators' ideas be "capable of being put into practice by many different teachers in many different situations."

4. Barrow & Woods (1975:181-9).

5. *SH-5749* [1988-89], II:415.

6. *Avot* 1:17 states that "not study but deed is the essential thing"; see also *LS*, VIII:109-10, Paragraph 10.

7. *SK-5749*, II:415.

8. These include forty of R. Schneerson's educational projects for practical implementation, which are listed in Rabbi Elyashiv Kaploun's *Takanot HaRabbi—Hora'ot V'Takanot HaRabbi L'Dor HaShevi'i* [The Lubavitcher Rebbe's Directives: Instructions and Ordinances by the Lubavitcher Rebbe for the Seventh Generation of Habad]. As well, *Chinuch L'Ma'aseh—Likkut Hora'ot V'Hadrachot HaRabbi MiLubavitch*

MeSichot—5748-5752 [Education in Practice—An Anthology of Teachings and Instructions of the Lubavitcher Rebbe, Delivered between 1987 and 1992] is an 86-page anthology edited by R. Levi Stolick and R. Nechemia Kaploun that lists over 200 of R. Schneerson's practical educational suggestions that he communicated between September 24th, 1987 and late February, 1992.

9. Journal entry of *Sivan* 8th, 5702 [May 24th, 1942], draft of an address to the lottery for *"Mishnah* by Heart" in *Reshimot*, I:380 [*Reshima* No. 13]. See also Zaklikowski & Greenberg (*eds.*) (1993):337-41 for the text of an address at an undated *farbrengen* of 1947-1948, where Sabbath-observant chess champion Samuel H. Reshevsky was present.

10. *SH-5749* [1988-89], I:29. Here Rabbi Schneerson wrote: "Even when...attending to other matters and on [one's] way, one encounters a child, one must realize that...this is Divinely ordained so that one will involve oneself with this child and influence the child. One must be aware of the responsibility related to this as one cannot be sure that one will ever meet this child again."

11. Zaklikowski & Greenberg (*eds.*) (1993):337-41.

12. *TM-HIT-5743* [1982-1983], III:1207ff; *TM-HIT-5747* [1986-1987], IV:233-6.

13. Address of *Nissan* 26th, 5740 [April 12th, 1980] in *SK-5740* [1979-1980], II:815-8.

14. Letter to R. Hendel Lieberman in *The Lamplighter*, Vol. 59:3, published by Chabad House, Caulfield, Melbourne, Australia.

15. *Ibid.*

16. *TM-HIT-5711* [1950-51], I:315-7.

17. Address of *Tevet* 7th, 5729 [December 28th, 1968] in *SK-5729* [1968-1969], I:252-8.

18. *SK-5736* [1975-6], II:33-7, address of *Nissan* 11th, 5736 [April 11th, 1976].

19. A succinctly presented sample of forty-four practical life-lessons derived by R. Schneerson from worldly phenomena are collected in an anthology entitled "Listening to Life's Messages" by D. S. Polter (*ed.*), 1997.

20. Address of *Shabbat Parashat Bamidbar, Sivan* 2nd, 5750 [May 26th, 1990], *TM-HIT-5750*, III:246, f.n. 48.

21. Address of *Shabbat Mevarchim HaChodesh Tammuz, Sivan* 23rd, 5750 [June 16th, 1990], *TM-HIT-5750*, III:364.

22. Address of *Shabbat Parashat Emor, Erev Lag B'Omer*, 5750 [1990]; *TM-HIT-5750*, III:179.

23. Address of *Cheshvan* 20th, 5744 [October 27th, 1983] in *LS*, XXV:309-11.

24. See address of *Shabbat Parashat Chayei Sara, Cheshvan* 22nd, 5751 [Nov. 10th, 1990] (*SH-5751*, I:135, f.n. 70.)

25. *LS*, XXV:309-11.

26. Address of *Shabbat Parshat Beha'alotecha, Sivan* 24th, 5749 [June 17th, 1989] (*TM-HIT-5749*, III:369).

27. Address of *Shabbat Parashat Chayei Sara, Cheshvan* 22nd, 5751 [Nov. 10th, 1990] (*TM-HIT-5751*, I:315, f.n. 71).

28. Likewise, he urged naming a baby on the first possible weekday Torah reading and not to delay until Shabbat. Address of *Shabbat Parashat Shelach, Shabbat Mevarchim Tammuz, Sivan* 21st, 5750 [June 24th, 1990] (*TM-HIT 5750*, III:364).

29. Address of *Shabbat Parshat Vayeishev, Kislev* 24th, 5749 [Dec. 3rd, 1988] (*TM-HIT-5749*, II:37-8).

30. Address of *Sivan* 9th, 5749 [June 12th, 1989] to the collective *Yechidut* (*TM-HIT-5749*, III:304).

31. Synopsis of address of third day of *Selichot, Ellul* 24th, 5751 [Sept. 3rd, 1991] to *Nshei U'Bnot Chabad* in *TM-HIT-5751*, IV:310-1.

32. *TM-HIT-5750*, I:181-2 and see address of *Shabbat Parashat Acharei, Nissan* 24th, 5749 [April 29th, 1989] (*TM-HIT-5749*, III:75), "as has been explained in detail at the outset of RSZ's *Laws of Torah Study.*"

33. See address of *Shabbat Parashat Chayei Sara, Cheshvan* 22nd, 5751 [Nov. 10th, 1990] (*SK-5751*, I:134, f.n. 68): "Indeed, our Sages have remarked, 'When does a child merit the World to Come?... From when he responds *Amen*, [as it is stated, (Isaiah, 26:2): Open the gates and let the righteous nation, guardians of faith, come.' Do not read *shomer emunim*—'guardian of faith' but rather *she'omer emunim*, meaning 'who recites *Amen*'].'" See *Chidushei Aggadot MaHaRSHA, Sanhedrin*, 110b.

34. Address of *Shabbat Parashat Chayei Sara, Cheshvan* 22nd, 5751 [Nov. 10th, 1990] (*SK-5751*, I:134, f.n. 66): "Generally at six years of age" (see *Ketubot*, 6a and elsewhere), even though more precisely "the legal requirement for the commencement of *chinuch* as a positive *mitzvah* is determined in the case of each child according to / contingent upon his intellectual development and his knowledge of each area according to its content" (*Shulchan Aruch* of RSZ, *Orach Chayim*, 343:3).

35. Address of *Ellul* 24th, 5734; Addresses of *Cheshvan* 20th and *Shabbat Parashat Chayei Sarah*, 5735 (in *LS*, XV:168ff); Addresses of *Shabbat Parashat Metzorah*, 5736 and *Shabbat Parashat Metzorah*, 5735 (in *LS*, XVII:146-7); Letter of *Iyar* 11th, 5735 (in *LS*, XVI:577); *LS*, XI:288; *SH-5750*, II:481; Letter of *Adar-Sheini* 28th, 5741 (in *LS*, XXI:382); Letter of *Cheshvan* 28th, 5735 (in *LS*, XI:288); Address of *Tishrei* 6th, 5735; *IK*, XIV, Letter 5,316.

36. *LS*, XVII:146.

37. *IK*, IV:155-6, Letter 897.

38. See *HaYom Yom*, entry of *Iyar* 4th.

39. *IK*, IX:181, Letter 2,803; *op. cit.*, V:174-5, Letter 1,378.

40. See address of *Shabbat Parashat Chayei Sara, Cheshvan* 22nd, 5751 [Nov. 10th, 1990] (*SH-5751*, I:135, f.n. 72 and address of *Shabbat Parashat Emor, Erev Lag B'Omer*, 5750; *TM-HIT-5750*, III:179-80.

41. Address of *Kislev* 19th, 5747 in *TM-HIT-5747*, II:37-9.

42. *LS*, XVII:146.
43. Numbers, 15:37-41.
44. *IK*, IV:155-6, Letter 897.
45. Address of *Erev Rosh Chodesh Sivan*, 5740 (Addenda to *LS*, XXIII:250*ff*).
46. Address of *Nissan* 11th, 5741 in *SK-5741*, III: 129*ff*; Pastoral letter of *Tishrei* 11th, 5742 (Addenda to *LS*, XXIV:583) and *op. cit.*, XXIII:296.
47. English letter of *Tevet* 26th, 5742 [Jan. 21st, 1982, in *Letters of the Rebbe*, VI: 190-4]; Address of Third Day of *Chol HaMoed Sukkot*, 5741 (*SK-5741*, I:176*ff*).
48. Addresses of *Shabbat Parashat Ekev*, *Menachem-Av* 20th and Saturday night, *Menachem-Av* 21st, 5740 [Aug. 3rd, 1980] in *SK-5740* [1979-80], III:880-903.
49. *Ibid*. See also address *Shabbat Parshat Re'ei*, 5740 in *SK-5740* [1979-80], III:934-41.
50. Founded in Israel in 1952 and in the United States and Canada in 1955.
51. Founded in Israel in 1952 and in the United States in 1953.
52. In Israel these are conducted in over 300 communities, each group attracting up to 400 participants.
53. *IK*, I:75-8, Letter 48; *op. cit.*, I:59-61, Letter 37; *op. cit.*, I:93-4, Letter 55 [Addenda to *LS*, XXVI:446].
54. *IK*, III:344; *op. cit.*, IV:357; *op. cit.*, I:322; *op. cit.*, XXII:380-2; *op. cit.*, XII:445; *op. cit.*, XIII:359; *op. cit.*, XIV:16; *op. cit*, XIV:404-6 & 409.
55. *Op. cit.*, VI:302-3, Letter 1,807.
56. *Op. cit.*, XIV:405-6, Letter 5,181 [Addenda to *LS*, XXII:397-8].
57. *Bar-Mitzvah* occurs at the age of 13, *Bat-Mitzvah* occurs at the age of 12.
58. This included the *Lag B'Omer* Parade which R. Schneerson would attend, speaking to the children himself and watching them as the parade with its floats and thousands of children passed by the dais.
59. Address of *Shevat* 8th, 5743 [Jan. 22nd, 1983] in *TM-HIT-5743*, II:859-60.
60. *IK*, III:355-7, Letter 657; *op. cit.*, IV:406-7, Letter 1,126; *op. cit.*, IV:454-5; Letter 1,177 [Addenda to *LS*, IX:306-7].
61. Address of Third Day of *Chol HaMo'ed Sukkot*, 5741 (in *SK-5741*, I:176*ff*); see English letter of *Tevet* 26th, 5742 [Jan. 21st, 1982].
62. See R. Schneerson's responsa to *The Moshiach Times*, cited in *Teshura MeSimchat HaNissu'in Shel Aharon David V'Nechama Dina Rabin*, *Ellul* 20th, 5759 [Souvenir Journal Celebrating the Wedding of Aron and Dinie Rabin, Sept. 1st, 1999]: 19-53; *Dvar Melech—Likut Tshuvot M'yuchadot Me'et Kvod Kdushat Admor Shlita*:4.
63. R. Schneerson's statement on education entitled *Some Basic Problems of Education* published in Rabbi Dr. Nissan Mindel's *The Letter and the Spirit: Letters by the Lubavitcher Rebbe*, III:41-6.
64. *Ibid*.
65. *Ibid*.

66. Addresses of *Kislev* 19th, 5743 [Dec. 5th, 1982] and second day of *Shavuot*, 5743 [May 19th, 1983].

67. See *SH-5749*, I:30-7. R. Schneerson sought to promote ethical monotheism, arguing that Jewish history had previously never allowed for this opportunity given the anti-Semitic feelings which prevailed at the time. To R. Schneerson, the comparative freedom of speech prevalent in the contemporary world rendered obligatory the promotion of this ideal. See also *LS*, IV:1094-5 and *op. cit.*, V:159-60.

68. In the 1980s, non-denominational groups in America founded societies based on the Noahide principles.

69. For details of this campaign, see Shemtov (*ed.*), 1996, *and Letters of the Secretariat of the Lubavitcher Rebbè* dated *Cheshvan* 24th, 5723 [Nov. 21st, 1962] and *Nissan* 26th, 5724 [April 8th, 1964].

70. Concerning these laws, President G.H.W. Bush (1989-90) wrote, "The principles of moral and ethical conduct that have formed the basis for all civilization come to us, in part, from the centuries-old Seven Noahide Laws. The Noahide Laws are actually seven commandments given to man by G-d... These commandments include prohibitions against murder, robbery, adultery, blasphemy, and greed, as well as the positive order to establish courts of justice."

71. English letter of *Shevat* 16th, 5724 [Jan. 30th, 1964] in *Letters by the Lubavitcher Rebbe*:275-6.

72. English letter of *Cheshvan* 15th, 5733 [Oct. 23rd, 1972] in *Letters from the Rebbe*, III:131-2, Letter 97.

73. R. Schneerson's letter of *Iyar* 18th, 5747 [May 17th, 1987] addressed to US president Ronald Reagan in Shemtov (*ed.*), 1994:54.

74. On November 20, 1987.

75. He spoke publicly and wrote in support of the introduction into public schools of the non-denominational Regents' Prayer, whose text read: "Almighty G-d, we acknowledge our dependence on Thee, and we beg Thy blessings upon us, our parents, our teachers, and our country."

76. English letters of *Cheshvan* 24th, 5723 [Nov. 21st, 1962] and *Nissan* 26th, 5724 [April 8th, 1964] in *Letters from the Rebbe*, IV:42-9, Letter 27 and *op. cit.*, 64-74, Letter 38.

77. *IK*, XXII:492.

78. Address of *Nissan* 11th, 5741 [April 15th, 1981] published in *SK-5741*, III:110-5, analyzing the March 30th attempted assassination of President Reagan two weeks prior.

79. From an address of the last day of *Pesach*, 5743 [1983] in *TM-HIT-5743*, III:1345, citing *Ethics of the Fathers*, 2:1.

80. Addresses of *Shevat* 10th, 5743 [Jan. 24th, 1983]; *Nissan* 11th, 5743 [March 25th, 1983]; Last Day of *Pesach*, 5743 [April 5th, 1983]; and *Tammuz* 12th, 5743 [June 23rd, 1983]; Addresses of *Tishrei* 6th, 5744 [Sept. 13th, 1983];

Kislev 19th, 5744 [Nov. 25th, 1983]; and *Nissan* 11th, 5744 [April 13th, 1984]; Address of *Tishrei* 6th, 5745 [Oct. 2nd, 1984].

81. Address of *Nissan* 18th, 5743 [April 1st, 1983] to Children Participating in *Tzivot HaShem* Rally, published in *TM-HIT-5743*, III:1293-1301, §50; *op. cit.*, 1345.

82. *TM-HIT-5745*, I:137.

83. English letter of *Tevet* 26th, 5742 [Jan. 21st, 1982] in *Letters of the Rebbe*, VI:190-4, Letter 133.

84. *IK*, IV:425-6, Letter 1,145.

85. *Op. cit.*, III:237-8, Letter 559.

86. *Op. cit.*, V:26-7, Letter 1,246.

87. *Op. cit.*, IV:483, Letter 1,200.

88. English letter of *Av* 22nd, 5739 [Aug. 15th, 1979] addressed to Dr. R. Wilkes of Coney Island Hospital, Brooklyn, in response to the latter's inquiry of August 9th, 1979, published in *Letters of the Rebbe*, II:206-10, Letter 97.

89. Address of *Shabbat Parashat Bamidbar*, 5739 [1979], Paragraph 60.

90. Address of *Adar-Sheini* 17th, 5738 [March 25th, 1978] in addenda to *LS*, XVI:625.

91. Address of *Cheshvan* 13th, 5750 [Nov. 11th, 1989] in *SH-5750*, I:108.

92. Address of *Ellul* 24th, 5748 [Sept. 6th, 1988] in *TM-HIT-5748*, IV:339 & 341-6

93. Address of *Av* 20th, 5737 [July 28th, 1977] in *SK-5737*, II:388-9.

94. Deuteronomy, 11:19.

95. *Reshimot*, II:260-8 [*Reshima* No. 30].

96. *TM*, III [5711, II]:85-92. §19-§27 & §29. Similarly, he required (*IK*, III:375-6, Letter 677) that all ensure kosher education for all boys, girls, and youth in Morocco, as well as making sure that these children would receive a kosher education in other countries after their emigration from Morocco.

97. *IK*, III:445, Letter 736. He believed (*op. cit.*, III:445, Letter 736) that this was particularly applicable to the education of those boys and girls in Israel as well as those migrating there and that saving these youths spiritually is an obligation upon every man and woman, with every individual duty-bound to assist this rescue to the fullest extent of their potential (*op. cit.*, IV:176-7, Letter 920). The educator's unique responsibility was to save tens of thousands of Jewish boys and girls from the terrible danger of denial of G-d (*op. cit.*, IV:121-2, Letter 865), where the greatest energies must be exerted to maintain a soul's connection to G-d (*op. cit.*, IV:176-7, Letter 920). Self-sacrifice and fearless resistance were called for, especially for the sake of education (*op. cit.*, IV:202-4, Letter 940) to protect innocent young boys and girls (*op. cit.*, IV:213-5, Letter 949; *op. cit.*, IV:216, Letter 950).

98. For examples, see *op. cit.*, XV:28-31, Letter 5,355 and *op. cit.*, XVII:339-41, Letter 6,490.

99. *Op. cit.*, VIII:227; *op. cit.*, XIV:511-2; *op. cit.*, XIV:525-6; *op. cit.*, XX:236; LS, XVI:553; *op. cit.*, XXII:356, *op. cit.*, 399, *op. cit.*, XXIV:347.

100. *IK*, III:254-5, Letter 572; *op. cit.*, XXI:126-7, Letter 7,881; *op. cit.*, XXIII:357, Letter 8,962.

101. Letter of *Ellul* 28th, 5730 [Sept. 29th, 1970]; unpublished letter of *Iyar* 1st, 5740 [April 17th, 1980] addressed to All Participants in a Dedication of the New Building of the Yeshiva College, Sydney, Australia.

102. *IK*, I:63-4, Letter 40.

103. *Op. cit.*, IV:371-3, Letter 1,090.

104. The Habad House, with its ongoing classes and lecture series, is widely recognized as a center of education. In Israel the Habad House lecture service arranges educational evenings for community groups. The Habad House also supplies supplementary Torah education programs, including seminars, preparation for *Bar-* and *Bat-Mitzvah*, library facilities, and vacation education programs.

105. Seligson, 1994:A19.

106. Kagan, 1988:98.

107. Letter to the Friends of Lubavitch in California, headed by Mr. Avrohom Lazaroff, dated June 26th, 1972 in Cunin (*ed.*) 1973:71. In a letter of *Adar* 19th, 5729 [March 9th, 1969] (addressed to the Friends of Lubavitch, Los Angeles, upon R. Schneerson's receipt of the key to the new Lubavitch Center), R. Schneerson expressed his hope that "the new edifice" truly be a center for various activities to spread goodness and holiness as embodied in the Torah. He expressed his desire that it be a centre in the fullest sense, namely, "that the spirit of the center...should reach out to the entire periphery and indeed beyond, to the entire West Coast."

108. Letter of July 29, 1972 to Rabbi Shlomo Cunin by S. Modell, associate professor of history at Los Angeles Valley College in Cunin (*ed.*) 1973:34. Prof. Modell wrote, "Habad can make a positive contribution to any college campus where Jewish students are in attendance." Similarly, Robert Tannenbaum, professor of development of social systems at the Graduate School of Management, University of California, Los Angeles, observed (cited in Cunin [*ed.*] 1973:32), "I have known some students who have been most positively affected by the type of experience—personally, socially, and religiously—provided them at Habad House, and I have heard indirectly about others. I also have been aware...of the large number of students who have found Habad House to be a most important centering point for their lives on campus—often, at times, that are personally critical to them." The Editorial of *The Bnai Brith Messenger* of June 16, 1972, reported, "on the UCLA campus they are provided the unique facilities of the Habad House—an inspiring center at which Jewish youths find themselves and project themselves" (cited in Cunin [*ed.*] 1973:30).

109. One example is the Habad Men's Residential Rehabilitation Program in Los Angeles. A women's rehabilitation program providing a comfortable environment for drug-dependent women was launched in 1987 and is termed Project Pride. Habad's *National Network of Clinically Based Drug Prevention and Education Centers* had grown to include twenty-eight cities across the United States by the year 1988 and was serving more than 50,000 people at that time.

110. Brod, 1988.

111. Countries included Australia, Austria, Belgium, Brazil, Canada, Chile, Colombia, England, France, Holland, Hong Kong, Italy, Mexico, Morocco, Paraguay, Peru, Romania, Scotland, South Africa, Spain, Switzerland, Tunisia, Uruguay, Venezuela, and West Germany. In 1993, a Habad House was opened in Thailand.

112. *SK-5736* [1975-76], II:633-8; address of *Av* 23rd, 5736 [Aug. 19th, 1976] addressed to the Israeli team participating in the 1976 Paraplegic Olympics.

113. *SK-5736* [1975-76], I:548-9; *LS*, XXV:514-5.

114. Hebrew/English letter of *Kislev* 15th, 5738 [Nov. 25th, 1977] in *Letters from the Rebbe*, II:187-9, Letter 87.

115. Pastoral letter of *Nissan* 11th, 5717 [May 12th, 1957] published in *IK*, XV:33-6.

116. R. Schneerson's view was predicated on the Midrashic statement (*Bamidbar Rabba*, 12:3) that G-d only requires of individuals according to their abilities. From this principle, R. Schneerson argued that negative circumstances are indicative of Divine bestowing of greater latent abilities.

117. *LS*, I:128, address of the Last Day of *Pesach*, *Nissan* 22nd, 5712 [April 17th, 1952]; *op. cit.*, I:27-53; Letter of *Nissan* 11th, 5712 [April 6th, 1952] in *IK*, II:6-8.

118. *Op. cit.*, I:128-9, Letter 78.

119. *Op. cit.*, I:163-4, Letter 91.

120. *Op. cit.*, I:214-5, Letter 120.

121. *Op. cit.*, I:128-9, Letter 78.

122. *Op. cit.*, I:127-8, Letter 77.

123. *Op. cit.*, I:66-7, Letter 42.

124. *Op. cit.*, IV:430-1, Letter 1,151.

125. *Op. cit.*, I:38-40, Letter 22.

126. Several of R. Schneerson's *Mitzvah* campaigns focused specifically on the Jewish woman. These included a *Shabbat* candle-lighting campaign, the campaign for observance of the laws of Family Purity, and the *Kashrut* Campaign.

127. Kagan (1988:55) noted that this organization was founded on the basic tenet that continuing intellectual and emotional growth through Torah study, particularly Hasidic teachings, were to be no less accessible to women than men. Indeed, these teachings seek to explain the uniqueness of the female role and the unique powers granted to her. In 1953, R.

Schneerson established branches of the same organization in the US and other countries.

128. R. Schneerson has been instrumental in establishing *mikva'ot* [pools for ritual immersion] in communities with small Jewish populations, including remote locations such as Utrecht in Holland, the island of Djerba off the coast of Tunisia, Marakhesh, Tangier in Morocco, Hobart in Tasmania (Australia), and Hong Kong (*Shemtov* [*ed.*], 1988).

129. *The Shamir Center for Advanced Technologies* in Jerusalem provides high-level jobs in departments such as computers, physics, and chemistry, while simultaneously running a high-level Torah study institute for newly arrived immigrants.

130. It is noteworthy that many Habad educators, are themselves Soviet emigres who are second- and third-generation Habad activists produced by RJIS's underground *yeshivot*.

131. *IK*, I:120-1, Letter 73.

132. *SK-5741* [1980-81, II], address of *Parshat Ki Tissa, 5741* [February 21st, 1981]: 513-5; *TM-HIT-5742* [1981-82], I, daytime address of *Simchat Torah,* 5742 [Oct. 21st, 1982]: 274-6.

133. *Ibid.*

134. *Bava Batra*:14a.

135. He noted that this was the case, given the widespread use as a symbol of Jewish affiliation by educational institutions. Besides this, the misrepresentation of the tablets appeared in children's reports, certificates, and merit awards.

136. *LS*, XXI:164-71.

137. Rabbi Yosef Kapach's edition of Maimonides' *Pirush HaMishnayot.* See Maimonides' *Mishneh Torah, Hilchot Beit HaBechira*, 3:9.

138. R. Schneerson suggested (*LS*, XXI:164-71) that the depiction of a *menorah* with curved branches at the Arch of Titus in Rome may have been due to either an artist's inaccurate depiction, or that Titus may not have accessed the actual *menorah* given that it was hidden at the time of the Roman conquest of Jerusalem or that the artist may have depicted a candelabra other than the Biblical candelabra of the Temple.

139. *IK*, IV:371-3, Letter 1,090.

140. *Op. cit.*, III:308-9, Letter 616.

141. *Ibid.*

142. *Op. cit.*, V:67, Letter of *Kislev* 8th, 5712 [Dec. 7th, 1951].

143. *Op. cit.*, V:66-8, Letter 1,281.

144. *Op. cit.*, XI:125, Letter 3,509.

145. *Op. cit.*, IV:425-6, Letter 1,145.

146. *Op. cit.*, 308-9, Letter 337.

147. These activities took place under the auspices of *Agudat Yisrael.*

148. *Op. cit.*, XXI:81, Letter 7,828. He believed (*op. cit.*, III:355-7, Letter 657)
     that an educator's personal frustration, which is temporary, does not com-
     pare to the damage suffered over many years and the entire lifetime of a
     student through his or her abandoning the educational calling.

149. While viewing the educational task to be the obligation of all, including
     those in other professions, R. Schneerson simultaneously supported the
     cause of pedagogic training for those who would take on the educational
     role in a professional capacity. See *op. cit.*, XV:353, Letter 5,698 of *Ellul* 1st,
     5717 [Aug. 28th, 1957].

150. R. Schneerson (*LS*, III:792-4, §13) believed that everyone shares a respon-
     sibility for education and not only the professional educator, in the same
     way that all must contribute to extinguishing a fire, not only professional
     fire-fighters. This analogy is in harmony with R. Schneerson's citation (*op.
     cit.*, I:98-102) of RJIS's utilization of a conflagrational metaphor, which
     likened the futility of compromising educational ideals to attempting to
     extinguish a fire with kerosene.

151. Pastoral letter of *Ellul* 18th, 5712 (Sept. 19th, 1952), in *IK*, I:6-7; *Letters by
     the Lubavitcher Rebbe, Tishrei-Adar*:5.

152. R. Schneerson spoke of the great responsibility that parents carry to exert
     influence on both their family and the community (*IK*, III:251-2, Letter
     570). In the case of family, their responsibility is to their children, who
     will build future Jewish homes (*op. cit.*, IV:176-7, Letter 920), and par-
     ents must therefore aspire to constantly improve their children's education
     (*op. cit.*, IV:31, Letter 792). In particular, a special responsibility is placed
     on a woman, as *akeret habayit* [mainstay of the home], upon whom are
     largely contingent the will and conduct of her husband and children (*op.
     cit.*, IV:10-1, Letter 775).

153. *Op. cit.*, VI:179-80, Letter 1,696.

154. *Op. cit.*, XXI:277, Letter 8,034.

155. *Op. cit.*, IV:298, Letter 1,024.

156. Landau, 1994.

157. Speigel (1975) observed, "A nod from the Rebbe will dispatch a disciple
     to the remotest corner of the world. Let the Rebbe cast a pebble in the
     Crown Heights section of Brooklyn where the Lubavitch movement has
     its headquarters, and the ripples reach Melbourne, London, Casablanca,
     Los Angeles and Jerusalem."

158. Sacks, 1990:68; 1993:75.

159. R. Schneerson was one of the first Jewish leaders to realize that modern
     communications were transforming the world into a global village and
     that educational initiatives could now take place on a scale previously
     unimaginable.

160. Sacks, 1994.

161. Goldberg (1989) noted that while two of R. Schneerson's contemporaries, R. Soloveitchik and R. Hutner, devoted themselves to "modern, secular Talmudic philosophic synthesis" and a focus on "an elite, Talmudic-pietistic training centre" respectively, R. Schneerson devoted his life to creating a worldwide Hasidic movement.

162. Miller, 1993.

163. Addresses of *Sivan* 12th, 5720 [June 7th, 1960], *Adar* 14th, 5721 [March 2nd, 1961], *Shevat* 29th, 5722 [Feb. 3rd, 1962], and multiple addresses until *Tishrei* 9th, 5747 [Oct. 12th, 1986] in *SK-5747*, I:27, Paragraph 8.

164. *LS*, XXI:452 and multiple addresses between *Adar* 14th, 5721 [March 2nd, 1961] (see *SK-5721*:124) and *Kislev* 21st, 5745 [Dec. 15th, 1984] (see *TM-HIT-5745*, II:915-6).

165. Already in July of 1994, the *New York Times* had observed, "The Lubavitch Hassidim, no strangers to zealously taking their message to Jews in other parts of the world, have also established an electronic outpost on the Internet." In 1995, Katzen alerted Habad Houses to the upcoming vast potential of educational outreach via the internet. http://www.chabad.org/library/article_cdo/aid/784112/jewish/The-Infancy-and-Growth-of-Judaism-on-the-Web.htm

166. For a detailed historical account of Habad educational institutions established between 1940 and 1950 by RJIS, including its central *Yeshivot* and branches throughout larger US cities, Girls' Schools, and Release Hour programs, see Levin, 1989:178-304 & 361-5.

167. Between the years 1950 and 1956, R. Schneerson founded day schools in North Africa (1950) and Israel and Australia (1952). He also founded elementary and high schools for girls in Australia and Canada (1956). He founded senior *Yeshivot* in New York and Toronto (1955), besides an agricultural school (1954) as well as a general vocational school in Israel (1955).

168. Senior *Yeshivot* in Melbourne (1967), Miami (1974), Seattle and New Haven (1976), Caracas (1977), Los Angeles (1978), Buenos Aires (1980), Casablanca (1981), and Johannesburg (1984). Advanced Torah academies for married students (*Kollelim*) were established in New York (1962), Melbourne (1969), and Montreal (1981). This list is far from exhaustive. A full list of educational institutions established by R. Schneerson is beyond the scope of this study.

169. An example of such growth is the Minnesota Habad community, which developed both an elementary school as well as a tertiary academy for girls, named *Beit Chana*, which specializes in courses for tertiary female students of limited Jewish background. It serves such students from throughout the US, South Africa, and Australia. A similar tertiary girls academy in New York, *Machon Chana*, provides ongoing education for graduates of *Beit Chana*. Similarly, R. Schneerson expanded Melbourne's Oholei Yosef Yitzchak Boys' High School into a *Yeshivah Gedolah* and

Beth Rivkah Ladies' College into an *Ohel Chana* Tertiary Seminary for
Girls. Eventually, the *Yeshivah Gedolah* led to the establishment of a *Kollel.*

170. Student analyses of his writings are collected in *Yagdil Torah* and other
such studies where Rabbinical students debate the precise meaning of R.
Schneerson's writings.

171. He emphasized that such activities were to take place exclusively outside
the *yeshivah*'s daily schedule or during vacation time only (*Yechidut* of
Rabbi N. Nemenov, the *Mashpia* of *Tomchei Temimim*, France, with R.
Schneerson).

172. Sacks, 1980.

173. In an early interview (Kranzler, 1951), R. Schneerson outlined his intended
initiatives and referred specifically to the "heavy decimation of Jewry over
the past decade or two." In a discussion with college students in 1960 (*SK-
5720* [1960]:408) he likened the task of contemporary Hasidism, in the
wake of the Holocaust, to the challenges faced by BST, in the face of the
Chmielnicki Massacres, which pre-empted the earliest beginnings of Hasidism. Similarly, in 1964, R. Schneerson wrote (Letter of *Cheshvan* 28th,
5725 [Nov. 3rd, 1964]) that "after so many Jews lost their lives in recent
years, among them the best and choicest of our people, the responsibility
of those whom G-d, in His mercy has spared, is increased many-fold..."
See *Rader*, 1979:203.

174. Kranzler, 1951.

175. Another of R. Schneerson's most successful initiatives, besides his successes in propagating the renaissance and growth of Orthodoxy itself
following its decimation in the Holocaust, was attainment of a character of
self-confidence of the entire Jewish nation. R. Schneerson's contemporary
American Orthodox Jewish leader and thinker, Rabbi J.B. Soloveitchik,
viewed Habad's achievement as imbuing Orthodoxy with a sense of pride.
He cited as an example consultation by the media with Orthodox authorities concerning Jewish issues while previously this had been the exclusive
domain of the Reform spokespeople. He believed that it was largely due
to Habad that orthodoxy had been projected into the media (Glitzenstein
& Steinsaltz, 1980:304). Handelman (1995) stated that "growing up in sub-
urban Chicago in the 1950s and '60s, we Jews kept a low profile. From the
Rebbe, I learned not to be ashamed, not to be afraid, that the world, in
fact, was yearning for the light of Torah."

176. Address of *Adar* 23rd, 5750 [March 20th, 1990] to Friends of Lubavitch
(*TM-HIT-5750*, II:433).

177. English letter of *Av* 22nd, 5739 [Aug. 15th, 1979] published in *Letters of the
Rebbe*, II:206-10, Letter 97.

178. *IK*, I:78-9, Letter 49.

179. *Op. cit.*, I:101-2, Letter 59.

180. *Op. cit.*, III:277-8, Letter 587.

181. *Reshimot*, III:145-50 [*Reshima* No. 59].
182. *IK*, V:26-7, Letter 1,246.
183. *Op. cit.*, IV:67-8, Letter 821.
184. *TM-HIT*, III [5711, II]:224-6.
185. *IK*, I:66-7, Letter 42 (Paragraph iv).
186. *IK*, III:104, Letter 482.
187. *IK*, III:355-7, Letter 657.
188. *Haggadah Shel Pesach Im Likkutei Ta'amim, Minhagim U'Biurim*:11.
189. *IK*, III:256-7, Letter 574.
190. *IK*, III:476-7, Letter 757.
191. *IK*, III:469-71, Letter 753 citing Talmud, *Berachot* 63b.
192. Correspondence of August 15, 1979, addressed to R. Wilkes. From Rabbi Schneerson's response, it is apparent that Wilkes had sought Rabbi Schneerson's opinion on the controversy surrounding the creation of "group homes for those children who are presently placed in an environment, often quite distant from the individual's home and community."
193. *Op. cit.*, III:316-7, Letter 623; *op. cit.*, IV:213-5, Letter 949 [Addenda to *LS*, XXIV:470-1]; *IK*, X:87, Letter 3,048; *op. cit.*, X:121-2, Letter 3,083; *op. cit.*, XII:354-5, Letter 4,169.
194. Included in the practical dimension is mastery of commonly recited blessings over food (*op. cit.*, IV:170-1, Letter 914) as well as other practical matters and areas of priority (*op. cit.*, IV:113-4, Letter 858).
195. *Op. cit.*, III:355-7, Letter 657.
196. Addresses of eve of First Day of *Rosh Chodesh Iyar*, 5736 [May 1st, 1976] and *Lag B'Omer*, 5736 [May 18th, 1976].
197. Undated monograph of 5704 [1943-4] entitled *Tochnit Limmudim* (a). *L'Mosdot Chinuch L'Na'arim* (b). *L'Mosdot Chinuch L'Na'arot MiShnat HaLimmudim HaRishona Ad Shnat HaLimmudim HaShminit* [Curriculum for Educational Institutions for (a). Young Boys (b). Young Girls—From the First Year until the Eighth Grade].
198. *SK-5748*, II:398-407.
199. *IK*, IV:357, Letter 1,076.
200. *Ibid.*
201. *Op. cit.*, IV:392-3, Letter 1,111 [Addenda to *LS*, XIII:300].
202. *IK*, IV:371-3, Letter 1,090 [Addenda to *LS*, VIII:368].
203. Communicated in a letter of *Av* 7th, 5711 [Aug. 9th, 1951] to Rabbi Yitzchak Dubov (*IK*, IV:406-7, Letter 1,126) recommending Habad *yeshivah* students do this through Great Britain in their vacation time.
204. *Op. cit.*, IV:371-3, Letter 1,090 [Addenda to *LS*, VIII:368].
205. Address of Last Day of Pesach, 5744 [April 24th, 1984] in *LS*, XXVII: 229-36; see also addresses of *Shabbat Parashat Kedoshim*, 5744 and *Shabbat Parashat Emor*, 5744; Address of the eve of *Sivan* 11th, 5744; Address of the evening of *Sivan* 12th, 5744; Address of the eve of *Kislev* 10th, 5745; Address

of *Shabbat Parashat Korach,* 5744; *TM-HIT-5745,* Address of *Nissan* 11th, 5745; and Addresss of the eve of *Tevet* 20th, 5749.

206. These can be seen throughout the world, especially in various areas of Israel, visiting soldiers on borders and lonely *Kibbutzim* and settlements as well as army bases and outposts in Israel. These mobile vans provide classes. On an average week, 400 classes are given to 17,000 persons, including soldiers, civilians, and children, through these "tanks."

207. *IK,* VI:283, Letter 1,789; *op. cit.,* VI:360-1, Letter 1,864.

208. *Op. cit.,* XIV:449, Letter 5,230.

209. *Op. cit.,* XVI:66-7, Letter 5,843.

210. *Op. cit.,* XXIV:47-8, Letter 9,071 [Addenda to *LS,* XI:196-8].

211. *LS,* XXIII:18-9; Address of *Shabbat Parashat Vayigash, Tevet* 5th, 5751 [Dec. 22nd, 1990]; *TM-HIT-5751,* II:90; *SK-5751,* I:90, footnote 47 and supra-notes & footnote 58; Address of *Shabbat Parashat Bamidbar, Sivan* 5th, 5751 [May 18th, 1991]; Address of *Shabbat Parashat Mishpatim, Shevat* 27th, 5752 [Feb. 1st, 1992].

Chapter 9

THE COHESIVENESS
AND INNOVATION
OF R. SCHNEERSON'S
EDUCATIONAL PHILOSOPHY

It seems clear that Rabbi Schneerson transcended all the
categories previously used to define the different aspects of
educational philosophy.

—Professor William Pinar[1]

In Chapter 9, this book identifies additional characteristics of a
significant and relevant educational philosophy. The first feature
is that its elements exist in relationship to each other, thereby confirming the existence of a cohesive educational philosophy rather
than merely being a conglomeration of unrelated elements. The
second feature is that the elements are united by meta-themes
from which they are derived and to which they pay homage. The
third feature is that the educational philosophy makes an innovative contribution to the broader society, with its impact being on a
cosmic scale.[2]

The connections between elements of R. Schneerson's philosophy of education have become evident through previous chapters.
While multiple examples of the inter-relatedness of themes exist,
a limited number of examples illustrates that such interactions
pervade the educational corpus with each element having direct
ramifications for other elements.

Education's Impact on Aims and Authority

R. Schneerson's understanding of the cosmic nature of education means that he views everything as educational, with all phenomena awaiting utilization for education purposes. This premise goes hand-in-hand with the principle that education is crucial to the fulfillment of creation and that education is fundamental to our lives. Similarly, R. Schneerson's understanding of the nature of education impacts profoundly on the aims of education. If everything we do and experience is educational, it follows that education must aim to produce a student who is sensitive to and capable of deriving uplifting lifelong lessons from all situations. Viewing education as a process that actualizes the human's self-fulfillment leads to an education which aims to produce students who live meaningful lives of moral excellence. If education is able to reveal the quintessential soul of the learner, it will initiate the learner into sanctity and not be satisfied with only a learner's acquisition of cognitive skills. Such understanding of the very nature of education will motivate higher education aims that include producing a student engaged in self-transformation and a learner who is aware of and in awe of a Higher Authority. Moreover, when education is critical to the Divine plan for the universe, educational authority is covenantal between students and their "Higher Calling," not simply contractual between teacher and learner.

R. Schneerson's employment of metaphors to communicate the nature of education has implications for the general aims of education. For example, his view of education as igniting the flame of the candelabra inspires an education that aims to produce a learner who seeks the maximal tangible realization of his or her potential, someone who will be altruistic rather than self-absorbed. The aim of producing an altruistic learner inspires usage of methodologies that encourage a learner to be an exemplar for other students, a person who will seek to illuminate their outer environment and thereby exert a positive influence on the broader society. Considering education to be the equivalent of nurturing a sapling, education can inspire an education curriculum that encourages a student who is aware of a Higher Authority, to seek to live a virtuous, altruistic life and thereby ensure continuity and perpetuation of values.

Education's Impact on Responsibility, Method, and Content

R. Schneerson's definition of the nature of education also has ramifications for the understanding of the responsibility for education, as well as the methodology and content of education. If everything is educational, it follows that a teacher has enormous responsibility because the very destiny of the universe depends on his or her educational efforts. The educator must display devotion to the educational calling and ensure that educational opportunities provided by the universe are fully utilized. If education is of universal significance, an educator simultaneously bears a responsibility to view his or her actions to be of universal importance. If education is by definition like a life-saving priority, then educator application to the task is essential, meaning that it is a concern that impacts beyond the hours of formal instruction, even transcending the constraints of the subject area. It also implies that the educator must be proactive and optimistic, rather than defeatist or complacent, investing enormous energy and ability in their educational calling and focusing primarily on the positive potential of the learner. At the same time, an educator bears a responsibility to ensure that educational ideals must not be compromised or diluted.

Similarly, metaphors created by R. Schneerson for education impact on the responsibility for education. For example, the critical importance of education implied by the life-saving metaphor leads to our understanding that an educator must engage in personal as well as professional self-improvement, both of which are prerequisites for success in influencing others. Other direct outcomes of R. Schneerson's metaphors for education include the educator's awareness that even minor advancements are highly significant, a focus on educator renewal of aspirations, as well as thoughtful contemplation of the soul of the learner.

R. Schneerson's understanding of the nature and aims of education impacts on his understanding of the ideal educational methodology. For example, R. Schneerson's understanding that "everything is educational" has implications for the educator's methodology of capturing a very wide range of teachable moments as and when they occur. The notion of education being an endeavor of cosmic significance with implications for the individual, the wider community, for cosmic redemption, and indeed a matter of life leads inexorably to a methodology where urgency and proactivity are essential. His conception of the aims of education, which include imbuing belief in a Higher Authority, inspiring a life of virtue and goodness, maximum realization of learner potential through ongoing student advancement, and his goal of producing a learner who engages in continuous self-transformation imply a methodology where an educator's idealism and devotion are key components and whereby they also teach by exemplifying ideals. Moreover, R. Schneerson's understanding of the responsibility for education leads to a methodology characterized by a sensitive, inclusive approach as well as a meticulous concern for detail and personal exemplification of ideals. These all culminate in an educator's positive perspective of the individual learner, including those learners requiring special education.

Furthermore, the aims of producing a learner who will, as an independent individual, live a life of altruism, transforming his or her fellow humans and influencing society and perpetuating his or her spiritual heritage to future generations, lead directly to the methodology that empowers students to become role models and consequently even educators and disciplinarians themselves.

Finally, R. Schneerson's understanding of the content of education is consistent with his definition of the nature of education. For example, if everything is educational, the integration of a variety of phenomena into the curriculum is completely acceptable. If everything is a matter of life, then the curriculum must address the purpose of life. If education is a Heavenly calling, the curriculum must include focus on values education and therefore introduce students to spirituality.

Other Reciprocal Ramifications

In turn, additional key elements are seen to be in harmony with other elements. For example, we see that R. Schneerson's views on the content of education and the inclusion of learning about spirituality and the supernatural reinforces the aims of education which aspire to produce a learner who transcends the limitations of the physical world. His views on the aims of education that seek to encourage virtuous conduct lead to a methodology which prioritizes course content over the language of instruction and a course content where spiritual edification precedes general studies in the curriculum. In addition, he advocated that matters regarding sexuality are taught in small groups of only one gender and with great sensitivity. A view of educational authority that is covenantal inspires aims that require student self-regulation and the methodology and practice where each student seeks a mentor. Adoption of an educational methodology where an urgency pervades leads to course content where the practical takes priority over the theoretical.

Indeed, an education that seeks to inspire the learner to live a virtuous, morally upright life implies that the educator has an educational responsibility to exemplify the ideals taught so there is no disconnect or discrepancy between what is taught and how the educator lives.

Meta-Themes in R. Schneerson's Educational Philosophy: A View from the Essence

At the heart of R. Schneerson's worldview is the meta-theme that unites all sub-themes, namely the Kabbalistic perception of the world from the elevated vantage-point of the essence of G-dliness [*Atzmut*], as opposed to G-d's manifestations or attributes. If we view life from this elevated vantage-point, there is special purpose in everything as "G-d is desirous of a dwelling place precisely in the lower realms."[3] This implies the inclusion and central role of precisely those dimensions furthest removed from spirituality. G-d's Infinity implies a concern that is not confined to the sublime and lofty, but rather it includes the minutiae of human existence. *Atzmut*, the ultimate expression of G-d's loftiness, specifically accommodates even the mundane and physical aspects of our lives and it is precisely the lower, more physical aspects of life that reach *Atzmut*, the Divine Essence. It follows that specifically those dimensions of life that are furthest removed from spirituality must be imbued with holiness.

Even remote features that are seemingly antithetical to spirituality can and must become vehicles that express Divinity. A derivative of the idea of adopting a view from *Atzmut* is R. Schneerson's focus on the *etzem* or the essence of a person or a phenomenon. This view looks beyond external forms and seeks the inner unity in all phenomena. In this system, there is a purpose in everything, whereby every phenomenon has a role to play in the Divine scheme. In educational terms, this means that all phenomena take on an educational dimension which is the starting point of R. Schneerson's educational discourse. It is this point that pre-empts and is axiomatic to many of the educational elements that emerge from it. This idea that everything is educational, a clear derivative of "*Atzmut* thinking," can be seen as the axiom that underpins R. Schneerson's understanding of the nature of education, leading to his delineation of aims of education that follow from this understanding, which has further implications for authority, responsibility, methodology, and content. In turn, these influence the practice of education that emerge from these elements. Interestingly, R. Schneerson's positive view of the individual is not the defining characteristic of his discourse but is indicative of the view derived from *Atzmut*. Furthermore, every individual is central to *Atzmut*, as a partner with

Atzmut in fulfilling the Divine scheme. This ideal is like the concept of *Hashgacha Pratit* or Divine Providence, where every phenomenon is Divinely orchestrated.

Since everything has a crucial role to play in the Divine scheme, education is all about positive engagement; thus, educators must see their role as one of constructive interaction rather than embracing an attitude of combat. Indeed, acceptance and an affirmative approach became the defining characteristics of contemporary Habad education and outreach under R. Schneerson's guidance. This concept does not, however, mean that for education, R. Schneerson adopted an exclusively benign approach. What it does mean is that even when educators are required to take on a disciplinary role, this corrective task should be seen as an integral aspect of what is ultimately a positive activity, and any punishment must never become an end in itself.

This *Atzmut* ideal implies that all of life is about being open to change and advancement of the soul, as well as to engaging in a lifelong process of ongoing self-transformation. Therefore, education is synonymous with lifelong learning, with every phenomenon, whether at a certain time or in a particular place, providing opportunities for the individual to leave behind whatever self-definition existed prior to this encounter and proceed to becoming someone different. In addition, education enables the student to integrate themselves with what is being learned. Living a G-dly life becomes a real possibility when education connects people with morality based on G-d's commands.

From Concealment to Revelation

Another meta-theme that characterized R. Schneerson's teachings was expounded by the foremost expert on Habad Hasidic philosophy, Rabbi Yoel Kahan, in a lecture[4] on the topic of "The Rebbe's Unique Contribution." At the beginning of his lecture, Rabbi Kahan stated that due to time constraints, he would convey a dominant meta-theme underlying all of R. Schneerson's thinking and initiatives, rather than engaging in a time-consuming explanation of many particular innovative aspects of Schneerson's thought.

Rabbi Kahan felt that R. Schneerson's understanding of creation at the opening of the Book of Genesis best encapsulated the meta-theme that pervaded his thinking. He argued that the meta-theme was to be found in R. Schneerson's understanding[5] of the pattern of G-d's inaugural creation of light on the first day, which is accompanied by the expression "...it was good"; the subsequent separation of higher and lower dimensions on the second day, with the omission of the phrase "...it was good"; and the formation of oceans and dry land on the third day, with an accompanying double expression of "...it was good." To R. Schneerson, based on Midrashic commentary,[6] the first stage is symbolic of a state where G-d is undisputably everything. The second day's separation of higher and lower realms is representative of our world where there is a separation of spiritual and material, enabling the existence of a dimension removed from the G-dly awareness of the first day. Because this second stage is symbolic of a world that enables a person to be completely unaware of G-d, mention of the expression "...it was good" is absent.

The third day symbolizes the drawing down of the spiritual to infuse the material and the elevation of the material to spiritual purposes. The pivotal factor in this amalgamation of spiritual and material is the human being, who brings together and merges the previously distinct domains of Heaven and Earth. Precisely because the third day's separation of ocean and dry land was for the purpose of enabling our world to be an abode for human beings where the synthesis of higher and lower would be possible and where transformation of our world into a dwelling place for the G-dly can occur, it is designated as doubly good.[7]

Rabbi Kahan pointed out examples of how this became emblematic of R. Schneerson's worldview and educational agenda. R. Schneerson's insistence that newly religious professionals maintain their former profession and infuse that area with spirituality stands in sharp contrast to those who advocated a lifetime of Torah study in *yeshivah* or *kollel* (post-graduate academy for Talmudic studies for married students). His insistence was a result of a view of the physical as awaiting spiritual input such as its utilization for G-dly ends. His ideal was a world where the seven Noahide Laws permeated the way people lead their lives with G-dly ideals. R. Schneerson's focus on *Mashiach*[8] can also be related to this meta-theme as the Messianic Era is seen as a time when the physical world is repaired, thereby bringing all elements of the universe to an acknowledgment of the existence of G-d and consequently transforming the world.

Rabbi Kahan cited various *Mitzvah* campaigns that were inaugurated by R. Schneerson which supported the objectives of this meta-theme. First, the *Tzedakka* or charity campaign, where people are encouraged to contribute coins to a charitable cause on a daily basis, whereby spending money on someone other than oneself thereby transforms the ingrained habit of focusing on personal financial resources for oneself to allocating some income for a higher purpose. Second, the *Tefillin* campaign merged the above and below because securing the *tefillin* on the arm, facing the heart, and on the head unites the domains of intellect, effected by the *tefillin* that rest on the head, and emotion as achieved by the *tefillin* facing one's heart with the lower, more mundane area of action realized by the *tefillin* bound to the arm.

Thus all three dimensions combine in synchronistic harmony, paralleling R. Schneerson's meta-theme that seeks the elimination of dissonance between the soul and body, spiritual and material. In practical terms, this means that education must strive to ensure that the spiritual is experienced in the physical; therefore the highest ideals are experienced and expressed in actions and deeds that occur at the present moment and precisely in our material world.

In a personal interview with Rabbi Yoel Kahan in 2015, he confirmed the centrality of this axiom to R. Schneerson's educational philosophy. In his explanation of the subject matter referred to by Rabbi Kahan,[9] R. Schneerson argued that education transcends its narrow, legal meaning, but rather entails an underlying broadly relevant obligation and responsibility. Rabbi Kahan explained that this notion, which he considered to be a pivotal aspect of R. Schneerson's perception of the nature of education and from which many of his understandings of education were derived, was itself an outgrowth of a meta-theme that pervades R. Schneerson's thought. This meta-theme is his worldview which stressed the *nekuda ham'achedet*, or the underlying dimension or the *etzem*, meaning "the essence," rather than external symptomatic manifestations. R. Kahan cited R. Schneerson's address of *Shabbat Parashat Shelach*, 5729 [June 14th, 1969],[10] where he proposed that the human preference for the essence or one underlying explanation is inextricably linked to the Divine unity that underlies all creation. R. Kahan noted that R. Schneerson garnered support for this concept from Biblical and Talmudic law.[11]

R. Schneerson's extensive discourse on the nature of a human being's spiritual capabilities defines the nature and aims of education. These lead inexorably to a redefinition of educational responsibilities and methodologies, having further implications for what is actually taught for concrete action that supports the most exalted ideals.[12]

Through the discovery of the interconnections of the previous educational elements and having illustrated that these elements are united by related meta-themes, the presence of a coherent educational philosophy is confirmed.

R. Schneerson's Educational Philosophy That Transcends Current Educational Thinking

In the course of delineating the pivotal elements of R. Schneerson's educational philosophy, several aspects of his philosophy go beyond conventional understandings of education and its practical application. The following pages provide a sample of these as they have previously appeared through these chapters in order to emphasize their significance.

Adopting the Broadest
Understanding of Education

R. Schneerson's acceptance of the broadest account of education, while based on the writings of his predecessors, is comprehensive when viewed against the backdrop of general discussion that commonly equates education with schooling. Moreover, as this book provides an all-encompassing account of education as the premise for much of R. Schneerson's educational philosophy, particularly its practical application, it appears to be a point of departure from more conventional understandings of education. For example, the breadth of R. Schneerson's educational vision that encompasses the newborn no less than the elderly and includes educational recommendations for both age groups as well as for the various stages in between shows the extensiveness of his educational philosophy and its broad application. Similarly, R. Schneerson's belief in limitless educational opportunities is one of many consequences of his inclusive understanding of the nature of education, a position that may appear extreme in the context of those educational theorists and their works which generally restrict their focus to schooling and university study. R. Schneerson repeatedly stated that in education, no moment is too early, no detail inconsequential, no interaction incidental, and no effort ever unproductive. Similarly, no teacher is too advanced to have outgrown the responsibility of seeking a moral mentor of his or her own. Indeed, no student is too uneducated that he or she cannot be a teacher of others at some level. Clearly, R. Schneerson's broad definition of the nature of education is axiomatic to the other elements of his educational philosophy.

Belief in the Learner

R. Schneerson's belief in learner potential goes beyond the usual parameters of contemporary educational thinking. He was insistent that people who are considered society's failures are never beyond hope, and in light of this viewpoint, he argued that society has a responsibility to address and not despair of the most challenging educational circumstances. We have seen that R. Schneerson argued for an inclusive approach for those considered by many to be unworthy of investment of serious educational effort.[13] He saw education of the elderly as no less vital than providing education for the youngest age groups, and the responsibility for educational advancement of every age group as essential to their wellbeing, such as those with Down-syndrome or students who exhibit rebellious or apathetic attitudes. That no setback or challenge was too daunting in R. Schneerson's thinking reinforces his broad application and approach to education.

Special Children

R. Schneerson's encouragement of the education of special children has been shown to be particularly innovative. With respect to special education, we have encountered R. Schneerson's belief that an optimistic approach is "a pre-condition for greater success" when he argued,

> Just as the said [positive] approach is "important from the viewpoint of and for the worker and educator, so it is important that the trainees themselves should be encouraged—both by word and the manner of their training—to feel confident that they are not, G-d forbid, "cases," much less unfortunate or hopeless cases, that their difficulty is considered . . . only temporary and that with a concerted effort of instructor and trainee the desired improvement could be speeded and enhanced.[14]

While particularly concerned "to avoid impressing the child with his or her handicap," at the same time R. Schneerson cautioned that "care should be taken not to exaggerate expectations through far-fetched promises, for false hopes inevitably result in deep disenchantment, loss of credibility, and other undesirable effects."[15] R. Schneerson's approach shows his inclusive and realistic attitude to the education of learners with special needs.

Empowering the Learner

While many other educational thinkers were focused on the learner's own development and paid little attention to the need for the learner to enlighten others,[16] R. Schneerson was insistent that a crucial component of education was agency and empowerment of the learners, enabling them to become agents of change. Professor Feuerstein confirmed[17] that R. Schneerson's application of this idea to Down-syndrome children, urging that they also be empowered to assume a leadership role, was a highly innovative suggestion, particularly when viewed against the backdrop of the educational thinking of 1979.

Moreover, R. Schneerson firmly believed in empowering young children and teenagers, recommending that students be empowered with the responsibility for maintaining discipline of other students. He urged that those students themselves, though not particularly disciplined, be included in this project, recommending a rotating system, whereby everyone for a month would take responsibility for this area. This again is a radical educational principle that recognizes the worth and possible contribution of every individual.

The Privilege of Engaging in Education

One idea repeatedly and prominently emphasized in R. Schneerson's discourse is the privilege of engagement in education,[18] showing that he considered education to involve enormous advantages, even special privilege for those concerned. R. Schneerson spoke of the great merit of "illuminating hearts and homes through education"[19] and asked, "What can resemble or equal the pleasure generated Above through education?"[20] Interestingly, this element of R. Schneerson's educational philosophy differed markedly from contemporary perceptions and preoccupations. Indeed, R. Schneerson[21] would observe that theirs was the "fortunate lot"[22] and a "blessed vocation,"[23] showing his reflection on the important role of educators to impact society positively.

The Urgency for Educational Action

To R. Schneerson, education is an endeavor of foremost importance demanding immediacy of response, an activity that is to be addressed energetically due to its extraordinary urgency in our unstable world.[24] R. Schneerson argued that every day that passes without full utilization of educational opportunities represents an irretrievable loss of time to effect change for the better.[25] R. Schneerson's educational thinking was focused on action, with a Habad imperative that abstract deliberations about education should inspire tangible initiatives.[26] While educational institutions can become complacent, R. Schneerson's educational philosophy demanded that people act energetically, even passionately, in pursuit of these significant educational goals.

Education for Virtue and Altruism

The ideal of virtue accompanied by piety was seen by R. Schneerson as a highly significant aim of education, which also includes the value of modesty.[27] This principle refers not only to physical modesty in our attire but also to the ideal of intellectual humility[28] and self-discipline, whereby the learner engages in self-cultivation to curb excessive ego and takes control of any self-centered perception of the superior status of his or her intellect. If left uncontrolled, intellectual arrogance can lead the individual to determining moral issues independent of Divine imperatives.[29] Indeed, R. Schneerson reminded us that during the Holocaust, many perpetrators of heinous crimes were the bearers of formal academic degrees. Moreover, student idealism, devotion, and self-sacrifice are expectations which R. Schneerson contended should be inspired by an education that aims for virtue and piety.[30]

R. Schneerson's emphasis on virtue in education, while compatible with the twenty-first century's increased interest in values education and social or emotional learning, would want student conduct to become the central and pivotal ideal to which the education process aspires, rather than a focus solely on academic achievement. It is also consistent with all constructive approaches to education which seek to contribute to healthy interpersonal and intrapersonal functioning by students. The introduction of a "Moment of Reflection" in all schools at the start of the school day was seen by R. Schneerson as a means to attaining this goal.

R. Schneerson noted the educator's awakening in the learner an aspiration to lead a life of altruism, thereby transforming his or her fellow human being and influencing the broader society, as a vital aim of the education process. So significant is this aim that R. Schneerson viewed its fulfillment through the learner's positive impact on other learners as an indispensible prerequisite for successful education. As a corollary of this pivotal educational goal, he considered the empowering of learners to be exemplars as an important aim of education.

Education for Resilient Learners

In light of the sometimes antagonistic attitude of society to values considered vital in the Abrahamic tradition, another educational aim enunciated by R. Schneerson was that of raising a learner who is undaunted by derision and who is capable of withstanding even opposition to his or her ideals or values. The student would be an exemplar so devoted to disseminating appropriate values that he or she will be undeterred by disrespect to their treasured values.

Broad Responsibility for Education

R. Schneerson's understanding of the educator's responsibility extends that responsibility to education that takes place off the school premises and outside school hours. During the school year, when students in an educational institution apply themselves with diligence to their studies, the obligation rests on their educators to be utterly focused on them, trying with all their power to ensure that their students' conduct and lifestyle are appropriate even after they leave school for the rest of the day.[31] To R. Schneerson, it follows even more that during summer vacation, educators should take an active interest with additional vigilance about the whereabouts and activities of their individual students, assisting them to conduct themselves in a correct, upright way. The current situation means a greater responsibility for educators to extend the breadth of the curriculum to include values education, as R. Schneerson believed that it is the inculcation of ethics and morals that serves to equip children to be decent and productive citizens.

In using the horticultural metaphor, the educator, as a sensitive gardener,[32] must nurture every individual[33] because only paying attention to the collective welfare of the class as a whole is insufficient. Besides addressing the educator's responsibility for the Down-syndrome learner, R. Schneerson was also insistent that there is a parallel responsibility for individuals facing physical disability,[34] detainees of corrective institutions,[35] the elderly,[36] the disenfranchised,[37] the disadvantaged,[38] and the antagonistic.[39] Society's educational responsibility includes justice and fairness in special education; overcoming the myths of learning disabilities; developing a capability perspective on impairment, disability and special needs; nurturing gifted children; and advancing average students.

The Highest Educational Ideal

In his 1991 call[40] for an education whereby the child is a living exemplification of the Messianic ideal, completely focused on contributing to its urgent realization, R. Schneerson introduced a potent educational value whose practical outcome is that the learner must view his or her consequent conscious thought, speech, or action as a crucial factor in bringing this Messianic ideal to fruition. R. Schneerson's call is consistent with the requirement legislated by Maimonides[41] that every individual view his or her ensuing action, speech, or thought as of crucial cosmic significance in a precariously balanced universe. Viewed in an educational context, R. Schneerson's call is an innovative application of Judaism's Messianic ideal and belief in cosmic redemption to the practical living of the learner.

R. Schneerson's Educational Philosophy

This book has closely examined R. Schneerson's substantial and significant educational corpus with a view to identifying whether it represents the manifestation of a cohesive and comprehensive educational philosophy.

Specifically, three related issues have been explored, namely:

- whether a cohesive educational philosophy exists within R. Schneerson's educational corpus;
- the extent to which R. Schneerson's recommendations for educational practice and policy are an expression of such an educational philosophy; and
- how the elements of such a philosophy are inter-related in a way that establishes that they comprise a cohesive educational philosophy rather than being isolated educational thoughts.

Having disclosed a comprehensive educational philosophy within R. Schneerson's corpus, this book has presented its original contribution by making explicit the pivotal elements of that philosophy and by demonstrating that R. Schneerson's previously undiscovered coherent educational philosophy has significant implications for contemporary educational practice.

In summary, it may be argued that while R. Schneerson's educational philosophy appears to have been previously over-shadowed by his outreach achievements, this book has uncovered the underlying inspiration for these attainments, particularly in the field of education. By establishing R. Schneerson as an educational thinker of broad significance, this book has also demonstrated a dimension of his intellectual contribution which has been largely eclipsed by the success of his global educational achievements. To R. Schneerson, because education has implications for the very future of humankind, he saw it as crucial to the creation of a more spiritual human being and a better world, which "will be filled with the knowledge of G-d as the waters cover the sea" (Isaiah, 11:9).

Notes

1. "Habad in the Academy" Conference at the University of Pennsylvania, March 28th-29th, 2012.
2. Bowen and Hobson, 1974, 10-3.
3. *Midrash Tanchuma*, Nasso 16.
4. On Sunday June 29th, 2014, there took place at the Kupferberg Center for the Arts, Queens College, NY, a day of analysis of R. Schneerson's contribution led by foremost scholars and experts on R. Schneerson's teachings entitled "Soul Encounters: A Journey of Connection, Reflection, and Upliftment."
5. See *SH-5750*, II:585 and at length in *SH-5752*, II:426-39.
6. *Bereishit Rabba*, III:11-2, cited by Rashi in his commentary to *Bereishit*, 1:5.
7. Besides detecting this paradigm in the Biblical account of the first three days of creation (*SH-5750*, II:584-70; *SH-5751*, I:62*ff*), R. Schneerson identified the same paradigm as evident in the first three verses of the account of the first day of creation (*IK*, VII:5-6, Letter 1,873 [Addenda to *LS*, IV:1247

and to *LS*, II:657-8) and in other Biblical contexts (*SH-5750*, II:587*ff* and *SH-5752*, II:423*ff*).

8. In a rare autobiographical disclosure (*IK*, XII:414), R. Schneerson wrote of his childhood years that "from the time that [he] attended *Cheder*, and even prior to this, [he] had begun to envisage the Future Redemption of the Jewish People, from their final exile—a Redemption of such standing that in its context, the suffering of exile, decrees and persecutions, will be comprehensible . . ."

9. Rabbi Kahan considered *LS*, VII:151, footnote 24 to be a pivotal expression of R. Schneerson's understanding of education.

10. See *SK-5729*, II:214-20.

11. Citing Exodus, 21:35-6, R. Schneerson derived evidence from the law of the habitually goring ox whose belligerence is ascribed to one underlying inappropriate characteristic, namely, its aggression, rather than assuming that disparate reasons motivated the three events. He cited other sources from Talmudic sources (*Talmud, Sanhedrin* 99b and the Rogatchover *Gaon*'s reference to the Jerusalem Talmud) to illustrate this concept.

12. Another view of the above-mentioned meta-themes underlying R. Schneerson's approach argue that these are predicated on the hypothesis that the agenda of each of the seven *Admorim* of Habad corresponds to one of the seven Kabbalistic *sephirot* or emotional attributes that define both Divinity and the individual human being. As such, R. Schneerson's agenda as the seventh *Admor*, would correspond to *Malchut* [Sovereignty], the seventh of the *sephirot*. *Malchut* finds its expression in tangible, practical actions which bind philosophy to action. Indeed, R. Schneerson's educational philosophy is connected to tangible action such as making a child's room a *Tzivot Hashem* room and thereby a mini-sanctuary. Another attribute of *Malchut* is its expression in "multiple vessels," which explains R. Schneerson's constant outpouring of educational initiatives.

13. It was only after the successes of R. Schneerson's pioneering outreach efforts to the unaffiliated (during the 1950s, 1960s, and 1970s) became unmistakably apparent that Orthodox Jewry beyond Habad in Israel and America began to include outreach in their agenda. Prior to that time, during the 1950s and 1960s, its religious leadership had quietly ridiculed Habad outreach to the unaffiliated and particularly its initiative to ensure that Jewish students who were hippies put on *tefillin*. Thereafter, these groups began their own *yeshivot* for returnees and S.E.E.D. programs paralleling those initiated by R. Schneerson and implemented by him in the decades prior. [Interview of November 29th, 1981 with Rabbi Yosef Wineberg (1917-2012).]

14. Correspondence of August 15th, 1979, addressed to R. Wilkes, the assistant program director of the Council for Retardation at Brooklyn's Coney Island Hospital. R. Schneerson's use of the term "retardation" in his

correspondence of 1979 can be understood in light of the reality that the A.A.M.R. (The American Association on Mental Retardation), which was founded in 1876, only changed its name in 2006 to A.A.I.D.D. (the American Association on Intellectual and Developmental Disability) (whereas in Australia, from 1980, the term "retardation" was no longer used). As Professor Foreman has stated, "The USA was ahead in practice but behind in the use of terminology" (interview with Professor Phil Foreman, March 20th, 2014). See *SH-5748*, II:590, addendum to second note to footnote 10, on R. Schneerson's address of *Shabbat Parshat Ekev, Av* 23rd, 5748 [Aug. 6th, 1988] where he employed the term "special children" and explained that "special children" is not a euphemism but rather a clarification of the true nature of the spiritual mettle of these individuals.

15. He expressed confidence that "a way can surely be found to avoid raising false hopes, yet giving guarded encouragement."

16. At the time of R. Schneerson's assumption of leadership of Habad, this attitude was prevalent among Jewish educators to the point that R. Schneerson dedicated a large number of his early addresses and pastoral letters to identifying the fallacy of this approach. (See *LS*, III:880.) [Interview of November 29th, 1981 with Rabbi Yosef Wineberg.]

17. Interviews with Professor Reuven Feuerstein, January 19th and 20th, 1998, in Sydney, Australia.

18. Brod & Friedman (*eds.*), 1989, and Solomon (*trans.*), 2009.

19. *IK*, IV:93-4, Letter 841.

20. *Op. cit.*, IV:113-4, Letter 858.

21. For examples, see *IK*, XV:28-31, Letter 5,355 and *IK*, XVII:339-41, Letter 6,490.

22. *Op. cit.*, VIII:227; *op. cit.*, XIV:511-2; *op. cit.*, XIV:525-6; *op. cit.*, XX:236; *LS*, XVI:553; *op. cit.*, XXII:356; *op. cit.*, 399; *op. cit.*, XXIV:347.

23. *Op. cit.*, III:254-5, Letter 572; *op. cit.*, XXI:126-7, Letter 7,881; *op. cit.*, XXIII:357, Letter 8,962.

24. *Op. cit.*, I:38-40, Letter 22.

25. *Op. cit.*, I:110-2, Letter 65.

26. *LS*, XXIX:9-17.

27. *IK*, IV:67-8, Letter 821.

28. *TM-HIT-5711* [5711, I] II:91-2 & 94-5, §13-§14 & §17.

29. *IK*, IV:216, Letter 950.

30. *Op. cit.*, IV:14-6, Letter 780.

31. *IK*, IV:371-3, Letter 1,090.

32. *Op. cit.*, I:82-3, Letter 52.

33. *Op. cit.*, I:81-2, Letter 51.

34. *SK-5736* [1975-76], II:633-8; Address of *Av* 23rd, 5736 [August 19th, 1976]; *SH-5748* [1988], II:590 addressed to the Israeli team participating in the 1976 Paraplegic Olympics. R. Schneerson elaborated on the principle that

a physical deficiency is indicative of a greater spiritual potential, enabling the individual to more than compensate for the deficiency.

35. *SK-5736* [1975-76], I:548-9; *LS*, XXV:514-5. This letter comprised a response to several correspondents who had sought R. Schneerson's advice on how to attain peace of mind, given their incarceration. R. Schneerson's response began by pointing out that the *Chanukkah* Candelabra is lit precisely after sunset, indicative of one's ability to attain "light" even in the "darkest of situations." R. Schneerson argued that through a positive attitude, the individual can overcome the most negative external circumstances and thus transcend these external constraints.

36. Addresses of *Shabbat* of *Av* 20th and Saturday night, *Av* 21st, 5740 [August 3rd, 1980] in *SK-5740* [1979-80], III:880-903.

37. Pastoral letter of *Nissan* 11th, 5717 [May 12th, 1957] in *IK*, XV:33-7.

38. R. Schneerson's view was predicated on the Midrashic statement (*Bamidbar Rabba*, 12:3) that G-d only requires of individuals according to their abilities. From this principle, R. Schneerson argued that negative circumstances are indicative of Divine bestowing of greater latent abilities.

39. *LS*, I:128, address of the Last Day of *Pesach*, *Nissan* 22nd, 5712 [April 17th, 1952]; Letter of *Nissan* 11th, 5712 [April 6th, 1952] in *IK*, V:308-9.

40. *SH-5752* [1991-92], I:41; Address of the Eve of *Simchat Torah*, 5752 [September 20th, 1991].

41. Maimonides, *Mishneh Torah, Laws of Teshuvah*, 3:4.

GLOSSARY OF TERMS

Admor (plural, *Admorim*)   An acrostic for the initial letters of *Adoneinu Moreinu V'Rabbeinu,* meaning "our master, teacher, and Rabbi." This is the term or title (mostly used in indirect speech) when referring to a Hasidic master or spiritual guide with a Hasidic following. See *Rebbe.*

Aggadah (adjective, *Aggadic*) Homiletic sections of the Talmud.

Ahavat Israel   Literally "love of one's fellow Israelite."

Aleph   First letter of the Hebrew alphabet.

Amidah   The standing, silent prayer which is of central importance in all Jewish prayers.

Anochi   "I"—first word of the Ten Commandments, Exodus, 20:2.

Atzmut   The Divine Essence.

Avodah   Literally "work" or "service"—Divine service through prayer and self-refinement.

Avot   Literally "fathers"—a reference to *Pirkei Avot* [*Ethics of the Fathers*].

Baal Shem Tov   Literally "Master of the Good Name"—R. Israel Baal Shem Tov, founder of Hasidism, also referred to in non-Hasidic circles by the abbreviation of *The Besht.*

Baal Teshuvah   Returnee to Jewish religious observance.
  (plural, *Baalei Teshuvah*)

Bar Mitzvah   Literally "son of a *Mitzvah*"—a male over the age of thirteen years, fully obligated in the fulfillment of the *Mitzvot.*

Bat Mitzvah   Literally "daughter of a *Mitzvah*"—a female over the age of twelve years, fully obligated in the fulfillment of the *Mitzvot.*

Beit   Second letter of the Hebrew alphabet.

Bittul   Self-abnegation or intellectual humility.

Chafetz Chayim   Literally "desiring life"—R. Israel Meir Kagan (1839-1933), named after his *magnum opus* of the same name.

Chanukkah   The Festival of Lights.

Chassidut   See *Hasidut.*

Cheder (plural, *Chadarim*)	Torah school for young children.
Chiddush (plural, *Chiddushim*)	Renewal or innovation.
Chinuch	Jewish religious education.
Chinuch Al Taharat HaKodesh	Authentic religious education.
Chochma	Wisdom—seminal thought or an intuitive flash of intellectual realization.
Daat	Knowledge; the conclusive aspect of the intellectual process.
Erev	Literally "the eve of"—the day prior to.
Ethics of the Fathers	One of the sixty-three tractates of the *Mishnah*, compiled in the Holy Land at the end of the second century CE, by Rabbi Judah the Prince. It details the Torah's views on ethics and interpersonal relationships. A sixth chapter was appended to *Ethics of the Fathers* so that one chapter could be studied on each of the six Sabbaths between *Passover* and *Shavuot*.
Farbrengen	An intimate gathering of Hasidim to discuss Hasidic philosophy, recount tales of *Admorim* and distinguished Hasidic personages, as well as to provide the opportunity to give one another moral exhortation where a Hasidic elder would often preside; a special occasion where the *Admor* would deliver a *ma'amar* often accompanied by *sichot* to his adherents. In the case of R. Schneerson, the *farbrengen* was a gathering attended by thousands, with weekday *farbrengens* transmitted worldwide.
Habad	Acronym for the initials of the three Hebrew words, *Hochmah, Binah,* and *Daat,* which refer to the three basic elements upon which the philosophy of Habad is founded, namely "wisdom," "understanding," and "knowledge."
Hadracha	Literally "guidance."
Haggadah	Text recited on the first two evenings of *Passover* at the *Seder* service.
Halacha (adjective, *Halachic*) (plural, *Halachot*)	Literally "the way"—Jewish Law.
Hasid	Adherent of the movement founded by BST.
Hasidut	Movement founded in the eighteenth century by BST; the philosophy and literature of this movement.

Haskalah	The "Enlightenment" Movement which began within Jewish society in the 1770s and which advocated assimilation and emancipation.
HaYom Yom	*From Day to Day*—R. Schneerson's collection of Habad aphorisms anthologized from the writings of RJIS.
Hitbonnenut	Contemplation.
Hochmah	See *Chochma.*
Hora'ah	Teaching, guidance, or instruction.
Igrot Kodesh	Thirty-two volumes of R. Schneerson's published Hebrew and Yiddish personal correspondence.
Kabbalah	Literally "received tradition"—the corpus of classical Jewish mystical teachings.
Kabbalist	Exponent of Kabbalah.
Kabbalistic	Pertaining to the Kabbalah.
Kabbalat Ol	Literally "acceptance of the yoke"—subordination to the Will of G-d.
Kashrut	Status whereby an item is considered to be *kosher.*
Kedusha	Sanctity.
Kfar Chabad	Official weekly Hebrew language journal of the Lubavitch Youth Organization, Israel.
Kfar Habad	Literally "Village of Habad"—a village founded by RJIS near Tzafaria, Israel.
Kohen	An Israelite priest.
Kollel (plural, *Kollelim*)	Post-graduate academy for Talmudic studies for married students.
Kosher	Fit for ritual use.
Likkut	An edited, highly structured essay based on R. Schneerson's address, but organized in a sequential manner.
Likkutei Amarim	RSZ's classic work, which encapsulates the principal doctrines of Habad thought. Also known by the first word of the work, *Tanya.*
Likkutei Sichot	Literally "A Collection of Addresses"—thirty-nine volumes of R. Schneerson's edited addresses, or *sichot,* delivered mainly at Hasidic gatherings.
Lubavitch	Literally "town of love"—Russian townlet in Belorussia, which was the center of Habad Hasidism from 1813 when R. Dovber Schneuri moved there from Liadi, until 1915 when RSB left it for Rostov; the name of this town has become synonymous with the term "Habad," to identify this particular branch of Hasidism.
Lubavitcher Rebbe	*Admor* of the Habad school of Hasidism.
Ma'amar (plural, *Ma'amarim*)	A formal dissertation of Habad philosophy by an *Admor.*

Ma'amarim Melukat	Six volumes of R. Schneerson's edited *ma'amarim.*
Maggid	Preacher.
Mashiach	The Messiah.
Mashpi'a (plural, *Mashpi'im*)	A mentor for spiritual matters; this is a specific educational position in Habad educational institutions.
Maskil (plural, *Maskilim*)	Exponent of the theoretical dimension of Habad philosophy.
Mechilta	Commentary on the Books of Exodus, Leviticus, Numbers, and Deuteronomy, authored by second-century Mishnaic authority R. Yishmael.
Melamed	A teacher of small children.
Menachem-Av	Literally "comforting father"—the month of the year in which there takes place the commemoration of the destruction of the Jerusalem temples.
Menorah	Candelabra.
Merkos L'Inyonei Chinuch	Literally "The Central [Committee] for Jewish Education"—Habad's educational organization over which R. Schneerson presided. Founded in 1941 by RJIS.
Mesibat Shabbat	Sabbath afternoon gatherings for children.
MeSichot	Literally "from the *sichot*"—edited transcripts of R. Schneerson's central Sabbath addresses, delivered between 1987 and 1992.
Mesirat nefesh	Self-sacrifice.
Metzuyan (plural, *Metzuyanim*)	Literally "an outstanding individual"—a term applied by R. Schneerson to individuals with a physical handicap.
Mezuza (plural, *Mezuzot*)	Parchment attached to doorways in the Jewish home.
Midrash (plural, *Midrashim*) (adjective, Midrashic)	A classical collection of Rabbinical homiletical teachings on the Torah.
Mishnah (adjective, Mishnaic)	A collection of paragraphs containing seminal statements of Rabbinic law. The *Mishnah*, together with its commentary (*Gemara*), constitutes the Talmud.
Mishneh Torah	*Magnum opus* by twelfth-century Rabbinic authority, codifier, philosopher, and physician R. Moses Maimonides (1135-1204).
Mitzva (plural, *Mitzvot*)	A religious obligation; one of the 613 Torah commandments.
M'kabel	Recipient of the *Mashpia's* influence.
Modeh Ani	Literally "I thank [You]..."—opening phrase of the first prayer recited upon rising in the morning.
Ner	A candle.
Niggun	Hasidic melody.

Nissan	Month of the year in which *Passover* falls.
Noahide Laws	According to Jewish tradition, seven commandments were given to humanity by G-d, as recorded in the Old Testament. The seven comprise prohibitions against idolatry, murder, robbery, adultery, blasphemy, and greed, as well as the positive order to establish courts of justice.
Ohr	Light.
Oonzer Kinder	Literally "our own children."
Oved (plural, *Ovdim*)	One who toils in the labor of self-refinement.
Parasha	Torah portion of the *Parshat Toldot*.
Pardes	Literally "an orchard"—a reference to levels of Torah interpretation ranging from the literal to the most esoteric.
Passover	Seven-day festival beginning on the 15th day of *Nissan*, commemorating the exodus from Egypt.
Pikuach Nefesh	The saving of human life.
Pilpul	Talmudic dialectics.
Pirkei Avot	Literally "Chapters of the Fathers"—a reference to the section of the *Mishnah* commonly known as *Ethics of the Fathers*.
Rashi	R. Shlomo Yitzchaki (1040-1105), leading commentator of Bible and Talmud.
Rayatz	Hebrew abbreviation for the name of RJIS.
Rebbe (plural, *Rebbe'im*)	A Yiddish term for a spiritual guide with a Hasidic following (derived from the Hebrew word *Rabi*, meaning "my teacher" or "my master"); alternative term for *Admor*.
Rebbitzen	Wife of a rabbi.
Reshimot	R. Schneerson's unedited, scholarly private notes.
Rosh Chodesh	First day of every Hebrew month (in some months also including the last day of the previous month).
Rosh HaShana	The Jewish New Year (literally "Head of the Year").
Seder	Literally "order"—family service held at home on the first two nights of *Passover*, to commemorate the exodus from Egypt.
Sefer HaMitzvot	Literally "The Book of the Commandments"—Maimonides' codification of the 613 Laws of the Torah.
Shabbat	The Jewish Sabbath.
Shaliach (plural, *Shluchim*)	Emissary of an *Admor*.
Shavuot	Literally "Weeks"—festival commemorating Sinaic revelation, see Leviticus, 23:9-22.
Shechina	The Divine Presence.
Shema	The daily declaration of G-d's unity.

Shlichut	Serving as an emissary for an *Admor* in an educational or religious outreach capacity.
Shlucha (plural, *Shluchot*)	Female emissary of an *Admor*.
Shofar	Ram's horn sounded on *Rosh HaShana*.
Shulchan Aruch	The Code of Jewish Law.
Sicha (plural, *Sichot*)	A talk by an *Admor*, less formal than a *ma'amar*.
Sichot Kodesh	Fifty volumes of unedited transcripts of R. Schneerson's addresses.
Siddur	Literally "order"—Prayer Book.
Simchat Torah	Festival of the Rejoicing of the Law immediately following *Sukkot*. This festival commemorates the conclusion and immediate recommencement of the annual Torah reading.
Siyum (plural, *Siyumim*)	Completion of the study of a Talmudic tractate.
Smicha	Rabbinical ordination.
Sofer	Religious scribe.
Sukkot	The Festival of Tabernacles.
Talmud	Compilation of Jewish law and Biblical exegesis.
(adjective, *Talmudic*)	Compilation of the Babylonian version was completed at the end of the fifth century. The Jerusalem Talmud was compiled in Israel at the end of the fourth century.
Talmud Torah	Literally "the study of Torah"—the term also applied to after-school religious instruction.
Tamim (plural, *Temimim*)	A student of Tomchei Temimim.
Tanya	See *Likutei Amarim*.
Targum	Interpretive Aramaic translation of the Pentateuch.
Tefilla	Prayer.
Tefillin	Black leather boxes containing small scrolls on which are written pivotal Biblical passages. These are placed on the arm and the forehead and worn daily by Jewish males over the age of thirteen.
Teshuvah	Literally "return"—the desire to change one's life and return to religious observance.
Tishrei	The month of the Jewish High Holy Days.
Tofe'ach Al M'nas L'Hatfiach	Saturation to the point whereby an item dampens other items with which it comes in contact.
Tomchei Temimim	Habad *Yeshivah* founded by RSB in 1897.
Torah	Literally "teaching"—the Pentateuch or five books of Moses. In its wider sense, this term refers to all Rabbinic commentary and law, based on the Old Testament, including contemporary exegesis.

Tzaddik (plural, *Tzaddikim*)	A totally righteous person; the leader of a Hasidic group.
Tzavta	To coalesce or to attach.
Tzedakah	Appropriation of a portion of one's wealth to the needy.
Tzemach Tzedek	Literally "The Flourishing of Righteousness"—title of the *magnum opus* of the third *Admor* of Habad.
Tzivot Hashem	Literally "The Army of Hashem"—a worldwide informal educational initiative for children under the age of *Bar-* and *Bat-Mitzvah.*
Yechidut	Intimate meeting of an instructional or inspirational nature between the *Admor* and his adherent in the *Admor's* private study, often, but not always taking place prior to a significant event in the lifetime of the adherent, such as birthdays, *Bar Mitzvah,* or weddings, or prior to taking up a communal position of significant duration, which would involve geographical isolation from the *Admor.*
Yeshivah (plural, *Yeshivot*)	Talmudic academy.
Yetzer hara	The inclination to act contrary to Divinity.
Yetzer Tov	The good inclination.
Yiddish	Language of Eastern European Jewry.
Yiddishe Heim	Literally "The Jewish Home"—quarterly journal of the Lubavitch Women's Organization.
Yiddishkeit	Judaism.
Yirat Shamayim	Piety or religious devotion [lit. "fear of Heaven"].
Zohar	Literally "radiance"—the central work of Jewish mystical teaching, organized as a commentary to the Torah.

REFERENCES CITED

Interviews and Lectures

Rabbi Mendel Feldman—Interview of 2007.

Professor Reuven Feuerstein—Interviews of January 19th & 20th, 1998.

Professor Phil. Foreman—Interview of March 20th, 2014.

Rabbi Moshe Pesach Goldman—Interviews between 2010 and 2014.

Rabbi Yitzchak D. Groner—Interview of June 30th, 1996.

Rabbi Yossi Jacobson—Lecture of July 11th, 2002 to the Habad fraternity of Sydney, Australia.

Rabbi Simon Jacobson—Lecture of September 21st, 2014 to the Habad House of Double Bay, Sydney, Australia.

Rabbi Yoel Kahan—Interview of Oct. 14th, 2015.

———— Lecture of June 29th, 2014 entitled "The Rebbe's Unique Contribution" delivered at "Soul Encounters: A Journey of Connection, Reflection and Upliftment" held at the Kupferberg Center for the Arts, Queens College, NY.

Rabbi Shalom Dovber Levin—Multiple interviews during 1995.

Professor Ramon Lewis—Interview of December 2006.

Rabbi Naftali Roth—Interviews of December 16th & 19th, 2011 during his visit to Sydney, Australia.

Chief Rabbi Jonathan Sacks—Lecture of Sept. 11th, 1994 entitled "Lubavitcher Rebbe Memorial Lecture" (London).

Professor Lawrence Schiffman—Lecture of June 29th, 2014 entitled "The Rebbe in the Jewish Hall of Fame: The Rebbe on the Backdrop of History's Greatest Scholars" delivered at "Soul Encounters: A Journey of Connection, Reflection and Upliftment" held at the Kupferberg Center for the Arts, Queens College, NY.

Rabbi Michoel Seligson—Interview of November, 1996.

Rabbi Elkana Shmotkin—Interview of February, 2000.

Rabbi Adin (Even-Yisrael) Steinsaltz—Interview by Mrs. B. Olidort
during the plenary session of "Soul Encounters: A Journey of
Connection, Reflection and Upliftment" held at the Kupferberg
Center for the Arts, Queens College, NY on June 29th, 2014.
Rabbi Yosef Wineberg—Interviews of Nov. 29th, 1991 & June 19th, 1996.
Rabbi Aaron Mordechai Zilberstrom—Interview of June 19th, 2006.

Works by Rabbi Schneerson's Predecessors

Rabbi Israel Baal Shem Tov

1981   Kaplan, A. L. *et al.* (*eds.*) *Torot U'Pitgamei HaBaal Shem Tov.*
(Published as Addenda to BST 2004) Kehot Publication Society,
Brooklyn, NY.

2004   *Keter Shemtov HaShalem.* (Re-edited by Rabbi J. Immanual
Schochet) Kehot Publication Society, Brooklyn, NY.

The Maggid of Mezeritch

2009   *Maggid D'varav L'Yaakov—Likutei Amarim* (Re-edited by Rabbi
J. Immanual Schochet) Kehot Publication Society, Brooklyn, NY.

(RSZ) Rabbi Schneur Zalman of Liadi

1900   *Likkutei Amarim-Tanya.* Vilna.

1968   *Hilchot Talmud Torah.* Kehot Publication Society, Brooklyn, NY.
(Reprint from Shklov 1794.)

1968   *Shulchan Aruch.* Kfar Habad. (Reprint from Kopys and Shklov
1814.)

1972   *Likkutei Torah.* Brooklyn, NY. (Reprint from Zhitomir 1848).

1972   *Torah Ohr.* Brooklyn, NY. (Reprint from Kopys 1837, and Lem-
berg 1851.)

2008-2017   *Likkutei Amarim-Tanya* (5 vols.) *Perakim 1-34 Im Pirush
Chasidut Mevu'eret.* Heichal Menachem, Brooklyn, NY.

(RSB) Rabbi Shalom Dovber Schneersohn

1986   *Torat Shalom:Sefer HaSichot.* (4th edition) Kehot Publication Society, Brooklyn, NY.

(RJIS) Rabbi Yosef Yitzchak (Joseph Isaac) Schneersohn

1957   *Ma'amar Klalei HaChinuch V'Hadracha. Kuntres Chai Ellul 5703*: 52-70. Kehot Publication Society, Brooklyn, NY. (Reprint from Brooklyn 1944 edition).

1980   *Likkutei Dibburim.* (Vols. 1-4, 5th edition) Kehot Publication Society, Brooklyn, NY.

1982-2014   *Igrot Kodesh—RJIS.* (Vols. 1-16) Kehot Publication Society, Brooklyn, NY.

1986   *Sefer HaSichot.* Kehot Publication Society, Brooklyn, NY.

1986-2018   *Sefer HaMa'amarim 5680-5711* [1919-1951]. (21 vols.) Kehot Publication Society, Brooklyn, NY.

1995   *Sefer HaSichot 5680-5711* (1919-1951). Kehot Publication Society, Brooklyn, NY.

1987-2012   Kaploun, U. *(Trans.) Likkutei Dibburim—An Anthology of Talks by Rabbi Yosef Yitzchak Schneersohn of Lubavitch.* (6 vols.) Kehot Publication Society, Brooklyn, NY.

1990   Danzinger, Y. E. *(Trans.) The Principles of Education and Guidance.* Kehot Publication Society, Brooklyn, NY.

Edited Primary Sources by Rabbi Menachem Mendel Schneerson (Hebrew/Yiddish)

1962-2001   *Likkutei Sichot Al Parshiyot HaShavuah, Chagim U'Moadim.* (39 vols.) Kehot Publication Society, Brooklyn, NY.

1977   *Kuntres Inyana Shel Torat HaChasidut Me'et Kvod Kedushat Admor Shlita Schneerson MiLubavitch.* (3rd ed., with addenda) Kehot Publication Society, Brooklyn, NY.

1987   *Haggada Shel Pesach Im Likkutei Ta'amim, Minhagim U'Biurim.* (19th expanded ed.) Kehot Publication Society, Brooklyn, NY.

1987-1992   *Sefer Ha'Ma'amarim—Meluket.* (6 vols., comprising 200 discourses, 2nd ed.) Kehot Publication Society, Brooklyn, NY.

1987-2009   *Igrot Kodesh*. Vols. 1-32. Kehot Publication Society, Brooklyn, NY.

1989-1993   *Sefer HaSichot 5747-5752/1986-1992*. (12 vols.) Kehot Publication Society, Brooklyn, NY.

1992   *Torat Menachem—Igrot Melech, Michtavim Klali'im L'Moadei HaShana* (Vols. 1 and 2) [Anthology of 182 pastoral letters penned by R. Schneerson between 1951 and 1992]. Kehot Publication Society, Brooklyn, NY.

2005   *HaYom Yom—From Day to Day, An Anthology of Aphorisms and Customs, Arranged According to the Days of the Year, Assembled from the Talks and Letters of Admor Rabbi Joseph Isaac Schneersohn of Lubavitch* (Rabbi Menachem M. Schneerson's collection of Hasidic aphorisms anthologized from the writings of *RJIS*). Kehot Publication Society, Brooklyn, NY.

Edited English-Language Primary Sources by Rabbi Menachem M. Schneerson

1979   *Letters by the Lubavitcher Rebbe*. Kehot Publication Society, Brooklyn, NY.

1981   *Letters by the Lubavitcher Rebbe to N'shei U'Bnos Chabad 1956-1978*. Kehot Publication Society, Brooklyn, NY.

1998-2005   *Letters from the Rebbe* (6 vols.) Otzar Sifrei Lubavitch, Brooklyn, NY.

1998-2018   *The Letter and the Spirit: Letters by the Lubavitcher Rebbe Selected and Arranged by His Personal Secretary Rabbi Dr. Nissan Mindel OBM.* (4 vols.) Nissan Mindel Publications, Brooklyn, NY.

Unedited Primary Sources by Rabbi Menachem M. Schneerson (Hebrew/Yiddish Transcripts)

1951-1981   *Sichot Kodesh—(transcripts)*. (41 vols.) Vaad Hanachot Temimim, Brooklyn, NY.

1981-1992   *Torat Menachem—Hitva'aduyot 5742-5752/1981-1992.* (43 vols.) Lahak Hanachot, Brooklyn, NY.

1992-2018   *Torat Menachem—Hitva'aduyot 5710-5731/1950-1971.* (Vols. 1-63.) Lahak Hanachot, Brooklyn, NY.

1994-1997   *Reshimot Kvod Kedushat Admor Menachem Mendel Schneerson MiLubavitch.* (6 vols.) Kehot Publication Society, Brooklyn, NY.

English Translations of Rabbi Menachem Mendel Schneerson's Primary Sources

1978   Greenberg, H. & Handelman, S. S. (*Trans.*) *On the Essence of Chassidus.* Kehot Publication Society, Brooklyn, NY.

1980-1992   Schochet, J. I. (*Trans.*) *Likkutei Sichot—An Anthology of Talks Relating to the Weekly Sections of the Torah and Special Occasions in the Jewish Calendar, by the Lubavitcher Rebbe, Rabbi Menachem M. Schneerson.* (5 vols.) Kehot Publication Society, Brooklyn, NY.

1980-1994   *Sichot in English.* (*Multiple translators.*) (51 vols.) Sichot in English, Brooklyn, NY.

1986   Sacks, J. (*Trans.*) *Torah Studies—Based on Excerpts of Talks by the Lubavitcher Rebbe, Rabbi Menachem Mendel Schneerson.* Lubavitch Foundation, London.

1988-1997   Tauber, Y. (*Trans.*) *The Week in Review on Jewish Thought and Its Contemporary Applications—From the Works and Talks of the Lubavitcher Rebbe Shlita.* Vad Hanochos HaTemimim, New York.

1990-1996   Wineberg, S. B. (*Trans.*) *The Chassidic Dimension—Interpretations of the Weekly Torah Readings and Festivals, Based on the Talks of the Lubavitcher Rebbe.* (3 vols.) Kehot Publication Society, Brooklyn, NY.

1993   Kaploun, U. (*Trans.*) *Proceeding Together: The Earliest Talks of the Lubavitcher Rebbe, Rabbi Menachem M. Schneerson.* (4 vols.) Sichot in English, Brooklyn, NY.

1999-2011   E. Tauger (*Trans.*) *I Will Write It in Their Hearts: A Treasury of Letters from the Lubavitcher Rebbe Rabbi Menachem M. Schneerson—Selections from Igros Kodesh.* Sichot in English, Brooklyn, NY.

Secondary References

Althaus, P. T. (*ed.*)

   1999 *Ben Yud-Gimmel L'Mitzvot: Bar-Mitzvah B'Or Chasidut Chabad V'Hadrachoteha* ["At Thirteen—(The Obligation to Observe) the Mizvot"]: *Bar-Mitzvah* in Light of Habad Hasidism and Its Directives"]. Machon Lubavitch, Lubavitch Youth Organization, Israel.

Anonymous Editor

   1972 *Igrot Kodesh—Kovetz 2: Inyanei Chinuch 5732. Tzeirei Agudat Chabad.* Kfar Habad, Israel.

Archambault, R. D. (*ed.*)

   1964 *John Dewey on Education: Selected Writings.* The Modern Library, Random House, NY.

   1965 *Philosophical Analysis and Education.* The Humanities Press, Inc., New York.

Bagnall, D.

   1994 "A Prophet Is Lost—Testing Times for Jewry's Messianic Movement." *The Bulletin,* July 5, 26.

Barrow, R.

   1994 "Analytic Philosophy." In *The International Encyclopedia of Education,* Husen, T. and Postlethwaite, T. N. (editors-in-chief). Pergamon, New York.

Barrow, R. & Woods, R. G.

   1975 *An Introduction to the Philosophy of Education.* Methuen, London & NY.

Belcove-Shalin, J. S.

   1995 *New World Hasidism: Ethnographic Studies of Hasidic Jews in America.* State University of New York Press, Albany.

Black, H. C.

   1954 "Practical Implications of a Philosophy of Education." *Educational Philosophy* 4, no. 4 (Oct.): 263-8.

Blau, T. (*ed.*)

   1991 *Klalei Rashi B'Pirusho Al HaTorah Al Pi Sichot Kvod Kedushat Admor Shlita MiLubavitch* (2 vols., 2nd edition). Kehot Publication Society, Israel.

Block, Y.

    2010   "Who Knows One—1961," *Living Torah*, Disc 80, Program 319. Jewish Educational Media, Brooklyn, NY.

Boteach, S.

    2002   *Judaism for Everyone: Renewing Your Life Through the Vibrant Lessons of Jewish Faith*. Basic Books, New York.

Bowen, J.

    1972   *A History of Western Education*. (Vol. 1.) *The Ancient World: Orient and Mediterranean*. Methuen, London.

Bowen, J. & Hobson, P. R.

    1974   *Theories of Education: Studies in Significant Innovation in Western Educational Thought*. John Wiley & Sons, Australasia.

Brickman, W. W.

    1999   "Historical Background." In A. B. Metzger's *The Heroic Struggle: The Arrest and Liberation of Rabbi Joseph Y. Schneersohn of Lubavitch in Soviet Russia*. Kehot Publication Society, Brooklyn, NY.

Brod, M. M. & Friedman, A. E. (*eds.*)

    1989   *HaMechanech: HaShlichut HaChinuchit L'Or Sichot U'Michtevei Kvod Kedushat Admor Shlita MiLubavitch* [The Educator: The Educational Assignment in the Light of the Addresses and Correspondence of the Lubavitcher Rebbe]. Machon Lubavitch, Kfar Habad, Israel.

Burbules, N. C.

    2000   "Philosophy of Education." In Moon, B., Ben-Peretz, M. & Brown, S., (*eds.*), *Routledge International Companion to Education*. Routledge, New York.

Bush, G.

    1989 & 1990   *Proclamation by the President of the United States of America Concerning Education Day USA, 1989 and 1990*. (Shemtov, L., ed., 1996.) American Friends of Lubavitch, Washington, DC.

Chazan, B. & Wexler, P.

    2012   "A Proposal: A New Conversation." Initial Conception of the "Chabad and the Academy" Conference held at the University of Pennsylvania in March 2012. Proposal electronically circulated to lecturers at the conference.

Clinton, B.

  1994   Letter of Condolence of June 12th, 1994, addressed to the Movement of Lubavitch and World Jewry. *Chabad Magazine.* June, 33.

  1995   Address of September 12th, 1995. (Shemtov, L., ed., 1996). American Friends of Lubavitch, Washington, DC.

Cohen, S. Y. (*ed.*)

  1975   *Likutei Hanhagot V'Halachot B'Chinuch Al Taharat HaKodesh.* Privately printed, Kiryat Malachi, Israel.

Cohen, Y.

  2001   *HaChinuch B'Mishnato Shel HaRabi: K'ta'ey Sichot, Michtavim, Yechiduyot U'Maynot Kodesh B'Inyanei Chinuch* [Education in the Teachings of the Rebbe: Excerpts of Addresses, Letters, Private Audiences, and Responsa Concerning Matters of Education.] Ufaratzta Publishing, Kfar Habad, Israel.

Cole, P. R.

  1931   *A History of Educational Thought.* Oxford University Press, London, Humphrey Milford.

Cowen, S.

  2014   "An Education in Shared Ethic: Common Values of Judaism, Christianity and Islam." In *Contemporary Politics and Social Policy through the Lens of Traditional Faith and Universal Ethics.* The Institute for Judaism and Civilization, Melbourne.

  2015   *The Philosophy and Practice of Universal Ethics: The Noahide Laws.* The Institute for Judaism and Civilization, Melbourne.

Craig, E. (*ed.*)

  2012   *Routledge Encyclopedia of Philosophy.* Routledge, London. Retrieved March 1, 2012, from http://www.rep.routledge.com/article/N015

Cunin, S. (*ed.*)

  1973   *Chabad Lubavitch Chassidism Today: A Pictorial Review of Vibrant Dynamic Judaism in Action.* Chabad-Lubavitch of California, Los Angeles.

Curren, R. (*ed.*)

  2003   *A Companion to the Philosophy of Education.* Blackwell, Malden, MA.

  2007   *Philosophy of Education: An Anthology.* Blackwell, Malden, MA.

2012 "Philosophy of Education." In E. Craig (*ed.*), *Routledge Encyclopedia of Philosophy*. London: Routledge. Retrieved March 01, 2012, from http://www.rep.routledge.com/article/N015.

D'Amato, A.

1994 Letter of Condolence. *Chabad Magazine* 1(4): 34.

Danzger, M. H.

1989 *Returning to Tradition—The Contemporary Revival of Orthodox Judaism.* Yale University Press, New Haven, CT.

Davidman, L.

1991 *Tradition in a Rootless World: Women Turn to Orthodox Judaism.* University of California Press, Berkeley.

Dennison, P. & G.

1985 *Personalized Whole Brain Integration.* Edu-Kinesthetics, Ventura, CA.

Dewey, J. D.

1934 "The Need for a Philosophy of Education." In R. D. Archambault (*ed.*), *John Dewey on Education: Selected Writings.* (1964). The Modern Library, Random House, New York.

Edel, A.

1956 "What Should Be the Aim and Content of a Philosophy of Education?" *Harvard Education Review* 26 (Spring): 119-26. Reprinted in C. J. Lucas (*ed.*) (1969:140-7).

Elias, M. E. & Arnold, H. (*eds.*)

2006 *The Educator's Guide to Emotional Intelligence and Academic Achievement: Social-Emotional Learning in the Classroom.* Corwin Press, Thousand Oaks, CA.

Einbender, M.

2014 "My Personal Emissary: Rabbi Mordechai Einbender." *Here's My Story.* July 5th, 2014. Jewish Educational Media, Brooklyn, NY.

Eliezrie, D.

2015 *The Secret of Chabad: Inside the World's Most Successful Jewish Movement.* Toby Press, New Milford, CT.

Fishkoff, S.

2003 *The Rebbe's Army: Inside the World of Chabad-Lubavitch.* Schocken Books, NY.

Ford, G.
  1975   Letter of January 17, 1975, cited in D. Zaklikowsky (*ed.*). *The Rebbe and President Ford.* http://www.chabad.org/therebbe/article_cdo/aid/461848/jewish/The-Rebbe-and-President-Ford.htm
Foreman, P.
  2009   *Education of Children with an Intellectual Disability: Research and Practice.* Information Age Publishing, Charlotte, NC.
Foreman, P. (*ed.*)
  2011   *Inclusion in Action.* Cengage Learning, Australia.
Freidman, A. E. (*ed.*)
  1982   *Biurim Al Pirkei Avot.* Kehot Publication Society, Brooklyn, NY.
Froebel, F.
  1826   *On the Education of Man.* Vienna.
Gardner, H.
  1983   *Frames of Mind: The Theory of Multiple Intelligences.* Basic Books, New York.
Giuliani, R.
  1994   Letter of Condolence. *Chabad Magazine* 34.
Glitzenstein, A. Ch. & Steinsaltz, A. (*eds.*),
  1980   *The Rebbe: Thirty Years of Leadership.* Vol. 1. The Commmittee for Publishing the 30-Year Jubilee Book, Kfar Habad, Israel.
Goldberg, H.
  1989   *Between Berlin and Slobodka: Jewish Transition Figures in Eastern Europe.* Ktav Publishing House, Hoboken, NJ.
Greenberg, Y. Y. & Zaklikowski, E. Y. (*eds.*)
  1993   *Yemei Breishit Yoman MiTkufat Kabalat HaNesiut Shel Kvod Kedushat Admor Shlita BeShanim 5710-5711 Al Pi Yomanim, Mikhtavim V'Zikhronot SheBichtav U'Baal Peh.* Kehot Publication Society, Brooklyn, NY.
Greene, V.
  2009   *Un-Expert Advice*, Living Torah, Disc 65, Program 258. Jewish Educational Media, Brooklyn, NY.
  2010   *One Little Apostrophe.* Living Torah, Disc 73, Program 289. Jewish Educational Media, Brooklyn, NY.
Gurewicz, S.
  2015   *Mr. G.—A Memoir.* The Lamm Jewish Library of Australia, Melbourne.

Haldane, J. (*ed.*).

2004 *Values, Education and the Human World.* Centre for Ethics, Philosophy and Public Affairs. The University of St. Andrews Press, Great Britain.

Handelman, S.

1995 "A Man Apart: The Legacy of the Lubavitcher Rebbe." *Crosscurrents: Religion and Intellectual Life* (Summer): 234-40.

2008 *Choosing a Thesis.* Living Torah, Disc 57, Program 226. Jewish Educational Media, Brooklyn, NY.

Hartman, Y.

1984 *HaChinuch B'Mishnat Chabad—M'vusas U'M'lukat MeSichot Kvod Kedushat Admor MiLubavitch* [Education in the Teachings of Habad: Anthologized from the Addresses of the Lubavitcher Rebbe]. Reshet Chinuch Chabad—Oholai Yosef Yitzchak, Kfar Chabad, Israel.

2007 *Keitzad Nchanech Et Yaldeinu* [How Shall We Educate Our Children?] (2 vols.) Reshet Chinuch Chabad—Oholai Yosef Yitzchak, Kfar Chabad, Israel.

Havlin, Y. Y. (*ed.*)

2007 *Sha'arei Chinuch: Bi'urim, Ha'arot V'Hadrachot B'Inyanei Chinuch* [The Portals of Education: Explanations, Elucidations, and Directives in Matters Pertaining to Education]. Kehot Publication Society, Machon Heichal Menachem, Jerusalem, Israel.

Hirst, P. H. (*ed.*)

1983 *Educational Philosophy and Its Foundation Disciplines.* Routledge & Kegan Paul, London.

Hirst, P. H. and Peters, R. S.

1970 *The Logic of Education.* Routledge & Kegan Paul, UK.

Hoffman, E.

1991 *Against All Odds—The Story of Lubavitch.* Simon & Schuster, New York.

Horne, H. H.

1932 *The Democratic Philosophy of Education; Companion to Dewey's "Democracy and Education"; Exposition and Comment.* Macmillan, New York.

Husen, T. and Postlethwaite, T. N. (editors-in-chief)

1994   *The International Encyclopedia of Education.* (8 vols.) Pergamon, New York.

Jacobs, L.

1972   *Hasidic Prayer.* Valentine, Mitchell & Co., London.

Kahan, Y.

1993   "Hakol Novei 'a MiNekuda Achat." *Kfar Habad Magazine,* 500: 33-8.

Kaploun, E.

2014   *Takanot HaRabbi* [The Rebbe's Directives]. Sifriyat Eshel, Kfar Chabad, Israel.

Kaploun, U.

1987   *Glossary to Likkutei Dibburim—An Anthology of Talks by Rabbi Yosef Yitzchak Schneersohn of Lubavitch,* 1:323-40. Kehot Publication Society, Brooklyn, NY.

Kaufman, D. R.

1991   *Rachel's Daughters: Newly Orthodox Jewish Women.* Rutgers University Press, New Brunswick, NJ.

Kessa, Y.

2007   *A Childhood Neighbor of the Rebbe Remembers.* Living Torah, Disc 34, Program 134. Jewish Educational Media, Brooklyn, NY.

Kilpatrick, W. H.

1924   "Tendencies in Educational Philosophy." In I. L. Kandel (*ed.*), *Twenty-Five Years of American Education.* Macmillan, New York.

Kleinberger, A. P.

1962   *HaMachshava HaPedagogit Shel HaMaharal MiPrague.* Magnus Press, The Hebrew University, Jerusalem.

Klein-Halevy, Y.

1994   "The Lubavitcher Rebbe." *Sydney Jewish News,* June 17th.

Kovacs, M.

1977   *The Dynamics of Commitment: The Process of Resocialization of Ba'alei Teshuvah—Jewish Students in Pursuit of Their Identity at the Rabbinical College of America* (*Lubavitch*). Union Graduate School, New York.

Kranzler, G.

1951   "A Visit with the New Lubavitcher Rebbe." *Orthodox Jewish Life,* September/October Edition, Tishrei, 5752.

Kraus, Y.
2007 *Ha-Shevi'i: Meshihiyut Ba-Dor Ha-Shevi'i Shel Habad.* Yediot
Acharonot, Tel Aviv, Israel.

Landau, D.
1994 "The Lubavitcher Rebbe: An Intellectual and Spiritual Giant."
Australian Jewish Times, June 17th.

Lau, I. M.
1994 Letter of Condolence. *Chabad Magazine,* June.

Lauffer, M. M. (*ed.*)
1987 *Betzail HaChochma—Reshimot V'Roshei Prakim MiDivrei Kvod
Kedushat Admor Shlita MiLubavitch Im Admorim, Rabbanim, Roshei Yeshivot U'Gedolei Torah.* Machon L'Hatzaot L'Ohr, Kollel
Avreichim Habad, Nachalat Har-Habad, Kiryat Malachi, Israel.

1991 *Klalei Rambam B'Sifro Mishna Torah—Yad HaChazaka Al Pi
Sichot U'Michtevei Kvod Kedushat Admor Shlita MiLubavitch.*
Kehot Publication Society, Kfar Habad, Israel.

Levin, S. B.
1989 *Toldot Chabad B'Rusyah Ha'Sovyetit* [History of Habad in the
USSR, 1917-1950]. Kehot Publication Society, Brooklyn, NY.

Levinson, M. and S.
2003 "'Getting Religion': Religion, Diversity, and Community in
Public and Private Schools." In Alan Wolfe (*ed.*), *School Choice:
The Moral Debate,* 110-18, 123-4, 305-6. Princeton University
Press, Princeton, NJ.

Levy, S.
1973 *Ethnic Boundedness and the Institutionalization of Charisma: A
Study of the Lubavitcher Hassidim.* Manuscript, University Mi-
crofilms, Ann Arbor.

Lincoln, Y. S. & Guba, E. G.
1985 *Naturalistic Enquiry.* Sage, Beverly Hills, CA.
1986 "But Is It Rigorous? Trustworthiness and Authenticity." In D. D.
Williams (*ed.*), *Naturalistic Evaluation.*

Loewenthal, N.
1990 *Communicating the Infinite: The Emergence of the Habad School.*
University of Chicago Press, Chicago.

294

References

Lucas, C. J. (ed.)

1969 What Is Philosophy of Education? MacMillan, Collier-MacMillan, London.

Mark, J.

1994 "A Life of Faith and Outreach." Australian Jewish News, June 16th.

Merrell, K. W. & Gueldner, B. A. (eds.)

2010 Social and Emotional Learning in the Classroom: Promoting Mental Health and Academic Success. Guilford Press, New York.

Merton, R. K.

1949 & 1968 "The Self-Fulfilling Prophecy." In Merton, Social Philosophy and Social Structure, 475-90. Free Press, New York.

Metzger, A. B. Z.

1999 The Heroic Struggle: The Arrest and Liberation of Rabbi Yosef Y. Schneersohn of Lubavitch in Soviet Russia. Kehot Publication Society, Brooklyn, NY.

Miller, Ch. (ed.)

1993 The Nechoma Greisman Anthology. Machon Chaya Mushka Women's Institute for Jewish Studies, Jerusalem.

Miller, M.

2014 Turning Judaism Outward: A Biography of the Rebbe, Menachem Mendel Schneerson. Gutnick Library of Jewish Classics, Kol Menachem, New York.

Moore, T. W.

1982 Philosophy of Education: An Introduction. Routledge & Kegan Paul, London.

Morris, B. J.

1995 "Agents or Victims of Religious Ideology? Approaches to Locating Hasidic Women in Feminist Studies." In J. S. Belcove-Shalin, 1995, 161-80.

Nixon, R.

1973 Letter of March 21st, 1972 cited in B. Z. & H. Rader (eds.), Challenge: An Encounter with Lubavitch-Chabad in Israel, 284. Lubavitch Foundation of Great Britain, London.

Omar, Y. Y. (ed.)

2000 HaShlichut HaChinuchit B'Igrot HaRabbi [The Educational Mission as Found in the Letters of the Rebbe]. Kehot Publication Society, Argentina.

Peters, R. S.

  1965 "Education as Initiation." In R. D. Archambault (*ed.*), *Philosophical Analysis and Education*, 87-111. Humanities Press, New York.

  1966 *Ethics and Education*. Allen and Unwin, London.

Peters, R. S. (*ed.*)

  1973 *The Philosophy of Education*. Oxford University Press, Oxford. (Includes R. S. Peters, J. Woods, and W. H. Dray, "Aims of Education: A Conceptual Enquiry," 11-57; and R. S. Peters, "The Justification of Education," 238-67.)

  1977 *John Dewey Reconsidered*. International Library of the Philosophy of Education. Routledge & Kegan Paul, London.

  1977 "John Dewey's Philosophy of Education." In R. S. Peters (*ed.*), *John Dewey Reconsidered*, International Library of the Philosophy of Education. Routledge & Kegan Paul, London.

  1983 "Philosophy of Education." In P. H. Hirst (*ed.*), *Educational Philosophy and Its Foundation Disciplines*, 30-61. Routledge & Kegan Paul, London.

Phillips, D. C.

  1994 "Philosophy of Education: Historical Overview." In T. Husen and T. Neville Postlethwaite (*eds.*), *The International Encyclopedia of Education*, 4447-56. 2nd ed. Pergamon Press, Oxford.

Polter, D. S.

  1997 *Listening to Life's Messages – Adapted from the Works of the Lubavitcher Rebbe Rabbi Menachem M. Schneerson*. Sichos in English, Brooklyn, NY.

Posner, Z. I.

  1994 Translator's Introductory Notes to *HaYom Yom—From Day to Day*. Kehot Publication Society, Brooklyn, NY.

Purdy, L.

  2000 "Educating Gifted Children." In R. Curren (*ed.*), *Philosophy of Education 1999*, 192-9. Philosophy of Education Society, Urbana, IL.

Rabenort, W. L.

  1911 *Spinoza as Educator*. Teachers' College, Columbia University Press, New York.

Rader, B. Z. and H. (*eds.*)

1970 *Challenge—An Encounter with Lubavitch-Chabad.* Lubavitch Foundation of Great Britain, London.

1973 *Challenge—An Encounter with Lubavitch-Chabad in Israel.* Lubavitch Foundation of Great Britain, London.

1979 *Return to Roots.* Lubavitch Foundation of Great Britain, London.

Ross, S.

1966 *The Meaning of Education.* Martinus Nijhoff, The Hague, Netherlands.

Rivkin, M. S. (*ed.*)

1974-1980 *The Uforatzta Journal.* Lubavitch Youth Organization, New York.

Rusk, R. R. & Scotland, J.

1979 *Doctrines of the Great Educators.* 5th ed. Macmillan, London.

Sacks, J.

1980 "In Search of the Soul: Thirty Years of the Lubavitcher Rebbe." *Jewish Chronicle* (London), February 1st.

1990 *Tradition in an Untraditional Age—Essays on Modern Jewish Thought.* Vallentine & Mitchell, London.

1994 "The Man Who Turned Judaism Outwards—A Personal Tribute to the Lubavitcher Rebbe." *Chabad Journal* (Albany, NY), June.

1995 "When Mysticism Saved the Jewish People: A Memorial Tribute to the Lubavitcher Rebbe." In *"Le'Ela: A Journal of Judaism Today* 39 (April, Pesach 5755): 4.

1997 *The Politics of Hope.* Jonathan Cape, London.

2000 *Future Tense: A Vision for Jews and Judaism in the Global Culture.* Jonathan Cape, London.

2004(a) "Education, Values and Religion—Political Society, Civil Society," in Haldane (*ed.*), 2004.

2004(b) "Language and Morals," in Haldane (*ed.*), 2004.

2006 *The Dignity of Difference: How to Avoid the Clash of Civilizations.* Continuum, New York.

2007 *Rabbi Jonathan Sacks's Haggadah: Hebrew and English Text with New Essays and Commentary.* Continuum, N.Y.

2014 "An Unparalleled Leader." *Jewish Action* (Summer).

2015 *Not In G-d's Name: Confronting Religious Violence.* Hodder and Stoughton, UK.

Scheffler, I.

1960 *The Language of Education*. Charles C. Thomas, Springfield, IL.

Seligson, M. A.

1994 "Genealogy and Brief Notes on the Descendants of Our *Rebbe'im*." *HaYom Yom*: A19-A40.

2001 *Mafte'ach Erech Chinuch B'Torat Rabbeinu—Melukat MiKrachei Sichot Kodesh 5710-5739 V'Od* [Index to the Entry of "Education" in the Torah Writings of Rabbi Menachem M. Schneerson, Collated from the Volumes of Transcripts of His Addresses Delivered between 1950 and 1979 and Other Occasions]. (Addendum to *HaShlichut HaChinuchit*). Kehot Publication Society, Buenos Aires, Argentina.

2012 *Mafte'chot L'Sichot Kodesh 5695-5752* [Indices to the Addresses of Rabbi Menachem M. Schneerson delivered between 1934-1935 and 1992]. Kehot Publication Society, Brooklyn, NY.

Shaffir, W.

1974 *Life in a Religious Community: The Lubavitcher Chassidim in Montreal*. Holt, Rinehart & Winston of Canada, Toronto.

Shemtov, L. (*ed.*)

1996 "Education Day USA, 1989 and 1990—A Proclamation by the President of the USA." In *Education Day USA—A Tribute and a Message*. American Friends of Lubavitch, Washington, DC.

Sherman-Swing, E.

1987 "In Memoriam: William W. Brickman, 1913-1986." *Comparative Education Review* 31: 1-6.

Shokeid, M.

1988 *Children of Circumstances: Israeli Emigrants in New York*. Cornell University Press, Ithaca, NY.

Siegel, H. (*ed.*)

2009 *The Oxford Handbook of Philosophy of Education*. Oxford University Press, Oxford.

Silova, I. and Brehm, W. C. (*eds.*)

2010 "William Brickman: His History, Our Story." *European Education* 42, no. 2: 85-101.

Silver, H. F., Strong R. W. & Perini, M. J.

1997 "Integrating Learning Styles and Multiple Intelligences." *Educational Leadership* 55, no. 1 (September): 22-7.

Solomon, A.

2000 *The Educational Teachings of Rabbi Menachem M. Schneerson.* Jason Aronson, Northvale, NJ.

2010 "William Brickman's Legacy in Jewish Education Worldwide." In I. Silova and W.C. Brehm (*eds.*), "William Brickman: His History, Our Story." *European Education* 42, no. 2: 85-101.

—————— (trans.).

2009 *The Educator's Privilege.* English translation of M.M. Brod & A.E. Friedman (*eds.*) (1989) Kehot Publication Society, Brooklyn, NY.

Spiegel, I.

1975 "The Rebbe: In His Torah There Is Room for All Jews." In *A Tribute to the Lubavitcher Rebbe Shlita* (reprinted from *The National Bnai Brith Monthly*). Lubavitch Youth Organization, Sydney.

Steinsaltz, (Even-Yisrael), A.

2014 *My Rebbe.* Koren Publishers, Jerusalem.

Strang, R.

1955 "Scholarship in Education." *School & Society* 81, no. 2060 (May 28): 161-4.

Swados, H.

1994 "He Could Melt a Blizzard." *New York Times,* op. ed., June 14th.

Tauber, R.T.

1997 *Self-Fulfilling Prophecy: A Practical Guide to Its Use in Education.* Praeger Publishers, Westport, CT.

Taylor, W. (*ed.*)

1984 *Metaphors of Education.* Studies in Education (new series) 14. Heinemann Educational Books, Institute of Education, University of London.

Terzi, L.

2005 *Justice and Equality in Education: Capability Perspective on Disability and Special Needs.* Continuum, New York.

Thompson, K.

1974 *Education and Philosophy: A Practical Approach.* Basil Blackwell, Oxford.

Underwood, B.J.

1948 "Spontaneous Recovery of Verbal Associations." *Journal of Experimental Psychology* 38: 428-39.

1957 "Interference and Forgetting." *Psychological Review* 64, no. 1: 49-60.

1969 "Attributes of Memory." *Psychological Review* 76, no. 6: 559-73.

Vitzhandler, S. (*ed.*)

2014 *Igeret HaChinuch: Hadracha Ma'asit L'Horim U'Mechanchim* [Epistle of Education: Practical Advice for Teachers and Educators]. Merkaz Hafatza Mamash, Israel.

Williams, D. D. (*ed.*)

1986 New Directions for Program Evaluation:Evaluation in Informal Science, Technology, Engineering, and Mathematics Education. *Naturalistic Evaluation* 1986, no. 30.

Zaklikowsky, D., (*ed.*)

2007 *The Rebbe and President Ford.* http://www.chabad.org/the rebbe/article_cdo/aid/461848/jewish/The-Rebbe-and-President-Ford.htm

Zamir, R.

1988 *Madrich Tochnit Avoda L'Gil HaRach* [Guide for a Program of Activites for Young (Pre-School) Children]. Privately published.

Zuriff, G. E.

1996 "The Myths of Learning Disabilities." *Public Affairs Quarterly* 10, no. 4 (October).

INDEX